IT NEVER ENDS

IT
NEVER
ENDS

A MEMOIR
WITH NICE MEMORIES!

TOM SCHARPLING

ABRAMS PRESS, NEW YORK

Library of Congress Control Number: 2020944993

ISBN: 978-1-4197-4792-2
eISBN: 978-1-64700-032-5

Printed and bound in the United States
10 9 8 7 6 5 4 3 2 1

ABRAMS The Art of Books
195 Broadway, New York, NY 10007
abramsbooks.com

To Sue and Tom, aka my parents.
One is gone, but both of you are with me every day.
You make every other so-called "parent" look
like a pile of discarded diapers.

CONTENTS

CHAPTER ONE

IT NEVER ENDS: THE BEGINNING

IN THE SUMMER of 2019 I was walking around a Midtown Manhattan bookstore with my friend Sammi Skolmoski, talking about the book that you're currently reading. Sammi was visiting from Chicago and we took a night to discuss some of the more philosophical aspects of writing a memoir. Sammi is a very funny writer and for years she has been saying that I should write a book. As much as I fantasized about someday becoming an author, I never felt ready. "A book is supposed to be a work of art," I would insist. "Have you actually seen the kinds of books that get published?" she would counter.

Yes, I know that football bro Rob "Gronk" Gronkowski is a published author. And Kiss bassist Gene Simmons has slapped his name on a half dozen bestsellers. But I grew up worshipping books. If I was ever going to write one it would need to be great! I'd rather die than have my name barfed onto the cover of one of those tomes with huge type that far too many comedians churn out. There was a point where famous people would compile their tweets into a book! Charging for tweets! The hubris!

People in my life would gently remind me that I needed to stop complaining about the ocean of undeserving clowns who proudly call themselves "author." Instead of moaning, it was my turn to BECOME one of those clowns! I thought about it for another two years—I'm sometimes slow with making decisions; you'll see it's a running theme throughout this book—before I finally acquiesced. So what made me change my mind? One day while floating around a bookstore, I decided to check out the "new releases" table. And sitting front and center was a self-help manual by DJ Khaled called *The Keys*. I never picked up the book but I'm assuming it consists of pages written by other authors with an occasional "DEEEEEE JAYYYYY KHALED" typed at the start of every chapter. This was the moment that I knew I had literally nothing to lose. If that buffoon could write a book, I could write a book. It was time for me to tell my story!

While I have read more than a million books—mostly rock and showbiz biographies—I had never actually written one, so I needed some help. Sammi dispensed some serious wisdom as we walked around the Union Square chain bookstore whose name I will not utter (it rhymes with Blarnes & Blowble and the branch we were in is located a few doors down from the final location of Andy Warhol's Factory, which is currently a PetSmart). We talked about the book's title. Sammi wanted to know exactly why I was calling this book *It Never Ends*.

I started to explain myself as we drifted past the Psychology section. I caught a glimpse of some of the titles scattered throughout the shelves and stopped dead in my tracks. "Look at this," I said, zeroing in on the books. "Any one of these would work as the title of my book."

Some of the titles included:

How I Stayed Alive When My Brain Was Trying to Kill Me
Maybe You Should Talk to Someone
The Trauma of Everyday Life

Duped
Let Me Not Be Mad
Going to Pieces without Falling Apart
The Invisible Gorilla
We've Been Too Patient
Are u ok?
Lost at Sea
Good Reasons for Bad Feelings
You Are Now Less Dumb

I turned to Sammi and said, "These are all perfectly good book titles, but it wouldn't be the same. I will tell you why I chose *It Never Ends*, but before I do, this bookstore has one of the only unlocked bathrooms in the city, so I'll be right back."

I excused myself and promptly entered the men's room. This particular Blarnes & Blowble featured a restroom that was wide-open to any New Yorker with the capacity to pretend they were shopping for a book. Every trip inside this bathroom was a spin of a disgraceful carnival wheel; where will it land this time? An open issue of *Penthouse* on the men's room floor? A bare-assed man pissing at the urinal with his pants and underwear lowered around his ankles?

Today delivered a special treat. Some mystery person was in the bathroom stall blasting an episode of Joe Rogan's podcast on their phone. I was tempted to knock on the door and ask the listener whether they knew that Joe's website sold *Star Wars*–related workout equipment like a Death Star slam ball and a "Han Solo frozen in carbonite" yoga mat, but opted instead to do my toilet business and not court my own toilet murder. I made a quick escape and rejoined Sammi, telling her the tale that led me to call this book *It Never Ends*.

If my stories were songs, this would be one of my biggest hits. It would be my "Hey Jude." My "Purple Rain." My "Despacito" (featuring Justin Bieber). The best stories feature a bunch of ridiculous elements that line up in a way that creates magic. I have told this tale on the radio and people love it so much that they regularly throw it in my face at any opportunity. It's that good of a story! On second thought this one should be my "Because the Night" since it involves punk legend Patti Smith.

The year was 2015. I was in San Francisco with my comedy partner Jon Wurster. We were being honored by the SF Sketchfest with an evening billed as "A SF Sketchfest Tribute to Scharpling & Wurster." For the uninitiated, I have been hosting a call-in radio show for the last twenty years called *The Best Show*. While most of the callers are real, Jon and I write and perform funny scripted calls within the body of the show. Jon will dial in as any number of beloved creations, like Philly Boy Roy (a lovable *Rocky*-loving meathead from Philadelphia) or Roland "the Gorch" Gorchnick (a violent senior citizen who claims the character of Fonzie was based on his days as a hoodlum back in the 1950s). We have spent years crafting literally hundreds of hours of comedy and now we were being honored for our dedication. It was a special night.

The Sketchfest organizers put us up in a nice hotel in the Japantown neighborhood for the length of our stay. On the first day, I was in the hotel elevator when I looked over and realized I was standing across from the one and only Patti Smith. Now there are famous people and there are legends. Jim Belushi is a famous person but most people wouldn't step across a puddle to tell him how much they enjoyed *According to Jim*. But Patti Smith is a legend, one of the true musical pioneers. She is a game changer who established an original voice early and never stopped pushing at her artistic margins. I was starstruck and I told everyone I saw that I had shared an elevator with her. They were all impressed because *she's Patti Smith*.

So imagine my shock when the next day I spotted Patti Smith floating through the marketplace that adjoined the hotel. By then I had learned she was performing a run of shows at the Fillmore, a venue located a couple of blocks from the hotel. Two encounters in two days, although "encounter" might be a strong word; I definitely saw her but she had no idea I was drawing air on this planet. Still—two times! That has to mean *something*, right?

I saw her a third time in the lobby. I was getting more starstruck with each sighting. It's something to see a musical legend actually existing within the same physical space as us mere mortals; when you stare at an album jacket the image is frozen in time. Only the music actually moves. So when you see the woman from the cover of *Easter* drift past you in real life, your perception shifts. Stardom is an extremely powerful thing.

The following day I was back in the lobby with Jon. We sat in comfortable chairs reviewing all the things we had planned for our tribute show that evening. And who do you think passed by on her way to the elevators? You get only one guess! Robert Loggia? Why would you use your one guess on Robert Loggia!? He's been dead for years! It was Patti Smith! This was the fourth time I spotted her and now I knew this was a sign. I had to say something to her. Jon watched me get up and follow her into the hotel elevator, the doors closing behind us.

I'm sure you're wondering whether I actually think that seeing another person staying at the same hotel is "a sign." No, I don't. I understand that every guest has to use the elevators to reach their hotel room and that if you plant yourself in the lobby for a few hours the odds of spotting someone more than once are considerably improved. But there's one thing you should know that informed my thinking at this point in my life: My father had passed away just three weeks earlier and I was, unsurprisingly, a disaster.

His death was a total shock; I spoke to him on a Friday night and by Sunday afternoon he was gone. People who haven't lost a parent have asked me what it feels like, and I can only describe it like this: The first piece of reality that you learn in your life is who is protecting you. For me it was my mother and my father. I lived my life believing that truth, until the day it changed. My entire life had been blown to pieces and I was still sorting through the rubble.

I didn't know what to do with myself after he died. Was I supposed to sit at home and stare at the wall? Should I just cry all day in my car? No, he would've hated that. So in a world that was spinning out of orbit I took control of the only thing I had any power over. I decided to fulfill all my professional commitments and try to soldier forward.

I was able to be physically present for these events but my brain was not functioning correctly. I had a hard time focusing, and I was clearly struggling with decision-making, as evidenced by me following Patti Smith into an elevator with the goal of "saying something to her."

The kicker is that I didn't actually have anything to say to her! As the elevator doors slid shut, I scrambled to figure out a question. It had to be a good one. None of this slobbering "I'm such a big fan" business would cut it. I needed to make her think, perhaps even surprise her with my insight. I was standing next to someone who had been interviewed thousands of times, so it was of paramount importance that I ask Patti Smith something she had *never* been asked before.

I started off with a smile and asked her how the Fillmore shows had been going. She pleasantly replied that they were going great; she was a little tired but the shows were worth it. The elevator doors would open in a matter of seconds, so it was time for THE BIG QUESTION! But what would it be? Out of nowhere the answer appeared in my sad brain in the form of a Memphis taxi. I knew what I was going to ask her.

A year earlier I had been in Memphis attending Gonerfest, an annual rock music festival hosted by an amazing record label called Goner Records. Gonerfest is one of the greatest things ever, with scores of bands playing throughout the city over the course of an extended weekend. We found ourselves in a taxi en route to one of the shows, and the cabbie was what you would call a "character." He was a grizzled guy well into his sixties, the kind of hack you only see in movies like *Taxi Driver* and *Taxi* and *D.C. Cab* and *Collateral* and television shows like *Taxi* and *Cash Cab* and *Hack*.

This weathered old salt knew the club we were heading to and started reminiscing about all the bands he had seen throughout the years. And he had seen them all: Led Zeppelin. The Faces. The Stooges. He was a walking (driving, actually) encyclopedia of rock history. I asked him who was the best band he had ever seen, and with zero hesitation he said, "Humble Pie, no question." Humble Pie was a '70s hard rock band fronted by Steve Marriott and Peter Frampton. They were great, but I had no idea they were the best. He sensed my surprise and explained why. "Steve would dance around and get the crowd going, and that voice! Nobody could sing like him. Trust me, everybody ripped them off."

As I stood across from Patti Smith, the unacknowledged greatness of Humble Pie echoed through my brain. I had my unique angle. I knew what I had to say.

"Can I ask you a question?" I said confidently.

"Uh, yeah," she replied.

"Did you ever see Humble Pie back in the day?"

As soon as the words left my mouth I knew I had royally fucked up. The question sounded insane and my use of "back in the day"—a phrase I had never once uttered before that moment—was just dumb icing on an idiotic cake. The look that overtook her face confirmed it: one part confusion, one part irritation, and a heaping dose of "get me the fuck out of this elevator." She stammered out a reply, doing the best she could to hang with my insane question.

"Um, no . . . that was before my time."

It doesn't matter that Humble Pie was *definitely* not before her time, but we are not here to litigate whether Patti Smith had the opportunity to see them in concert in the early 1970s. All of this is beside the point because I had clearly freaked her out. I tried to recover, blathering something about Steve Marriott, but thankfully the elevator doors flew open and she stepped out. I'm 99 percent sure she got off on a floor that wasn't even hers just to get away from me.

I stood there in the wake of my blunder and pressed the button that returned me to the lobby. I stepped out like the human manifestation of the blood pouring from the elevator in *The Shining* and sat back down with Jon. He excitedly asked how it went. I told him the story. He looked sad for me, most likely assuming that he would be the third and final soul on this planet to know that this incident ever took place.

But I couldn't hold back. I told the story on the next episode of *The Best Show*. People immediately responded to it; perhaps it was the universality of saying something stupid to someone you're desperate to impress, or maybe people just like hearing about someone royally eating shit. Either way, we've all been there before, and I've found that sharing these moments is the only way we can collectively realize that our mouths are forever one teeny-tiny step away from disaster.

One of the reasons I called the book *It Never Ends* rose out of the immediate aftermath of the Patti Smith story. As I stepped off that elevator, it dawned on me: *This has happened to me before.* And unlike the Patti Smith story, this story is one I was more or less prepared to take to the grave.

The year was 1983. Pac-Man was president of the United States and it was illegal to not be able to solve a Rubik's Cube. I was a young lad of thirteen or so. By this point in my life I was a rabid music fan, buying albums and poring over old issues of *Rolling Stone* and *Creem* as if my life depended on it. It wasn't long before I started begging my parents to let me see live shows. And for some reason they said yes, seeing nothing wrong with letting a child walk into a show without accompaniment. I could say, "That's just how it was back then," but it kinda wasn't how it was back then. Maybe my parents trusted me because I carried myself like a junior adult instead of the little kid I still was, but even a smart thirteen-year-old is still a thirteen-year-old. This misinterpreted maturity would lead to a lot of problems as time went on, but for now it made things pretty awesome. I saw as many concerts as I could. I saw the Fixx at Six Flags after riding the log flume all afternoon. I took my sister to see Rick Springfield at what was then the Brendan Byrne Arena in East Rutherford, New Jersey, and was treated to Sparks as the opening band. (They were both awesome and I will stand by Rick Springfield until the day I croak.) I managed to see R.E.M. play a Rutgers University food court right as their first album, *Murmur*, had been released. I was equal parts hypnotized and terrified; back then Michael Stipe sported long stringy hair that completely obscured his face, and when he mumbled, "Welcome to hell," before the band launched into "Radio Free Europe" my thirteen-year-old self was never the same.

One of the concerts I saw around this time was Marshall Crenshaw performing at Princeton University. Marshall Crenshaw is a bespectacled singer-songwriter whose music has a slight 1950s/pre-Beatles bent; his most famous song is probably "Someday, Someway" from his debut album. He played Buddy Holly in the movie *La Bamba*. He's a talented guy and I really liked his first two records.

I bought a ticket and walked inside, where there was a stage planted at the far end of the gymnasium. The audience was composed almost entirely of Princeton students. I was harboring plans to attend Princeton after high school, so the notion of having concerts like this right on campus made the school even more appealing. The show wasn't too crowded, so I was able to inch my way to the front with relative ease. The show was great. But instead of just watching and enjoying, my brain posited a question that in retrospect was bonkers.

I wonder if I can get Marshall Crenshaw's autograph.

It's not an inherently stupid notion to get an autograph. But it most certainly is stupid to attempt to get one DURING THE CONCERT. You'd think I would've realized this. I had seen enough movies and shows where fans crowded the backstage exit of a theater in hopes of landing an autograph, but I had never seen a single depiction in which someone tried to get their record signed in the middle of a performance. But my brain took me where it took me. I confidently pulled a ballpoint pen from my jacket pocket and slid the ticket beneath the clip. I looked at it admiringly; Crenshaw could reach for the ticket to sign it and the pen would already be a part of the exchange! Always thinking, Tom!

I maneuvered to the lip of the stage and planted myself directly in front of Crenshaw. I waited until he finished playing the song— I'm not an idiot!—and as he stepped back up to the mic, I saw my window. I extended my arm upward, level with his shin. After a long moment Marshall Crenshaw finally looked down and noticed me. It took him a couple of seconds to process the scene in front of him, but after a beat it dawned on him that this skinny little kid was trying to get an autograph in the middle of a show. He looked me straight in the eye and said in a tone dripping with confounded derision, "I'm not signing that now!"

My arm slinked downward and I backed away from the stage, becoming another anonymous person in the crowd. I probably wasn't *that* anonymous since I was the only child in attendance, but still. If anyone working in the Princeton University admissions department had been there that night looking for "Princeton material," they would've run a big red line through my name, noting that I "lacked basic social skills."

Oh, if only that innocent child knew that thirty-plus years later he would experience the same exact dynamic all over again. Literally nothing changed! It didn't matter how much I achieved. Whether figuring life out as a thirteen-year-old or on the eve of receiving a tribute concert in my midforties, I was still the same person.

So the book is called *It Never Ends* because it never does end. Things do have a tendency to reoccur over and over throughout my life. Sometimes it's funny and can be laughed away or turned into ridiculous stories for the radio show. Other times the events are tragic and heartbreaking. But the constant *is* their constancy! Now if only the guy in the elevator with Patti Smith could've forewarned the Tom Scharpling of 2017 that while literally everyone else in the first few rows of the Nick Cave concert at the Beacon Theatre would be gleefully snapping pics on their phones, Nick would for some reason decide he needed to swat *my* phone to the floor . . .

CHAPTER TWO

SO WHO IS THIS TOM SCHARPLING ANYWAY?

So YEAH, I hemmed and hawed about whether I would write a book. But from the second I agreed, I knew the dramatic shape that the book would take. There was only one way to tell my story, and it would go something like this:

- Act I: The book will start off funny and the reader will laugh.
- Act II: The book will become incredibly sad and the reader will cry.
- Act III: The book will get funny again and the reader will laugh but now they will also be cheering me on the way they cheered for lovable underdogs like Rocky or Seabiscuit or Rudy.

My goal is that upon finishing this book you will have no choice but to rise from your seat and slow clap while looking at the cover, muttering under your breath, "That SOB did it. He really did it!"

This is the only reaction I want from every single reader; anything less is a failure. Why would I want such a dynamic reaction? Because it is my story! It's a tale of triumph, of sadness, of overcoming the odds. But mostly it is a story about me getting mad at dumb stuff that happened to me or me making dumb stuff happen that made other people mad. Either which way, it is my life. And because I'm the one living it, the details sometimes feel like an endless blur, like living inside a tornado that never dissipates.

Every story has a backstory, so this is as good a place as any to fill in some of the blanks. This will be the part where I tell you who I am so we can all move forward in full possession of the greatest commodity known to humankind: CONTEXT. So many of the world's problems stem from a lack of context. If you can't understand who someone is, you will struggle to understand why they do the things they do.

One thing before we begin: I promise not to start telling my story one second earlier than I need to. There are few things more annoying than a memoir that starts generations before the subject was even born. Nobody cares that Paul Reiser's ancestors fought the Visigoths! (This probably isn't accurate. I didn't get much schooling, something that will become very apparent throughout this book.) If I don't give a flying fuck about my own great-grandparents coming to America, there is no reason you should!

So, who is Tom Scharpling? Great question. I'm sure some of you are probably asking that right now. Look, I know I'm not a household name. My level of fame hovers somewhere between the astronaut who wore the diaper and the hype guy in the Mighty Mighty Bosstones. I have a sizable and devoted audience that listens to *The Best Show* every week. They are called "Friends of Tom" and I don't need to introduce myself to them. But for the rest of you, here is some basic info:

- I was born and raised in New Jersey. It's a strange thing growing up in the Garden State, halfway between New

York City and Philadelphia. You always feel like you need to align your identity with one of these cities because saying you're from New Jersey is the punch line that keeps on giving. But you can't. If you're from New Jersey, you're from New Jersey. It's like a tattoo you didn't ask for.

- I come from humble stock. My family has been self-employed for generations, building fences and running small retail stores. My parents owned a T-shirt shop, so some of my favorite moments as a child consisted of getting the latest and greatest iron-ons. Trust me, no child ever rocked a HOMEWORK IS HAZARDOUS TO MY HEALTH shirt with as much panache as Young Tom.

- My family didn't always have a lot of money because my mother suffered through major health problems that required surgeries and transfusions and hospitalizations. The medical bills were astronomical and the insurance companies were pure evil, and too many times our family got crushed beneath the weight of the expenses.

- I was the first member of my family to attend college. Sure, it was a community college, but that counts! Right?

- When I announced to the people in my life that I wanted to write comedy for a living, I received a silent thud of confusion and disappointment in return. My parents had no idea what to make of this because there were no "show folk" in my bloodline. The closest anyone came to writing comedy would be that HOMEWORK IS HAZARDOUS TO MY HEALTH shirt I sported so amazingly as a child.

- My first big job was writing on the hit television show *Monk.* I was on board for the entire run, from the pilot up until the final episode eight seasons later.

- In 2000 I started hosting a radio show called *The Best Show on WFMU*. This call-in comedy program was the best thing that could've happened to me in terms of comedy. It is the purest form of expression and it's still my favorite thing to do.

In terms of chronology, we're going to bounce around a bit. I don't want this thing to have a linear narrative, so you don't have to wait for me to grow up and get to the good stuff. Nobody enjoyed waiting for Darth Vader to stop being eight years old in those prequels, so I'm not going to make you wait either.

I have a few goals in mind with this book. As I stated I will make you laugh and cry and cheer. I will also pass along some showbiz wisdom I have accumulated over the years. I will most likely attempt to settle a few scores with some jerks that have done me wrong, but I will do it with fairness and perspective; I know I carry my share of the responsibility for any relationship or situation that has gone south. I will also teach you how I managed to draw my own name for my family's Secret Santa for five years straight and why I pulled off such a stultifyingly stupid achievement.

One of my core goals in writing this book is to be honest. And if I'm being completely honest, I admit there's a sizable part of me that doesn't want to be. I actually said no to writing a book for years because of fear. Yes, I have been pretty confessional on *The Best Show* but I have definitely kept the darker parts of my life to myself. I didn't share the stories because of the pain and embarrassment they caused me. I'm not talking about the Marshall Crenshaw story because as embarrassing as it was, it is ultimately the tale of a dumb kid not understanding concert etiquette. The stuff I've been swallowing for the whole of my life has shaped every part of my existence and identity. I can count on one hand the people outside my immediate family who know some of these stories and I'd still have a couple of fingers left over.

The safe version of this book would be just the funny stories, but that would be me taking the easy way out and it would ultimately be a bit of a lie. I've finally grown enough to arrive at a place where I can tell my story. I actually feel like I have to tell it if I'm to keep going forward. I can't hold this stuff back anymore and I can't continue to bottle it up.

Don't get me wrong: This book is still going to be funny! I promise you that. But the sad stuff needs to be included. Think of this as the part of a roller-coaster ride where the safety bar slides across your chest. Once you hear that click, there is no turning back. The ride goes where it's gonna go, no matter how much you scream. Hopefully it brings you back safely, but the whole point of a scary ride is the possibility of this thing killing you. The odds are you'll live, but it's not worth it if you're 100 percent sure you'll survive the experience. There's always a chance that the ride will fly off the tracks.

I think I'll survive this. Wait a minute—I don't think this bar is fastened tight enough! Hey, amusement park employee, can you check this to make sure I'm not gonna fall out of the ride? Hey! Kid! Stop eating that churro and pay attention to—

Click!

CHAPTER THREE

AN EVENING WITH THE PIANO MAN

WE LIVE IN a complicated world. Things change without warning and we too often find ourselves hanging on for dear life as it whips curveball after curveball at our heads. Thankfully there are a handful of evergreen truths that we can always rely on to grant us footing when chaos overtakes us. Things like:

> Water is wet.
> The sky is blue.
> Billy Joel sucks.

I know that some people reading this are going to disagree with the third of my truths but I'm sorry—it's just the way it is. And yes, I've heard all the arguments: Billy Joel has sold a billion records! His songs are playing on an endless loop pretty much anywhere you go! He has been selling out Madison Square Garden since forever! But none of this changes the fact that Billy Joel sucks. I wish I could do something about it, but I'm not in charge of stuff like this. Maybe you should speak to the manager?

Yes, it is undeniable that he has been wildly successful. Beej (my pet name for Billy) has been racking up massive hits since the mid-'70s, and while he stopped releasing new music in the early '90s, his legacy only continues to grow. For anyone currently screaming at this book, ask yourself these two questions:

1) When has being successful been the yardstick for quality?

2) Do you think Billy Joel is great because he's great, or is it because his music has been tattooed on your brain since you started drawing air and you can't tell which way is up?

I personally can't remember a single day of my life without knowing Billy Joel existed. He's always been there, like that filthy-looking pizzeria that you ignore because there are actual good pizzerias right around the corner. But somehow it stays in business, polluting the community with low-grade slices year after year. Billy Joel is like a shitty version of the monolith in the beginning of *2001: A Space Odyssey*, but instead of teaching monkeys to beat each other to death it coaches a sea of dunces to scream "AND CAPTAIN JACK WILL GET YOU HIGH TONIGHT!" on command.

A few years ago, my lawyer told me that it would be beneficial for me to start a production company. Not like I'm a hotshot or anything; it would just be a semi-prudent thing to do when it comes to receiving paychecks and paying taxes. I realized that this business decision created a very exciting opportunity: If I formed a production company I would get to pick a funny production company name! I could join the pantheon of great funny television production company names throughout history!

Think about all those end credits on your favorite TV shows throughout your life.

There's "Sit, Ubu, sit." There's the meowing cat on *The Mary Tyler Moore Show*. The desperate Unabomber-esque screeds that

Chuck Lorre slaps on the end of his shows. Now it was my turn. I thought long and hard about what to name my production company. And then it hit me: I would call it BILLY JOEL SUCKS PRODUCTIONS. In a flash I saw my future play out before me: I sell a show. It gets the green light. We film the pilot. It tests well. Maybe people don't like one of the supporting actors, but that's what testing is for, right? So we recast. I arrange a lunch with the actor to tell them we're gonna go in a different direction. It's a difficult meeting but I do it anyway because firing someone over the phone is cowardly.

I'm getting off track here. The show gets picked up to series and hits the air. Somewhere out on Long Island, Billy Joel sits in his mansion. It is enormous and imposing, probably decorated with a lot of nautical stuff. An old diver's helmet and a shell vaguely shaped like a piano that Billy found while walking the beach at Amagansett sit on a coffee table that also serves as a leg rest for Beej's tired feet.

He lazily flips through the channels on his massive flat-screen television before settling on a show—MY show! He watches it. He likes it! The credits start to roll. Billy leans forward. He wants to know who is responsible for this show that just entertained him.

And that's when my title card pops up on his screen, dropping an image of, I don't know, Billy Joel on a toilet or something, with the words BILLY JOEL SUCKS PRODUCTIONS splashed big and bright across his television.

Billy's shoulders slump and a pained grimace overtakes his face. "Oh, come on," he defeatedly mutters to himself.

The Alexa on Billy's coffee table springs to life, robotically asking, "Did you say something, Billy?"

Billy sighs. "No, Downeaster Alexa, I was just talking to myself." He hesitates, then says quietly, "Play 'Scenes from an Italian Restaurant' three times in a row."

As the sound of his own voice drifts from his speakers, Joel leans back and lets out an anguished groan. He asks himself, "What did I ever do to the creator of *Grandpa Hoops*?"

That's my show! It's about an old dude who gets hit by lightning during reconstructive knee surgery and suddenly finds that he can dunk. He gets signed by the Brooklyn Nets to a contract and becomes a sensation, bringing an old-timey playing style to the modern-day NBA. It's *Rookie of the Year* meets *Eddie* with just a pinch of *Synecdoche, New York*.

When I pitched this idea to my lawyer he informed me that you cannot use someone else's name as your production company without permission. Dreams die so easily sometimes and another one faded away with a whimper that afternoon.

Let me say at this juncture that I sincerely believe Billy Joel is a nice enough guy in real life. I listened to the audiobook of his authorized biography and I respect him as a person. He wasn't handed anything, he did the work, he cracked the code, then stayed in the game and he's still doing it. Billy Joel is perfectly harmless, unless you happen to be a Long Island house near a road that Billy Joel drives down regularly.

But my mailman is a nice enough guy and I wouldn't want to hear his band! And as a sidebar: CAN YOU STOP LEAVING PACKAGES SITTING ON THE PORCH WHEN IT IS CLEAR NOBODY IS HOME? JUST STICK THEM IN THE BUSHES!

The point of this chapter isn't for me to evaluate Billy's music or my mailman or my production company. I want to tell you about the first time I went into New York City without parental supervision.

I was fourteen at the time, in the process of closing out a completely mediocre middle school run. My grades were horrible and I was pretty much invisible to everyone except a few like-minded dorks whose purpose was to make fun of everyone whose social status outranked us, which was pretty much everybody.

It was not pretty. If my school status was measured on a seven-tiered chart, I would've landed somewhere on the lower end of the sixth tier. I wasn't at the absolute bottom of the charts but I was just one embarrassing moment—me spilling a bowl of cafeteria soup on my unexpectant crotch, earning me a not-clever but accurate nick-name like "Soup Crotch"—away from the cellar. So I was more than a little shocked when a classmate named Dave asked me if I wanted to see Billy Joel at Madison Square Garden. Dave and two of my classmates—William and Keith—had an extra ticket. Dave was cool, one of the rare birds that managed to have half-decent musical taste while excelling at sports.

William and Keith were another story. They were straight-up jocks, cool guys that threw Actual Parties and drank beer with older kids. I had never been to any of their parties and I wasn't a part of their world. I thought guys like William and Keith kinda sucked, to be honest. They seemed to have everything figured out but they weren't funny or interesting. I'm pretty sure they felt the same way about me, if they had any idea I was even sharing a school with them.

It didn't dawn on me until now that this trio must've asked every-one at our school to take the ticket off their hands. I'm sure I was somewhat aware of this home truth back then but at that point any conflict would've been drowned out by the opportunity to see an actual rock concert in New York City without my parents.

I wasn't a big Billy Joel fan by any stretch. I had one or two of his albums and considered him to be perfectly fine, but definitely not one of my faves. I remember enjoying his album *Glass Houses*, which was Billy's answer to punk. I'm not sure what question he thought punk was asking him. Or why punk would even be talking to him. But answer he did, with hardcore slammers like "You May Be Right" and "It's Still Rock and Roll to Me," punk chestnuts that got the pits moshing from coast to coast.

We took a New Jersey Transit train from New Brunswick into Penn Station. I had actually spent plenty of time in New York City by this point; my parents would go into "the city" (how every New Jerseyan refers to NYC) to buy wholesale T-shirts in the garment district for their T-shirt store. Afterward we would head over to Katz's Deli on Houston Street to eat oversized sandwiches. It was here that I learned the value of tipping: If you dropped a dollar in the tip cup while placing your order you would be rewarded with a huge plate of the greatest pickles on earth.

We would all sit down to eat, staring at the endless framed photos of celebrities that covered every inch of the restaurant. "Dad, it's Mr. T holding a pastrami sandwich! And look! There's that up-and-coming weatherman Al Roker!" Eating at Katz's might be my favorite childhood memory, along with the time my family saw a young couple get into a lovers' quarrel in a local McDonald's parking lot. I must've been six or seven at the time but I remember it like it was yesterday, which is a miracle considering my sputtering brain. (More on this later!) The woman jumped out of the car and started whipping a bagful of cheeseburgers one at a time at the guy's Camaro. The burgers hit both the car and the window of the McDonald's. I recall a hamburger patty sliding down, leaving a streak of ketchup in its wake. It was my version of the baby stroller rolling down the steps in *Battleship Potemkin*, an iconic image forever burned into my mind. I was in paradise.

We stepped off the train and found ourselves in Midtown Manhattan. This was 1984, so NYC was still only a handful of years removed from the Son of Sam and the blackout and all the other things that New Yorkers from that era have fetishized into oblivion. We had a few hours to kill, so I assumed we would walk around and look at crap like the Empire State Building until the MSG doors opened.

But William had other ideas. "Let's go to Times Square."

Times Square?! That area of New York that is all peep booths and porno theaters? Why did he want to go to Times Square?

"I want to buy a switchblade."

Now just remember, I'm pretty much a child at this point. This was my first time in Manhattan without my parents. And now our self-appointed leader has declared that we will be heading directly into the belly of the beast? I was terrified but I didn't know what other options I had. I was punching so far above my weight by merely hanging with these guys that I didn't want to blow it by whining about how if we went to Times Square we could end up on the wrong end of a dude like Ramrod, the star of the exploitation pay-cable classic *Vice Squad*.

So we walked the dozen or so blocks into Times Square. It might've seen even worse days, but it was still incredibly scummy. Almost impossible to imagine that M&M'S World would someday rise from its sleazy ashes. And at this point I wonder what my parents were thinking sending a fourteen-year-old to New York City without adult supervision. Hadn't they seen *Vice Squad*?!

We landed on a corner and looked around, a quartet of clearly dumb, clearly suburban children overwhelmed by what was in front of them. But this didn't stop William from immediately transforming into Travis Bickle Jr. Somehow he managed to fit into the mosaic of sleaze and depravity; he looked around like he was there to conduct Street Business. And within seconds, a sketchy guy ran up to us.

The guy looked William up and down before asking what he needed. William told him he wanted a switchblade, zero hesitation in his voice. I had no idea why he would want a switchblade—did he plan on puncturing an offending kickball during gym class?—but to his credit, he somehow knew how to ask for one. I was impressed.

The street guy answered. "Okay, a switchblade. Thirty dollars."

This was too pricey for William, who somehow knew the going rate for a switchblade. "No," he answered firmly.

"Okay, twenty dollars," our concierge of scum countered.

William agreed. Twenty dollars for a switchblade.

"Okay, wait here," the guy said as he ran off.

We waited a couple of minutes. Then our guy came running toward us clutching a rolled-up paper bag. He was clearly in a panic. Was he on the run from the cops? Were we about to be accessories to a crime?!

"Gimme the money! Gimme the money!" he shouted as his head frantically swiveled from side to side. William handed him the cash as the guy pulled up William's pant leg and stuffed the paper bag into his sock—which I'm sure was a dopey white tube sock with three stripes at the top—before pulling his pants down over the contraband. The guy ran off in a flash, returning to his sleazy origins.

We were now buzzing. Look, I had never even seen a switchblade in person, let alone tried to buy one. But a kid my age had just navigated a sea of depravity and got a switchblade at the price he demanded. The gulf between me and the cool kids was wider than ever but for the first time I was a party to the action. I was in the shit and it was invigorating. William declared that we couldn't inspect the switchblade out in the open, so our underage foursome navigated the mean streets of NYC until we found a nearby department store.

William hurried into the men's room and stood in front of a urinal as we all hovered near the door. He pulled the paper bag from his sock and reached inside. We couldn't see a thing, but William's reaction told the tale. The bathroom was quiet for a second, until he yelled "SHIT!" and stomped out past us. I approached the urinal. Lying at its base was a Mounds bar.

I remember feeling an immediate rush of satisfaction. Mr. Cool himself had just majorly eaten shit, overpaying for a candy bar by about nineteen bucks. And it wasn't bad enough that two of his fellow jocks had witnessed it; the whole debacle happened in the presence of me! One of the losers! I saw a kid who was raised to believe he was better than everyone else turf out harder than either of us could have ever imagined.

We slowly made our way back toward Madison Square Garden, William leaking enthusiasm for the concert with every passing minute. Crowds were already forming on 34th Street, a sea of Joel-heads waiting to receive communion from their raccoon-eyed deity. Mixed among the throngs were a few scalpers hoping to flip unwanted tickets for a fast score.

William decided to cash out early. He stepped up to one of the scalpers and said, "I've got one." The scalper checked out William's ticket before handing it back to him with a superior laugh. "No thanks. That is literally the worst seat in Madison Square Garden." He wasn't wrong. Upon entering the arena we quickly discovered our seats were in the last row of the upper deck directly behind the stage. We were in the section that most performers simply don't put on the market because the seats are so undeniably shitty. But Billy Joel didn't play by the rules, apparently feeling that it was perfectly fine for somebody to buy a ticket to one of his shows only to see the back of his drummer, Liberty DeVitto, for the entire night.

William had now lost two times in a couple of hours and decided that his only option was to chase a good time no matter what. He returned from the concession stand holding a beer the size of a bucket and immediately started chugging. And just in case you forgot, William was FOURTEEN YEARS OLD, tops. Did he look old? No! He looked like a somewhat muscular fourteen-year-old! Nevertheless, William downed the vat of beer with the confident expertise of a dad on a riding lawnmower.

The concert started. Was it good? I don't know. At that point in my life it was enough that I was at Madison Square Garden watching a real concert without my parents. I had been to shows in New Jersey but this felt like a big deal. I do remember really not liking *An Innocent Man*, Billy's most recent album at the time. This was his "remember the good old days" album. It had one song that was like a terrible version of a Four Seasons song, that other song that was like a terrible version of a Temptations song, and one number that can only be described as "even worse doo-wop."

Halfway into the show, Billy ambled to the back end of the stage to face our sad portion of the crowd. We were no longer looking at the drummer's bald spot. We were face-to-face with Billy himself. He stepped up to a lone keyboard and played a song just for us, the suckers in the worst seats in the house. I think it was "Just the Way You Are," maybe his most nauseating song. Once the number finished he bounded back to the front of the stage to entertain the rest of the audience with unobstructed sight lines.

Things only got worse with William. He got his hands on a second beer and was getting drunker by the minute. His once-impressive chugging had slowed down and he eventually slumped forward in his seat, his beer lazily spilling all over the tour program Dave had just purchased. Dave was pissed off but there was no getting through to William. Our rock concert experience was falling apart fast. But they say that a problem never comes along without a gift in its hand, and our gift arrived in the form of an enterprising young security guard. He approached us with a sense of duty. Was he there to lend some aid to the fourteen-year-old suffering from alcohol poisoning? Fuck no! He asked if we wanted to see the concert from the floor. Why, yes! Yes we did!

He said that for ten bucks a head he could get us into some prime floor seats for the remainder of the concert. The three of us slapped the money in his hand—William was now completely immobile and uninterested—and promptly followed him through a series of stairwells and corridors. Before we knew it we were on the floor of Madison Square Garden, directly in the middle of the action. Everyone was dancing and singing along to the music. And standing right in front of us on the stage was the Piano Man himself. We watched the concert the way it was meant to be seen. And everything was admittedly pretty great!

This lasted for about two minutes. Another security guard—clearly not a member of "Operation Sneak Jersey Douchebags onto the Garden Floor"—asked to see our tickets. We showed him our sorry stubs and were immediately bounced back to the upper deck. We returned to find William literally sleeping in his seat, passed out from all that Michelob. We found the first security guard and to his credit he gave us a refund. Actually, "to his credit" might be a little generous. He must've taken one look at us and realized that these kids had the Crybaby Gene coursing through their DNA and would shoot their mouths off to his boss.

The rest of the show went by in a blur. William slowly awoke from his beer-soaked haze and we made our way back to Penn

Station. Everyone was tired and more than a little uneasy about the day we had just spent together. I said goodbye to my concert-mates once the train pulled back into New Brunswick. Nothing changed in regard to my social standing. I was never invited to any of their parties, spending the rest of the summer decidedly outside their orbit.

But things did change between me and William. He would go on to be shitty to all my peers, pulling rank the way only a high school jock can. But I always got a pass. He would say hi to me and actually treated me with a modicum of decency. I was exempt because he never forgot that *I knew.*

CHAPTER FOUR

HIGH SCHOOL

HALFWAY THROUGH EIGHTH grade I attended a high school basketball game in my hometown. I have no idea why I was there. At this point in my life I was interested in two things: music and comedy. I bought records with increasingly frantic regularity, obsessively checking out bands that I read about in music magazines. I was rapidly putting together a record collection and a musical aesthetic, although at the time I was just as likely to buy an Emerson, Lake & Palmer album as I was to pick up something by Hüsker Dü or Frankie Goes to Hollywood. I was just as enthusiastic about comedy. I had a small TV in my room, so I watched whatever I wanted whenever I wanted. I remember seeing the first episode of David Letterman and feeling like there was finally a talk show that was made for me, one that crapped on anything and everything. *SCTV* was another huge influence, one that I've never really outgrown. It's funny when you look at yourself super deep into adulthood to realize you're just a slightly creakier version of your thirteen-year-old self.

I liked basketball but I preferred watching the NBA to actually participating in the sport. I had never felt any connection to school sports; I saw no appeal to a sport played by kids who had to beg parking lot creeps to buy them a six-pack. I really have no clue what I was doing at this game. Something else must've been going down; maybe I'd heard a rumor that the refs were going to reveal the name of the new Indiana Jones movie during halftime?

I was sitting in the bleachers with a few friends. Nothing specific jumps out at me regarding the actual game, but I'll assume the players were terrible and the play was horrible and the score was 7–4 after three quarters of play. During a break in what passed for "the action," our group was approached by a cluster of older kids led by a high school junior named Donald.

Donald was a mountain of a young man, simultaneously overweight and muscular, bringing to mind a trashy suburban Kingpin from *Daredevil*. Donald lived in a run-down apartment complex a few blocks from my house, the kind of place you hesitated before walking through alone. I'm sure a couple of my stolen bikes ended up in some sort of junior chop shop in the bowels of the Hamilton Apartments. Nobody called Donald by his given name. Everybody called him "Doodles." I have no idea how he got his nickname and I was too scared to ask.

Doodles hovered over our lowly pack of eighth graders with a menacing intent.

"You guys're in eighth grade, right?"

Yeah, someone in our group answered.

"So next year you graduate from middle school."

Another muted confirmation before Doodles got down to business.

"Let me tell you what's up. We're gonna get you guys. If you go to Middlesex High, *he's* gonna get you." Doodles pointed at one of his crew, a scary kid named Kenny. I think Kenny might've punched a fist into his open palm at this point, but that sounds like something I saw a bully do in a movie.

"And if you go to Vo-Tech," Doodles continued, "*I'm* gonna get you."

And with that they strutted away. I'm sure none of them ever gave a second thought to their threats. But that night an all-encompassing fear overtook me. I was terrified! I didn't want to get got!

This also marked the first time I gave any consideration to attending Vo-Tech. For those not in the know, "Vo-Tech" is a vocational/technical school. They teach kids trades like automotive repair and welding, which—surprise!—are not skills that I had any interest in. At that point in my life, the closest thing I had to a technical skill was running up the score on Asteroids by leaving one small rock intact and zipping my ship in a fast upward motion so I could blow up the invading spaceships over and over.

But that night I lay in bed, wondering about which school I would attend for the next four years of my life, based solely on how brutal a punishment would be meted out by Doodles and his crew. *Sure, I always assumed I'd attend high school after middle school. And yeah, if I go to Vo-Tech I probably won't be playing a whole lot of Dungeons & Dragons or focusing on things I'm good at, like reading or writing. But perhaps Doodles will bestow a kindness upon me if I polish his welding mask.*

I'm not putting down Vo-Tech. They teach real life skills, and I'm sure kids graduated vocational school more prepared to become actual adults than anyone at my school. The only thing of any value that I took away from high school was my ability to type. I was great at it. I'm not too shabby these days, but man, you should've seen me back then. I'm not exaggerating when I say I was a typing artist; Fred Astaire's feet never graced a floor as elegantly as my digits danced across those keys. But other than that, high school was a straight-up bust. That dump would've been better off teaching some of those actual Vo-Tech skills. At the very least I could defend myself against Kenny if I knew my way around an impact wrench.

I eventually settled on attending high school. But once I got there, the true horror quickly became apparent: Kenny was not going to be the problem. I don't know if I ever saw him again. Come to think of it, Kenny looked considerably older than anyone else in my high school. Kind of like John Travolta's crew in *Grease*, a collection of sweaty midthirties actors sucking in their guts as the gang dances around the auto-body shop singing "Greased Lightning," the whole time silently praying that their trick knee doesn't give out mid-shimmy. Maybe Kenny was pulling a *21 Jump Street* at my school but I never got confirmation.

No, the problem was every meathead football player kicking off their junior and senior years. They were huntsmen and the incoming class of freshman boys all sported targets on our backs. The bullying started early. I'd hear stories of my classmates getting shoved into lockers and knocked around in the hallways by the older kids but I hadn't seen any of it firsthand, so I hoped this was just faulty reporting from my fellow children.

I learned that the rumors were all too true about a month into the school year. My pathetic crew was sitting in the cafeteria during lunch, eating our gruel and drinking our swill. Suddenly a line of football players stood in the cafeteria doorway, scanning the room. Each of these sacks of chuck was bigger than the next, and all of them were completely menacing. They looked like the cast of *Dazed and Confused* if it was populated with actual ugly high school jocks instead of Ben Affleck. After a horrible beat they zeroed in on our table.

The group I ran with in high school was a very singular lot. We weren't popular. (What?! No way!) We weren't athletes. We weren't burnouts, smoking cigarettes in the parking lot. And we weren't particularly smart. It was a true "bottom of the barrel" situation, a cluster of misfits whose only talent was to make fun of the popular kids and athletes and burnouts and jocks and smart kids while wishing the whole time that any of us would be invited to be a part of literally ANYTHING.

We were chum in the water. They approached our table and told us that in a few minutes we would be running a race out on the football field, so we'd better get our asses outside pronto. Next thing you know, there we were, lined up along the end zone, wondering what was going to happen.

One of these vicious pricks stood out. His name was Ronny Daly and he was particularly cruel; the bullying was clearly filling a void in his soul. Ronny looked kind of like Jay Jay French from Twisted Sister, the guy in the band with the rooster haircut and tinted aviator shades. I always thought Twisted Sister sucked shit, but their guitarist's resemblance to Ronny only heightened my dislike.

Ronny told us to line up as he explained the rules of the competition. The race was to the opposite end of the football field and back, and we had better try hard *or else*. I was ready to try hard, because I didn't want to get sucker punched in the hallway. I decided that I would run this race as if my life depended on it. Look out, Flo Jo, here comes Tom Jo!

One of the apes screamed "GO!" and I would not be denied. I ran as fast as I could, bolting ahead of my friends. I reached the far end of the football field and began running back toward the starting point, looking at some of my classmates still lumbering through the first half of the race. They'd have to sort out who was coming in second, but that wasn't my problem. I was gonna win this race! And as I crossed the finish line, I felt a surge of security. I was safe.

Ronny Daly pointed at me as if I were a steer at a cattle auction. "You. You came in first, so get ready for the next round."

The next round?! I was sucking air like nobody's business, and now I had to run again? *Come on, Ronny, you're a football player— you've never heard of bye weeks?* Thankfully a luxury car pulled into the parking lot alongside the football field and the school principal got out. I guess he had seen enough. The jocks slowly dispersed and I never had to run that second race. But the bullying was just getting started. The meatheads would pick on us on a near-daily basis. Making us sing songs in the cafeteria. Making us "hold our packages" as we lined up to wish a popular freshman girl "happy birthday." She laughed and they hooted and howled as we shrunk deeper into our individual and collective pits of shame. What could we do? Any notion of standing up to these buffoons was yanked off the table when a fellow freshman named Chris got ambushed.

The way I heard it, Chris was at the ShopRite—probably buying some off-brand orange soda like high schoolers do—when he was intercepted by Ronny and a couple of other jocks. They trapped him against the front window of the store and told him to climb on top of the long row of shopping carts stacked against the glass. They wanted him to dance. Chris scoffed at the notion—it was nighttime! Outside of school grounds! The rules of bullying didn't apply!—and made a move to walk past them.

That's when one of the guys unleashed a karate-style kick and caught Chris square in the throat. There's always one high school dickhead that studies martial arts just so they can beat up people in unexpected ways. "Yeah, that's right—I just knocked you out with a spin kick! Hold on, what's that you say? I'm only supposed to use this for self-defense? But did you *see* me kick that dude in the throat? It was sick!" So Chris climbed his way on top of the shopping carts and did a dance.

There was no break from the bullies; we had to be on guard at all times. The first thing to go was lunch. We could no longer eat in the cafeteria, where we were sitting ducks waiting to get plucked.

Sometimes we'd eat in the school library, hunching around the corner so a jock passing down the hall couldn't see us through the rectangular glass panels on the library doors. This was nobody's idea of a good time, but it kept us off the football field. The true low point was when someone in our group mentioned that his mom worked in an office directly next to the high school, so we started hiding in the backseat of her parked car, shoving our sad lunches into our sadder faces.

I would assume that you—or anyone with a semi-functional moral compass—would be asking themselves: WHERE WERE THE TEACHERS DURING ALL THIS? And to that I answer, "GOOD

QUESTION!" I remember that a couple of the gym teachers thought it was legitimately hilarious whenever the seniors went after us. But there was one school employee on our side: Mrs. King, the librarian. One lunch period we were hiding in the library when a couple of jocks decided to stick their heads in. They found us sitting with our bag lunches splayed open, a look of knowing doom spreading across our faces. They told us to get to the cafeteria immediately.

Mrs. King saw all this go down and promptly lost her shit. She screamed, "THESE BOYS AREN'T GOING ANYWHERE! LEAVE THEM ALONE! GET OUT!!" and the jocks sheepishly left us in the library. I would imagine one of them did the sneaky throat-slit gesture behind her back to say, "You nerds are dead!" but my faulty memory can't confirm it.

Look, I wasn't doing myself any favors back then. I come from humble working stock, generation after generation of self-employed working stiffs that made enough money to put food on the table and keep a roof over our heads. This is how my parents had learned to survive, and I was ultimately no different; when I hit thirteen I did what every newly christened teenager does and promptly got a job bussing tables at the town diner. At one point I was logging about twenty hours a week, completely under the table. Sure, I was missing out on being a child but I was flush with cash. The Emerson, Lake & Palmer records flowed like water!

But there was an undeniable dollars-for-dignity exchange going on. It's not a good look when your classmates watch you wipe down tables and lug plastic tubs filled with their dirty dishes with hands stained by someone else's ketchup. That job lasted for about two years, until I finally had my fill of getting yelled at by Bill, the owner, a guy who looked like Peter Cushing if he were an angry Greek grill jockey. Bill once screamed at me in front of the entire staff for asking one of the cooks to put a few fried onions on the free hamburger the diner generously included in my employment package, which did wonders for my thirteen-year-old self-esteem.

But self-esteem was clearly low on the list of priorities for Young Tom, because I started working as a janitor's assistant at my high school during my freshman year.

Let that sink in for a second. For a few days a week I would empty trash cans and clean the hallways at my own high school. You could feasibly sit next to me in science class, just another high school student, and then a couple of hours later pass me in the hallway, now dressed in dark blue zip-up janitor wear, spraying toxic chemicals on my oversized push broom. It was a real superhero-type transformation, kind of like what it must be like to go to school with Spider-Man, except I must've gotten bitten by a radioactive mop.

But they say membership has its privileges. And being a charter member in the High School Student's Janitor Society afforded me one very distinct benefit: I had keys to every classroom, and that meant I could root through every unlocked file cabinet and drawer and snoop to my heart's content.

And snoop I did. I flipped through teachers' grade books and folders. I discovered the essays students wrote at the outset of the school year in which they told the story of their life, an apparent effort by the English teacher to get to know their pupils better. But any chance to gain a leg up on the bullies wasn't going to be found here, primarily because my classmates were all boring. The dumb jocks wrote about stuff from the worldview of a dumb jock. I don't know if I thought I'd find some magic bullet—*"The sad truth about my life is that I'm a bully because I suffer from something doctors call 'Ken Doll Syndrome,' which means I have no genitals to speak of. You're the only one I've ever told about this, dearest teacher. If any of my classmates ever found out about this I'd be ruined"*—but it was all as boring as a postcard a kid would send from summer camp.

Even seeing the grades was meaningless—*Oh, wow! Russell is only getting a C+ in Algebra!* And I certainly wasn't going to change any of the grades; I was just there for observation, like those perverts at a hotel that walk extra slowly past the fitness center. Besides, those hallways weren't going to buff themselves, so I set down the grade book and returned to the push broom.

One of the side effects of getting bullied is the rising climate of meanness among the victims. We had tons of pent-up frustration and sadness, and it needed to go somewhere. So we made fun of one another. It was brutal, nerds positively destroying fellow nerds over any personal flaw or difference. This was around the time I realized that I was able to generate funny thoughts and comments at a more effective level than most of my classmates, so I could demolish my crew of friends with surprising ease. But they dished it out more viciously than I did, and their relative lack of verbal skills led them to create a physical game that satisfied their desperate need to hurt anyone because they were tired of getting hurt.

The game they invented was called "Pen Wars," which is not much more than what it sounds like. In a nutshell, you would take a pen and draw on an unsuspecting "friend" when they least expected it. I was a marginal participant in this majestic sport, occasionally sneaking up alongside a friend and marking up their arm before scampering away like a mischievous elf. Thankfully I didn't go all the way in on Pen Wars; I remember watching my peers literally stabbing at each other with markers, aiming for their opponent's foreheads. I wasn't the only one watching; I recall seeing looks on the faces of some nonparticipants in school, and it made me feel like such a failure to be even vaguely associated with this crowd. When the student who is also a high school janitor thinks you're a loser, you've got some real problems.

The avenues available to strike back at the actual bullies were virtually nonexistent. One of the only moves at my disposal played to all my strengths, which at that point were being funny and being a little crafty: prank phone calls. I started dialing up the homes of these jocks. The action generally went down at my friend Edward's house, because he had a phone extension so the non-pranker could listen in. Once his parents went to bed, out came the phone book and the party got underway.

The best pranks were aimed at the parents of the bullies. I'm not saying that they were necessarily fooled by any of the calls, but just knowing that you could create a little chaos for these dipshit meathead bullies provided a well-needed taste of power. The jerks who spawned the jerks who were making my life a nonstop horror show were finally getting theirs. A call would generally go something like this:

[*The phone rings*]

BULLY'S MOTHER [*groggy*]: Hello?

YOUNG TOM [*trying to sound old*]: Uh, yes. Hello. This is Officer Albertson from the police department. I'm calling about your son.

BULLY'S MOTHER: Wait, who is this?

YOUNG TOM: Officer Albertson. I'm a police officer. I'm an adult. We picked your son up tonight. He was selling drugs in the McDonald's parking lot.

BULLY'S MOTHER [*yelling*]: Glenn, pick up!

[*A phone extension picks up*]

BULLY'S FATHER: It's two in the morning, who is this?

YOUNG TOM: I'm a policeman. Officer—

BULLY'S FATHER: You're not a cop. Who is this?

YOUNG TOM: I'm, uh . . . YOUR SON IS A PIECE OF SHIT!

[*Tom hangs up, laughing victoriously*]

What were you expecting, a battery of Dorothy Parker bon mots? I was a freshman in high school fighting back against the villains beneath cover of night, like a dial tone Batman. And the parents of these bullies weren't the only people getting pranked; we dialed up gas stations and Dunkin' Donuts and 800 numbers, which clearly paved the way for my love of radio pranks and phone calls and all the ridiculousness that I'm still involved in.

But it wasn't all candy bars and cream soda; at the core of every prank phone call is one defining statement: I AM GOING TO WASTE YOUR TIME, PERSON FOOLISH ENOUGH TO PICK UP THEIR OWN PHONE WHEN IT RANG. Most of the time it was ridiculous; I never did anything horrible like breathing heavy or making threats. No sex or violence over here, just good old-fashioned phone hijinks. Although one time I realized I was not the dial tone Batman I thought I was. I was more of a dial tone Joker. Or maybe a dial tone Riddler—I'm not sure what the difference is; I grew up reading Marvel. But needless to say I was the bad guy.

It started when I noticed a "Harrison, George" listed in the phone book. I had stumbled across a gold mine and quickly dialed. The groggy person on the other end—remember, this call is going down between 1:00 and 3:00 A.M.—answered, unsure of what exactly was happening. I asked if I had reached George, and the guy said yes. Then I broke out the heavy comedy guns by asking if Paul McCartney was also there. I could hear the life drain out of George's voice as he wearily replied, "Please don't do this." The reality of this guy's situation hit me like a ton of bricks and I immediately stammered out a sincere "I'm so sorry" before he hung up.

If the prank phone call was a coward's way of enacting revenge, I was presented with a slightly more in-person opportunity to zing the jocks at a midnight screening of *The Rocky Horror Picture Show*. Like so many disaffected suburban youths in the 1980s, I invariably found my way to my local movie theater to experience the *Rocky Horror* phenomenon. For those who don't know, *The Rocky Horror Picture Show* was a musical that combined science fiction and horror and gender fluidity and a young Susan Sarandon and Tim Curry. The movie bombed during its initial release but found a second life on the midnight movie circuit, where the audience would dress up like the characters and shout out dirty replies to the film dialogue and throw stuff at the screen. It was the '80s equivalent of cramming into a phone booth or eating goldfish on a flagpole. You know, the dumb stuff that bored kids do.

Every midsize town had some kind of *Rocky Horror* screening on Friday and Saturday nights. Our local production wasn't as extravagant as New York City's, which was rumored to conclude in a full blood orgy in which an unsuspecting first-timer (known as a "virgin") would be literally sacrificed on an altar. But it wasn't nothing; the cast of local enthusiasts dressed like the characters and danced and jumped around at the base of the screen in sync with the film.

After seeing the movie a few times, I kinda knew the *Rocky Horror* thing wasn't really speaking to me. But it was something to do on a Friday night, and I was getting a handle on some of the lines the regulars would shout at the movie. The final time I saw the film I noticed that a group of the football players from my school were entering the theater, with Ronny Daly leading the way. "Why are they here?" I asked my friend. "This isn't their scene!" I slumped down in my seat, praying that they wouldn't spot me. The last thing I needed was to get the shit beat out of me in the movie theater parking lot as the guy playing Dr. Frank N. Furter looked on. Thankfully the lights went down before they caught me.

I had dodged a bullet by not getting spotted by the jocks. But something rattled around in my head—this was an opportunity for some revenge. I knew I had to do it. I was going to throw out a *Rocky Horror* zinger aimed squarely at my aggressors!

For those who don't know the movie, Brad and Janet are two normies whose car breaks down in a rainstorm. They hoof it to a nearby castle for help. One of the horror dudes in the castle, named Riff Raff, greets them at the door and says, "You're all wet." Janet replies, "Yes, it's raining." There's a slight pause, and Brad chimes in with a "Yes."

I saw my chance and like Steve Winwood commanded, I took it. Here's how the scene played out that night:

RIFF RAFF: You're all wet.
JANET: Yes, it's raining.

YOUNG TOM [*screaming at the screen*]: IS RONNY DALY
  AN ASSHOLE?!?!
BRAD: Yes.

It was a magical moment. I shouted out my joke during a particularly quiet stretch of the movie, so it ran unopposed. If Ronny was paying attention, there is no way he didn't hear it. The triumph of sticking the landing was immediately replaced by abject terror, as I waited to see if Ronny Daly would begin patrolling the aisles looking for his accuser. I slumped down in my seat and waited. And I kept waiting, because a whole lot of nothing happened. I watched the rest of the movie with my friends in peace and we slid out of the theater to safety with no confrontation from any of the football shitbags.

The remainder of my freshman year was wildly anticlimactic. The bullying eventually slowed down to a trickle. There were no more races and we were able to eat in the cafeteria without trouble. Once in a while an unknowing dweeb would get his books slapped out of his hand in a crowded hallway, but the threat had passed. The reality of the situation was that the jocks had other things on their minds. Once these dummies were done with football and basketball and baseball, they had to face the harsh reality of leaving the cocoon of high school to find themselves back at the bottom of their own ladder, whether that meant becoming a freshman in college or trying to find a job in the real world.

As my freshman year concluded, I forewarned a friend one year younger than me to watch out, because high school was brutal. He was going to get picked on, so he should make his peace with the unending nightmare that was right around the corner. But the bullying never came for him. It somehow stopped with our class, as if that crop of seniors was the problem. Or maybe *we* were the problem, a group of freshmen so annoying that something had to be done. Whatever the case might have been, I recently found out that Ronny Daly is the principal of an elementary school in a neighboring state. I'm tempted to show up at his place of work and walk him out to the football field and make him race against himself as the children under his charge watch and laugh. Then I'd ask the kids, "Is your principal an asshole?" A helicopter would land at the fifty-yard line and Barry Bostwick would step out and reprise his performance as Brad, saying in a definitive voice, "Yes," before getting back into the chopper and returning to Los Angeles.

CHAPTER FIVE

IT ALL FALLS APART

I SETTLED INTO the rhythm of a high school sophomore. Everything was a grey smear of mediocrity; I had no interest in any subject outside my beloved typing class, and it showed in my grades. I was in educational free fall, going from "outstanding student" to "okay student" to "student that needs to apply himself." It was like being washed up before you even got started:

> *"You had a good run, kid. But your arm is shot. You just don't have the fastball anymore."*
>
> *"What!? But I only threw two pitches! How can it be over already?"*
>
> *"It just is. Hit the showers, kid."*

It's not like school held some great fascination for me anyway. Like I said, I was interested in only music and comedy. However, my love of music never really went past fandom; the thought of actually *making* music didn't add up. It wasn't for lack of trying: I started learning bass guitar but didn't have the guts to do much with it outside my bedroom. The notion of getting together with other kids and starting a band was absolutely terrifying. There was an attempt at some sort of group that didn't go much further than a few practices and a handful of songs played in the drummer's driveway as a loose cluster of classmates looked on with palpable indifference. There's nothing more embarrassing than watching a group of virgins play "Feel Like Making Love," unless you're actually *in* the band of virgins. You feel like making love, eh? No shit, you're fourteen and all you think about is Lacey Underall's scene from *Caddyshack*.

Unlike music, comedy was always something I knew I could actually create, but I didn't have any idea how or where to do it. I never had a desire to do stand-up but I knew I was funny in a way that most other kids weren't. I could connect a concept to a person and thread thoughts together and they usually made people laugh. My attempts at comedy were expressed in strange ways. There was a social studies project that our teacher assigned to the class: We would break off into groups of four and write a slavery-based story that was to take place during the Civil War. (Nice assignment, weird white teacher!) I immediately overcame my mopey shyness and took the reins. If ever there was an assignment in my wheelhouse, this was it.

I devised a story about a vicious plantation owner that treated his slaves with cruelty. The slaves united and staged a revolt, eventually chasing the slave owner into a barn. In an attempt to escape, the plantation owner fell into a cotton gin. The cotton gin was churning out bale after bale of cotton in perfectly formed cubes that rolled down a conveyor belt. Suddenly the cotton gin sputtered and sparked as it spit out the plantation owner, who had been squished into the shape of a bloody cotton-bale-size cube.

Please keep in mind that I didn't—and still don't!—know what a cotton gin looks like or how it works. It also seems safe to assume that they didn't have conveyor belts in the 1860s. But none of that mattered to me. I had come up with an amazing story. It had action, violence, thrills, and a happy ending. I was bloodily rewriting history, combining the brutality of Tarantino with the cartoonish comeuppance of Bugs Bunny.

None of the other students took the creative initiative that I had, and they lazily read their presentations to the rest of the class, receiving a middling response. I felt good, knowing that our team had a masterpiece up our sleeves. Our names were called and we sat at the front of the classroom. I started reading our story and immediately felt something I had never experienced: the slow car-crash vibe of truly bombing. Every moment was vivid, from the looks of confusion on my classmates' faces to the disappointment in my teacher's eyes. Literally nobody liked the story. The members of my team began to distance themselves from my Civil War epic by staring at their hands. My memory is extremely rickety in so many ways—you'll find out why soon enough!—but I can recall how the air felt in that classroom as if it happened last week. We bombed and we bombed *hard*. And this was the moment I launched my career in comedy.

My real problems had to do with my mental health. I always had a passing relationship with sadness for most of my life. As an adult I try to focus on moving forward and finding solutions for the future instead of getting stuck in the past, but so much of that sunny attitude is a conscious counterbalance, me working over-time to offset my natural unhappiness. So much of it goes back to growing up with my mom being sick. I'm not gonna go too far into details because it's her story to tell, but for most of my life she has dealt with a series of blood-related diseases that have kept her in near-constant pain and distress.

A couple of things about my mother: She is literally the strongest person I know. Nobody comes close. Her health issues should've taken her out years ago. The sheer number of surgeries and proce-dures and transfusions she underwent throughout her life would've been enough to convince anybody else to give up. But she always refused to fold. No matter how much pain she was in, she would be up and about, doing whatever had to be done. Only in quiet moments would she reveal how much pain she was truly in, her arms covered with violent bruises that are one of the many brutal side effects of a blood disorder.

She also has an insane work ethic. I remember my mom lying in a hospital getting a transfusion only to drag herself to her feet and head to work as soon as the IV was detached. So much of who I am comes directly from her, from the desire to outwork any situation to the ridiculous competitive drive. She basically willed herself to stay alive. It's not hard to see how I landed on the name *The Best Show* once you get a handle on who my mother is.

As grateful as I am to have had her as my mom, it really messes with your head wondering whether today is the day your mother finally dies. It kept me in a constant state of fear, and that degree of panic hardwired a sense of fatalism into me. To this day every time the phone rings my brain automatically assumes that something terrible has happened. I have always been ready for the other shoe to drop, always waiting for everything to fall apart.

KIDS ARE RESILIENT. They can gather whatever terrible or bizarre thing is happening in their world and spin it into something that they can handle. This is what got me through so much of my life; I took all the fear and panic and pressure and just swallowed it, accepting my circumstances as nothing more than "that's how it is." The most pronounced example of this is my relationship with hospitals. I spent so much time in the hospital while my mother was getting operations or transfusions, hour after hour of waiting and worrying. The only option was to recontextualize all of this, so with a little brain magic the hospital suddenly became my friend.

I would carry around whichever science fiction book I was reading along with a notebook and just wander the entirety of the hospital, floor after floor, wing after wing. My mind would run wild.

I would create adventures, mysteries that I had to solve, a detective searching for something hidden away somewhere within this building.

I somehow twisted this ability to distract myself from the real world into a belief that I *enjoyed* spending time in hospitals. They were kinda like shopping malls that sold hospital beds and dying humans, right? I would grab some cheese crackers and a can of Coke from the bank of vending machines near the gift shop, wander the halls and just (sick) people watch. It's a good time, right? It wasn't until a few years ago that I finally allowed myself to put two and two together and consciously acknowledge that I FUCKING HATE HOSPITALS. I could never admit that back then. My mom was sick, and I wasn't gonna be the one to rock the boat.

I channeled all this frustration into trying to be as well-behaved as humanly possible. I would clean the house, do the dishes, mop the floor; I'd do whatever I could to make things easier for my mother. My sister Jill and I were so nauseatingly GOOD that one Mischief Night—the evening before Halloween when suburban kids whip eggs and toilet paper at houses and cars—we decided to stage our own anti–Mischief Night by anonymously raking the lawn of the old lady who lived a few houses down. I now realize I would've been better off spraying some shaving cream around the neighborhood, but what could I do? I was a born people pleaser, baby!

All these circumstances created a desire within me to do whatever I could to help. The immediate means of achieving this was to get a job and start working; if I had my own money I wouldn't be part of the problem. So I got a paper route at twelve, which kicked off my life as a member of the American workforce. Before long I was slinging dirty plates at the aforementioned diner, which led to me shoving a broom at my aforementioned high school. As I said, these gigs were a nightmare for my self-esteem, but they paid me enough that I didn't need a whole lot from my parents, since things were hard enough for them on the financial front.

My mother's medical bills were staggering. If our family hadn't been buried beneath piles of debt we would've been solidly middle class, but when you're racking up tens of thousands of dollars in bills for every surgery and procedure under the sun, the only direction is down. My parents worked so fucking hard, breaking their backs round the clock just to keep it all afloat. Those bills were a never-ending nightmare, but my parents kept my sister's and my life as normal as they could.

We always had food and we got to do a lot of the same stuff that other kids got to do. And I was positively swimming in HOMEWORK IS HAZARDOUS TO MY HEALTH T-shirts. But the line keeping our family from ruin was thin. Anyone with a working knowledge of human brains can surmise that swallowing these particular brands of pain and frustration and sadness without any outlet will create a pressure cooker situation in a kid.

It all started falling apart in middle school. I was taking a test in science class. I finished up early, walked my paper to the front of the classroom, and returned to my desk. I put my head down for a minute, only to realize that my neck had seized up. I could not move. I was literally paralyzed! A wave of terror took over, equal parts *Why can't I move my neck?* and *How do I ask for help without my jerkoff classmates making fun of me?* I decided that screaming in horror wasn't the answer, so I kept my head down and sat perfectly still, trying to block out the pain.

Eventually the period bell rang and the classroom cleared. The teacher must've noticed that one of the young dummies was still sitting at his desk with his head down. As he approached I croaked out a limp "I can't move." The school nurse was summoned and I was transferred to a wheelchair, then rolled dramatically down the hallway with my head bent to the side, past the entire school. So much for my plan to keep this situation under the radar!

My mother rushed to the school and drove me to the hospital. A doctor checked me out and determined there was nothing identifiably wrong with my neck. They gave me some pills and a foam neck brace that wouldn't have been out of place on a sitcom in which a middle school student fakes a neck injury to get out of gym class. From that day on I dealt with a bum neck. It is completely stress-activated: If something goes wrong in my life, my neck and shoulders turn into cement, and if I rotate my neck a certain way it sounds like an LP that has finished playing—the crackle of the run-on groove repeating over and over. And if I rotate my neck the opposite way it says, "Oh sweet Satan, sweet Satan, bow to your overlord." I am proud to be a human backward masking machine, one of my most celebrated accomplishments.

My emotional issues lay dormant for a couple of years before a sweeping wave of sadness rolled in. I could get so despondent so quickly, feeling the entirety of everything at once. Yes, I know that this is something teens go through. Robert Smith wouldn't be living in a castle called "Sad Teen Manor" if our collective angst wasn't bankrolling his dressage horses. I know that a part of me liked having any sort of identity, and being a morose sixteen-year-old into Depeche Mode and Cabaret Voltaire definitely distanced me from the pack during the Reign of Springsteen, a definite challenge for a kid growing up in the Garden State during the 1980s. But my sadness quickly became something that I had no control over during the summer between my sophomore and junior years.

When you live in New Jersey there is but one family summer vacation option: the Jersey Shore. My parents would blow our vacation budget on a small shore house a block or so from the beach, a place that would consist of a couple of bedrooms, an all-purpose living/dining room, and a small kitchen. They would invite friends and relatives down for short stays within our weeklong getaway, with everybody stacked on top of one another. The overcrowding didn't matter because we spent our days on the beach and boardwalk. I swam. I played video games. I ate garbage. I played a boardwalk game in which you try to get a too-small ring to land perfectly over the mouth of a too-large glass jug, all in the hopes of winning a framed mirror with an unlicensed Van Halen logo screen printed across it. It was heaven.

I would usually sleep on the living room couch during these trips, which was perfectly fine by me. The windows would all be open and the ocean air was cool and fresh. But this is when things started to get weird for me. I started seeing things that weren't there. It began with water. As I tried to fall asleep, the room would slowly fill up with water, as if high tide had overshot the beach and rolled all the way into our rental house. But something in my mind overrode these hallucinations, assuring me that everything would be okay, that none of this was real. And I liked the ocean. So as frightening as it all was, I could handle it.

Within a few nights the water was replaced by bugs. Wave after wave of cockroaches and worms slipped beneath the front door until they blanketed the floor, a steadily rising sea of insects all clustered together, cresting and falling, rolling back and forth like the ocean. I lay stone-still on the couch; unlike the water, the bugs scared the shit out of me. They rose upward to the lip of the couch cushion. One false move and the insects would keep rising until I was enveloped. I couldn't move. They were everywhere. A tangible sense of dying crept into my brain. I didn't want to die.

My parents promptly got me a therapist, and he handed me a pile of pills. The medication kept things relatively under control. I didn't see the bugs anymore, but I didn't feel like doing a whole lot either. My world felt flattened like a pancake; I was kinda just *there*, sleepily shuffling through the remains of my summer, heading into my junior year, living life as if I were isolated behind a sheet of plexiglass.

DURING MY JUNIOR YEAR my shop teacher had a meltdown. It was the highlight of an otherwise bleak year, and as I look back it might've been the highlight of my entire life.

For the purposes of this book we will refer to him as "Mr. Morris." It pains me to change his name because his actual name is weirdly hilarious and makes the story even funnier. If you ever run into me, ask me what his real name is and maybe I'll tell you. Mr. Morris was a first-year teacher and was certainly a nice enough guy. He probably wasn't a day over thirty-four yet he might as well have been pushing sixty, a man positively glistening with the magnificence that is the Defeated American Worker, one of those guys whose every action screams, "YES, I AM FULLY AWARE THAT I BLEW IT." Mr. Morris would constantly remind his students that he "was in industry" before he took a job teaching high school, as if he was doing us all some cosmic favor by entering the educational system. He wielded this phrase as some sort of gift to us, but every kid thought the same thing: *Why aren't you* still *in industry?* Clearly something went wrong somewhere, but we never got any answers.

Mr. Morris was desperate to be liked, which is poison for a teacher. Students will like you, sure. But they like you *as a teacher.* If they think you're cool, that means you're cool *for a teacher*, not cool the way the guy working the jug toss on the boardwalk is cool. (Side note: How did I not know that those Van Halen mirrors existed solely for coke-snorting purposes? You can't comb your hair in one because the VH logo is in the way!)

The high school kids that grew out their hair and smoked cigarettes and wore flannel were called "burnouts" at our high school. Very motivating, I know. Really gave these kids something to strive for. I had virtually nothing in common with them outside of an appreciation for Led Zeppelin, and like most everything else at this point in my life, I was scared of them. But the burnouts were buddy-buddy with Mr. Morris. They would hang out in his classroom every chance they could, whether they had shop or not.

Morris tried to narrow the generational gulf between himself and his cheap-cigarette-smoking charges by indulging their hangouts and letting them play Judas Priest tapes on a boom box in the corner of the classroom. Before long they were brothers in arms: the seventeen-year-olds looking for a safe place to smoke ditch weed during school hours and the teacher desperate for a taste of the validation he clearly missed out on during his own youth. But like too many things of beauty, this was fated to end far too early.

One day Mr. Morris started drinking with the burnouts during lunch period. I can only imagine the cheap booze these underage dirtbags kept stashed in the trunks of their Camaros, but whatever they were pounding did the trick because by the time I got to shop class immediately after lunch Mr. Morris was FUCKING HAMMERED. He teetered at the front of the classroom, drunkenly attempting to teach as if nothing was out of sorts. He stood at the chalkboard, slurring his speech, lecturing us about how he used to be someone before he took this job. He returned to his tried-and-true "I was in industry" over and over, but now it was a sad soliloquy. Years later when I saw *Fargo* and Jerry Lundegaard pathetically declared to his father-in-law that "it's my deal here," all I could think of was Mr. Morris.

As I look back on it, Mr. Morris's collapse was the culmination of all the sadness and frustration in a sad guy finally bubbling over at precisely the wrong time. But back then it was the greatest thing I had ever seen in my life. I got to witness the rarest of all the rare birds, the Halley's Comet of education: a drunk teacher. As the class proceeded he started raging in all his glory, stumbling around the room, ranting like a dictator on the wrong end of a military coup. At some point someone hit play on the boom box so Mr. Morris now had side two of *Screaming for Vengeance* as his soundtrack. The classroom bell rang and it was time for me to head to study hall, my final class of the day. I thought quickly and got Mr. Morris to write me a note saying that I needed to spend my last period in shop class. There was no way I was missing the final reel of this movie.

I dropped the note off and hustled back to shop class. But in the short time I was gone the bloom had already fallen off the rose. Mr. Morris didn't look so hot anymore. His ranting had been downgraded to some quiet muttering as he sat unsteadily on a workshop stool. Then he rose to his feet and lunged himself toward a large steel garbage can. He promptly started throwing up into the can, wave after wave of bright red vomit launching from his overworked guts. After he finished barfing, he staggered into his small office and slammed the door behind him. A few minutes later the vice principal entered the workshop, the Judas Priest tape got shut off, and we were all hustled down the hall, far away from the scene of the crime.

We never saw Mr. Morris again.

I WASN'T IN MUCH of a position to judge Mr. Morris because my own brain wasn't making too many great decisions either. My mental health didn't really improve over the next year. I still had friends and lived the life of a relatively normal teenager. I worked a lot, bought records, and watched as many movies as I could on the fancy new Betamax video player I had purchased with my savings. But beneath the surface I was numb most of the time. I would get profoundly sad over the smallest things. An overwhelming hopelessness creeped into just about every aspect of my life and never went away. I was still taking a multitude of pills and the medication felt like an invisible hand that kept me pinned into place. I saw my therapist all the time, but as my senior year started, nothing ever seemed to get better.

As far as college plans went, I assumed I'd end up at Rutgers University, the college most middling New Jersey kids end up at. But I hadn't applied to Rutgers, or any other college for that matter. How could I focus on school when my brain was steadily slipping away from me?

During one therapy session I told my therapist that I couldn't take it anymore. Nothing mattered. I couldn't see any reason to keep going on. I hesitated before dropping what I knew was an atomic bomb: I told him that I wanted to kill myself. He asked me if I really meant what I had just said: Did I really want to kill myself? I said yes and he quickly arranged a meeting at a facility on the Rutgers campus. It was all a little unclear but my mother took me over for a consultation. Once I entered the facility they said they weren't going to let me leave. They gave me a choice: I could volunteer to be there for a month, or I could decline and they'd have me committed for at least a couple of months.

I weighed my options and chose to make a break for it. I ran toward the exit, but there were more of them than me, and they pinned me down. No matter how much I struggled I could not break free. I gave in and granted them permission to keep me there. The doors slammed shut behind my mother as she went home to tell my father that their son was now in a mental institution. I told you I was gonna end up at Rutgers, har har!

The ward was teeming with juvenile delinquents, legitimately bad kids who were locked in alongside me for setting things on fire and beating the shit out of teachers. So why the fuck was I locked in here? I had nothing in common with these kids! I was trying to kill myself, not other people! But once those doors were locked, it didn't matter how little we had in common. We were all passengers on the same shitty cruise.

The initial feeling that overtook me was one of extreme guilt. After a lifetime of behaving, suddenly I was a Bad Kid. That wasn't who I was, but with just a few words, I managed to turn my family upside down. It felt horrible to know how much damage I was inflicting on my parents; they had enough to worry about without having to figure out whether I was going to hurt myself. And how would they pay for my meltdown? I had made a huge mess, but all the guilt was quickly dwarfed by the waves of fear brought on by being locked in a mental institution with the cast of *Over the Edge*.

One thing that I possessed that separated me from the rest of these kids was a sense of survival. Even in my medicated state, I still had an innate ability to assess a situation and figure out how to stay afloat. It is a skill that comes from being a people pleaser at such a young age: I developed an ability to analyze any predicament with an eye toward simply staying alive. It didn't take long for me to get a handle on how things worked at the hospital. The staff was overwhelmed by the aggressively bad kids, so they had no choice but to reward good behavior. And good behavior is something I had a surplus of. Remember, I was the goody two-shoes that raked my neighbor's yard on Mischief Night!

I promptly tapped into my default setting and became as good as I could humanly be all the time. I did what was asked of me. I took every pill without hesitation and participated in every therapy session. And every single doctor and nurse on that ward fell for it. Before long I was granted special privileges for good behavior, and allowed to eat in the downstairs cafeteria with the hospital staff and walk around different floors of the building. I had cracked the code to this shithole and I ran with it, turning up the good behavior at every opportunity.

But was I getting better? FUCK NO! My survival instincts had merely kicked in. I didn't start this game but I figured out how to play it. They got exactly what they wanted to hear from me and nothing more. I still had a voice in my head whispering terrifying things to me, telling me that I needed to die, that I was a bad person. But if I wanted to get out of the hospital, I knew I couldn't tell a soul about it. I hosted a master class in giving the doctors what they wanted, and I was correct in assuming that the staff was so busy dealing with the future Fonzies in the facility that a nice quiet kid saying all the right things got marked down as a success. After a month or so they released me, smack-dab in the middle of December. Me and the voices in my head were going home for the holidays!

I EXPERIENCED A SURGE of improvement once I got home, most likely because I wasn't trapped in a fucking mental ward anymore. But I also felt embarrassed about the whole ordeal. What would I tell my classmates when I went back to school after the holiday break? Did they already know? How would I ever cobble together a "normal" senior year if everybody knew me as the kid that got locked up in the loony bin? A growing dread hung over my head, but for the time being I was just happy to be home again.

My family spent a portion of Christmas Day at my uncle's house. I sat by myself on a stool at his wet bar in the corner of the rec room, desperately wishing things could go back to how they had been; I just wanted Christmas to feel like it used to when I was a kid. I stared at a one-panel *New Yorker*–style comic framed on the wall next to the bar. It depicted a man that looked a lot like my uncle in bed with his golf clubs. His wife stood angrily in the doorway. Beneath the drawing was a caption that said something like, "Hey, you're the one who said I had to choose between you and my golf clubs!" I remember thinking two things: How insulted is my aunt by this cartoon and does my uncle actually have sex with his golf clubs?

Just then my uncle walked by and asked how I was. I started talking into my chest, trying to explain that I was having an okay time but I was a little nervous because I had been . . . away. He patted me on the shoulder and said, "You don't have to talk about it." Not in a way that meant "Hey, don't force yourself to relive the horror you just went through," but more like "Please don't talk to me about this—I came down here to get drunk." He filled his glass and rejoined the family.

I attempted a return to school in the New Year but I just couldn't do it. The sadness rolled right back in and I couldn't handle anything. I stopped going to high school and spent the next couple of months with my parents at their store, reading and sleeping in the back room while they sold WHERE'S THE BEEF? T-shirts. While my classmates were charting out their post–high school lives I was slowly transforming into an overmedicated blob. The only thing that stood out during this stretch was the upcoming high school talent show. A few of the guys I had jammed with were going to start a new band but I was so out of it that nobody asked me to join.

But that didn't mean I wasn't contemplating a performance of my own. I had come up with an idea for a comedy routine: I would walk onstage with an acoustic guitar and start to strum a sincere song. Midway through the number, I would smash the guitar over my head until it was a pile of firewood. (Whoa, looks like we got a young Andy Kaufman over here!) But that was not meant to be. I wasn't in any shape to do a whole lot of anything.

The night of the talent show arrived but I didn't go. I stayed home and watched television. My parents had gone out for dinner and my sister wasn't at home. I'm sure I had told everyone that I was fine to be alone for a little bit. And on the surface I'm sure I thought I was okay. But that fucking voice in my head stayed home with me that night as well.

I can remember getting up off the couch as if I was in a trance. I walked to the hallway closet and found a bottle of pills. I opened the bottle and emptied the contents into my mouth. I staggered out of the house, got into my shitbox of a car, and drove to the high school. I wasn't thinking about anything, just acting as if I was under some sort of spell. I parked alongside the school and got out of the car. I remember walking down the hallway of the school and feeling like the corridor was endless. I saw the principal at the far end of the hallway but before I could say anything I fell to the floor and everything went black.

The next thing I remember was the bright overhead light of an emergency room shining in my eyes. I was lying on a table. I struggled to get free, but I was being held down or I was strapped down. Either way I couldn't move. Someone was shoving a tube down my throat. And once again everything went black.

As I said before, it was my dream to attend Princeton University for as long as I can remember. My first hero was Princeton graduate and New York Knicks star Bill Bradley. When I was little I always wore a Knicks jacket and would ask my parents if people thought I was on the team. (These days it would be an improvement if the Knicks signed a six-year-old with no handle and a terrible jumper.)

Princeton always felt like it would be my future. But that dream died hard, replaced by me ending up in a Princeton mental institution. But this time I wasn't dumped into the relative cakewalk that was the Rutgers facility. I was stuck at a place called Princeton House and it was no laughing matter.

For starters, I was the only young person in there. All the other patients were adults. These were seriously damaged people, dead-eyed and drooling. This place wasn't the first stop on anybody's mental illness tour. People ambled around in a drug-induced haze, smiling weakly but saying nothing. One old lady in a wheelchair would just scream in terror all day long. I was scared to my core. I desperately wanted to go home. I would sit at the bank of payphones in the communal room calling my parents at work, begging them to get me out of there. *"I won't do anything dumb! I won't try to kill myself again! I promise! Please, just get me out of here!"* But they had no choice. Their kid swallowed a bottle of pills and they had no idea what to do. I can't blame them.

I had a new psychiatrist in my life, a jovial older guy that years later I realized looked way too much like the leader of the Hale-Bopp comet cult. I liked him; when he found out I was a big fan of David Letterman during one of our sessions he popped a videotape into a player. It was my therapist on *Late Night*! He was a member of the studio audience and asked Letterman a funny scripted question during an audience Q&A bit. He was actually funny and it made me trust him a little more. After getting to know my story he sat my parents down and discussed my health. In his opinion I would be dead of kidney failure before my thirtieth birthday if I continued to consume the massive amounts of medication I was currently taking. He felt there was one option that could make a difference: He wanted me to undergo a full course of electroconvulsive therapy.

WHEN LOU REED was seventeen he was given electroconvulsive therapy (ECT) to treat his depression. It scarred him for the rest of his life and the impact of the experience crept into so much of his writing, most notably a song on 1974's *Sally Can't Dance* called "Kill Your Sons":

All your two-bit psychiatrists are giving you electroshock
They say, they let you live at home, with Mom and Dad
Instead of mental hospitals
But every time you tried to read a book
You couldn't get to page seventeen
'Cause you forgot where you were
So you couldn't even read
Don't you know, they're gonna kill your sons
Don't you know, they're gonna kill, kill your sons
They're gonna kill, kill your sons
Until they run run run run run run run run away

I didn't get it as bad as Lou—his treatment took place in 1959 and by accounts was seriously barbaric—but trust me when I say I get what Lou is singing about all too well. I paid a serious price for the treatment, one that will be a part of me for the rest of my life.

The way ECT works is you get electrodes hooked up to your head and receive an electrical charge. The goal is to send the brain into seizure to alter your chemistry in an attempt to reverse the symptoms of depression. These days ECT has become a relatively benign affair. For a lot of people it's an outpatient procedure; they get a treatment and go on with their lives as if nothing happened. Carrie Fisher and Kitty Dukakis have been advocates for it, but they received treatments in the twenty-first century. My treatments were much closer to Lou's, much more violent and arbitrary.

Look, I can only speak for myself when it comes to the subject of ECT. It is a highly stigmatized treatment with its share of champions and critics. I went through it and I survived it. I do believe it helped me. But my experience was BRUTAL and I bear its scars every day of my life.

Over the course of a month or so I was getting two treatments a week. My memory is foggy but I remember getting wheeled into a room at the facility. They put something in my mouth so I wouldn't bite my tongue during the procedure. They gave me an anesthetic and I faded into a haze. When I woke up it felt like I had been hit by a truck. I was a husk of myself. I could literally smell burnt hair on my head, and my mouth tasted like hot metal. They would basically pour me back into my hospital bed and I would sleep for ages. The experience truly beat the life out of me. I felt like a piece of my soul was removed every time I came out the other end.

Not having anyone my own age at the hospital was hard, but one of the most heart-wrenching aspects to the experience was occasionally getting a glimpse of the college students on the other side of the facility. They weren't patients, merely participants in clinical trials. The students were there to grab some quick cash in exchange for becoming human lab rats for a couple of days. They would poke their heads into our side of the facility to stare at the crazy people. It felt like being in a zoo, my life reduced to just another spectacle.

I underwent treatments for about six weeks and after some time I started to feel a little better. It was like the fog was getting blasted out of my brain, which is kind of what actually happened. As ugly as the procedure could be, I didn't feel an unyielding compulsion to kill myself anymore. I also developed a level of trust with my psychiatrist. We talked at length about all sorts of subjects and became bonded over this experience. He was a funny and interesting guy, the embodiment of everything I liked about Princeton, a man who was equal parts smart and practical. I knew he was working hard to keep me alive and I let him know that.

My high school graduation took place during my hospitalization and my parents arranged for me to walk with my class, checking me out for a few hours and taking me to the football field on which the bullies had made me race four years earlier. When they called my name I walked to the podium and was handed a diploma that I hadn't earned; all told I had probably attended two months of my senior year. Any tutoring that took place in the hospital was an absolute joke. It's interesting to have become a college graduate that didn't actually graduate from high school in the same way that it would be interesting to be a driving instructor who never took the time to learn about parallel parking.

I didn't talk to many of my classmates that day because I was pretty freaked out by all of it. I always wondered what they thought about the kid who hadn't been around for months suddenly appearing at graduation. I'm sure there was whispering about where I had been and I took all of it to heart. The odds are most of them didn't care beyond a very narrow point, since they were facing down their own uncertain futures, but I've never been able to get past the fear of someone calling me crazy. That feeling has only grown over the course of my adult life, twisting itself into a terror that can loom very large over my mental state.

I was sent home at the end of June. I have no recollection of a lot of that summer. Actually there are tons of things that I don't have any recollection of, because the primary side effect of ECT is memory loss. Even proponents of the treatment concede that memory loss is an unfortunate result; Carrie Fisher said that "the truly negative thing about ECT is that it's incredibly hungry and the only thing it has a taste for is memory." Most people experience a temporary loss of memory around the time of their treatments. Sometimes the memories return, sometimes they don't.

But some patients suffer more extensive memory loss. That's where I ended up. Basically, I have lost most of my memories from the first eighteen years of my life. The stuff just isn't there. I can't recall the names of so many of my relatives. I don't remember family vacations, and I couldn't tell you names of kids that I went to school with. I remember the names of only a couple of teachers from all my years of schooling. A few months ago my mother brought up the time I got my hand crushed under a heavy piece of equipment at my parents' screen printing shop. My hand swelled up like a balloon and my parents rushed me to the emergency room in a panic. But she could've made the story up for all I knew; I had zero recollection of something that no kid would ever forget. If I look through family photos or page through a high school yearbook, it's like going down someone else's memory lane. The pictures are proof that these things did take place but I might as well be looking at photos from someone else's life. No spark of recognition; I'd be faking it to pretend otherwise. An ECT patient named Marilyn Rice perfectly summed up the feeling of living with chunks of your memory missing: "You don't know you've lost it until you need it."

Have you ever tried to open some files on your computer only to be met by a window that says something like "CANNOT OPEN FILE"? You keep clicking it over and over and the windows pile on top of one another across your screen. Suddenly it dawns on you that the computer you've relied on for every aspect of your life might be on the blink. The stuff is maybe in there somewhere but it's out of reach. That's my brain, baby!

Some people might wonder how I can claim such severe memory loss while telling complete stories like the Billy Joel show or my high school adventures. All I can say is that the difference is the frequency with which I have told and retold those stories throughout my life. I memorized the Billy Joel story and I held on to it. Whenever I recount that story it is like threading back a lifeline into my past. I know in my head and heart that it happened, and I can feel it. But any memory that wasn't deliberately maintained has either been compromised—I can recall details and moments to varying degrees of success—or wiped clean. One of the most frustrating parts of this is the arbitrary nature of what my brain held on to. Can I remember playing organized baseball or being a Cub Scout? Barely if at all. But I have never forgotten for one day in my life that Baltimora was the singer of "Tarzan Boy" or that there were three Thompson Twins: Tom Bailey, Joe Leeway, and Alannah Currie. If anybody reading this wants to trade brains with me, please write to me care of Abrams Books.

I can count on one hand the number of people I've told about the hospital stays or the shock treatments. None of my friends knew.

It has been a secret that I buried in the back of my mind because I have been so embarrassed by it. And how could I not be? I was locked in two different institutions for months at a time. Things got so dire that doctors had to literally inflict brain damage on me to get my suicidal urges to retreat. And as a result of this I was turned into an incomplete person whose childhood memories have been erased.

Any sort of public admission regarding this part of my life would be a declaration about my defective brain. It would be me admitting that underneath all the funny guy trappings I was crazy. A terrifying proposition, but not nearly as scary as the fear that it could all happen again. There were no guarantees that this recovery would be permanent, so why would I tell anyone that my mental problems could very well return? This embarrassment mutated into a shame that grew larger and stronger over the years to where I would become terrified to even think about what I had gone through. So I denied it, I deflected it, I tried to move on. But you don't get to tell your past to go away. It followed me, the shadow growing taller and taller with each passing year.

Look, the intellectual side of my brain gets it. I was sick! It wasn't my fault! So I got help. And the truth is that it *worked*—the voice in my head eased up from a scream to a low murmur and the depression diminished. I paid a pretty huge price by losing so much of my memory. But I'm still alive and I'm happy and I make my living doing creative things with the same brain that got zapped over and over. All things considered, I'll take it.

But it took a long time to arrive at this place of acceptance. For years I felt like everything had been taken from me. I was nothing more than a crazy person who got their head cooked because they were so fucked up, but now I'm supposed to just go forward and figure out how to become an adult like nothing happened? I'm supposed to start dating and go to college and get a job? I was still a husk of myself, exhausted and confused. I wasn't much of a threat to myself anymore but at that point I wasn't much of anything.

And I had no idea that the worst was yet to come. I was about to discover a new level of debasement and humiliation that made going through electroconvulsive therapy look like a pie-eating contest. The voice in my head that drove me to do horrible things returned for one more nightmarish appearance, compelling me to do something truly terrible.

That summer I auditioned for the New Monkees.

CHAPTER SIX

A STORY OF UNQUALIFIED TRIUMPH #1

So the New Monkees, huh?

I'm gonna hit the pause button before jumping into that. It's simply too much to slide from my electroconvulsive therapy stories directly into this next disturbing chapter. I refuse to let this book plummet toward a level of sadness that would make Lars von Trier weep into his kerchief. I'm calling this audible because when push comes to shove my life is NOT sad! Yes, I've had a few curveballs tossed my way. But on the whole, I'm a relatively happy person and I'm pretty good at focusing on the positive side of most things. This book shall not become a testament to whining. Okay, maybe it'll have some whining in it because I am *very* good at it. But there will be other stuff as well!

From this point on, when the stories make it seem like this book should've been called *The Passion of the Tom*, I'm going to pivot. Every once in a while we will take a break from the struggle for an injection of relentless positivity. I'm talking about a story of UNQUALIFIED TRIUMPH.

At the beginning of 2015 Jon Wurster and I planned to perform some live shows. We had done a smattering of brief stage appearances over the years, but this was the first time we would attempt to headline a full-length live event. It was a daunting prospect, primarily because our comedic dynamic had been built around the simple act of conversation between two people. It is all sound and no visual, and since I'm not the second coming of Spalding Gray, merely sitting in front of an audience just wouldn't cut it.

So many fears swirled around my head. Would our comedy feel like a sitcom in a live setting, with audience members hooting and hollering? Would we find ourselves trapped inside an indie comedy version of *Seinfeld* whenever Kramer threw open Jerry's apartment door? And that's assuming people would actually enjoy what we were doing! We could very well eat a big bag of shit onstage! Nobody knew what the future held.

Over the next few weeks we wrote a live show. It was strange to construct something so elaborate without having answers to questions like "What do people want to see us do onstage?" or "What does it actually feel like to get hit by a piece of rotten fruit?" But we trusted that our experience and instincts would lead us through the darkness. I distinctly remember Jon and I turning to each other and wondering how long the show we had just written would actually take to perform. There was the possibility that we had scripted something that would take more than four hours to perform, which is about two hours more than anyone needs from any performer ever. There was also the opposite reality in which we would burn through all our material in under an hour. What would we do then? High-five everyone in the audience like a wrestler on their way to the ring? See how long we could keep a hacky sack session going?

The backup plan was the refuge of every under-talented nitwit who steps onto a stage: an audience Q&A segment. Whenever a show has a Q&A segment please realize that means the performer didn't have enough material.

Our first shows were booked at the Bell House, a fantastic venue in an area of Brooklyn best known for garbage truck storage. The first show sold out instantly, so we added another. That one sold out, so we added a third show, then a fourth show. They all sold out, two shows a night across two nights, more than 1,400 tickets! Even though there was a ton of goodwill aimed our way, we still had to deliver. And if you're wondering whether we delivered, you clearly forgot the name of this chapter! The shows were an UNQUALIFIED TRIUMPH! We didn't have a fucking thing to worry about! The shows were awesome and the crowds were fantastic. Years of validation washed over us like a warm wave of kindness; every laugh that we had been unable to hear over the radio was now sent our way loud and clear. UNQUALIFIED TRIUMPH!

We did more shows throughout the year. Chicago, Seattle, Portland, San Francisco, and Los Angeles. ALL OF THEM UNQUALIFIED TRIUMPHS except for a couple of triumphs that had slight qualifiers attached. But on the whole it was beautiful; a total validation of what Jon and I had built. We decided to end 2015 with a mid-December performance in Philadelphia.

Philly holds a special place in *Best Show* lore. Jon grew up just outside the city and the most beloved character from the show is Philly Boy Roy, a goon who revels in everything trashy that the City of Brotherly Love has to offer: Peanut Chews, Frank's Soda, Utz Potato Chips, and most of all his precious Wawa convenience stores. For our Philadelphia debut we knew that we had to "go for it," just like Rocky did in all his fights against people of color or communists.

We sold out Union Transfer, a place that held more than nine hundred people. The audience had spoken, so we would pull out all the stops and give them the biggest and bestest show we could dream up. No detail was too small: I spent hours before the show driving around Philadelphia looking for miniature Peanut Chews so Roy could toss them into the crowd during his appearance. To my shock, no grocery store in the city had them in stock. How could we look our audience in the face without bags of Philly's most prized candy on hand? Thankfully I found a grocery store in South Jersey that had mini Peanut Chews in stock and I promptly purchased enough to fill a wheelbarrow.

You're asking yourself, *So how was the show?* JESUS CHRIST I JUST REMINDED YOU THE CHAPTER WAS ABOUT UNQUALIFIED TRIUMPHS JUST THREE PARAGRAPHS AGO! It was the best! Everything got plus-size that night for max Philadelphia impact. In all the previous shows, Philly Boy Roy made his entrance by walking through the audience, but tonight he was seated in the balcony like an emperor. Two muscle-bound pals of ours carried him to the stage as the crowd went bonkers. Our friend and amazing rock star Kurt Vile joined us later in the evening and was hilarious. All the pieces were lining up.

Since the show was so close to Christmas we decided to lean into the yuletide spirit. Philly Boy Roy mentioned during his segment that he had a Christmas wish but he was aware that it would never come true: He wanted Philly punk legends the Dead Milkmen to perform live at the show, but it was impossible because the band was on tour. The crowd gave him a sympathetic "awwww" and the moment drifted by without much notice. But little did they know that the Dead Milkmen were not on tour. They were backstage and ready to join our show as secret surprise show-ending guests!

As we wrapped things up, Philly Boy Roy came back out to say goodbye and to sadly reiterate that his Christmas wish would go ungranted. But before he could mope off into the Philadelphia night, Santa Claus and two elves—played by *Best Show* producers AP Mike, Pat Byrne, and Jason "Dudio" Gore—arrived to inform Roy that his wish would be granted! The Dead Milkmen ran out and played a thrilling version of "Punk Rock Girl" with Roy assisting on vocals! I spent my time launching T-shirts into (and at) the crowd with a giant slingshot. It was the highlight of my performing life!

After the show, Jon and I hung out at the merch table and shook hands and took photos and signed anything that people wanted to throw in front of us. We were blown away by the outpouring of love. It's one thing to get a nice email from a listener saying how much the radio show means to them, but it's a whole other ball of wax to have people tell you to your face how your art has helped them. It's a gift to make things that make people feel better or give them hope during dark times. I know I can moan about anything from the quality of a men's room hand dryer to the shitty pizza in Toronto, but I know which side my bread is karmically buttered on, and I never take it lightly.

A couple of hours later my car was loaded up with show props and I drove off into the Philly night feeling like the king of the world. As I approached the entrance to the highway, I realized I should pay a visit to "the little boys' room," as Rocky said in *Rocky V*, so I pulled into the parking lot of a casino located in the middle of town. Yes, there's a casino smack-dab in the middle of Philadelphia. We live in strange times.

I like hanging out in casinos. I find it incredibly relaxing to spend an hour or so dicking around on a slot machine while watching desperate gamblers drunkenly stagger around looking for whatever might cap the void for just one night. I would've loved nothing more than to stay but I was mindful that my car was loaded with valuable stuff and I didn't want some Philly goon breaking my car window to grab my Gary the Squirrel puppet.

I hastily made my way through the casino. I located the restroom and did some restroom business, but on my way out of the building, I noticed an unoccupied *Sex and the City* slot machine a mere ten feet from the exit. The game was beckoning me with its siren song—better known as the theme from *Sex and the City*—so I slowed my pace and decided to spend a few more minutes in the casino.

My love of the *Sex and the City* slot machine is well established. I have talked about it on the radio for years. And while there is no way to be "good" at a slot machine, I have deluded myself into believing I am *seriously* good at the *Sex and the City* slot machine. Maybe it's my love of the show itself, a program that I have watched and enjoyed for years. (And I know what you're wondering: Is Tom a "Samantha" or is he a "Carrie"? Is he a "Charlotte"? Could he possibly be a "Miranda"? Truth be told, I'm probably more of a "Bitsy von Muffling" crossed with a splash of "Keith Travers.") Sure, the show is a manipulative tourist trap for dreamers from around the globe, leading suckers to believe they can buy designer shoes and live in a killer apartment on a sex columnist's salary. But I too am a dreamer, one who believes in the slot machine version of the *SATC* dream. I fed a twenty-dollar bill into the machine and started to play.

If you're wondering whether I lost money on the slot machine, I didn't. I am serious about the "unqualified" part of "unqualified triumph." If I lost my shirt at the casino, this story would've stopped with me driving away from the club or I would've leapt to the part where I rewarded myself with a Wawa cheese hoagie an hour later. The reality is that I played the slot machine for a couple of minutes before drawing three diamond-encrusted hearts, which launched me into the bonus round. I was greeted by the voice of "Mr. Big," the eternal love interest of Carrie Bradshaw. "Great job, kid," he told me smarmily.

Then I made a few selections from the touch screen, the machine went crazy, and before I knew it I had won almost $700! I hit the CASH OUT button faster than I have ever hit any button in my life, took my money, and ran back to my car. Less than fifteen minutes had passed in total.

An hour later, I pulled into that Wawa I mentioned earlier, got myself a cheese hoagie and some sort of soft drink and probably a snack (most likely an M&M cookie but I cannot for the life of me find the receipt), paying with one of the twenties the casino had reluctantly handed me. I spread the sandwich wrapper across my lap and pulled back onto the New Jersey Turnpike, intermittently eating while going 85 mph. If there is a better example of an unqualified triumph, I have yet to experience it.

CHAPTER SEVEN

I AUDITIONED FOR THE NEW MONKEES

THIS IS THE story of two hurricanes. One ran roughshod over the entirety of New Jersey while the other raged only within my head. One was created by warm water rising over the ocean and the other grew from a little well-intentioned confusion and mounds of bad judgment. Both left a trail of destruction in their wake but both also provided an opportunity to pick up the pieces and rebuild all that had been destroyed.

Let's start with the real one. New Jersey was in fact clobbered by two hurricanes in a one-year period. It was insane, some real "God is punishing you" business. Maybe we were too flush with hubris after *The Sopranos* and needed to be taken down a few pegs? Hurricane Irene struck in August 2011, followed by Hurricane Sandy in October 2012. Sandy really did a number on the Garden State: The roller coaster on the Seaside Heights boardwalk got tipped into the Atlantic, where it lay like a pathetic spider bobbing in the grey water. More than two million households lost power. Lots of people died. And perhaps worst of all, Chris Christie became a national celebrity by flaunting his collection of dumb fleece jackets every time he held a press conference in front of a fallen tree.

But when it comes to the House of Tom, Irene did a lot more damage. Torrents of rain and winds topping out at 70 mph thumped my house for what seemed like an eternity. The worst moment of enduring a hurricane is when night rolls in and you cannot get a good look at what's happening outside. It is like walking through a haunted house with your eyes closed; you are fully aware that scary stuff is going on around you but you pray that an out-of-work actor in a goblin mask doesn't touch you. Massive tree branches in the distance cracked and crashed to the ground, and I hoped that the branches extending above my house would make it through the night.

The darkness eventually lifted and the rain slowly began to ease. My home had gotten through the worst hurricane ever to hit New Jersey relatively unscathed: A neighbor's tree crushed a backyard fence but that was nothing compared to what happened to the rest of the state. But any sense of relief vanished as soon as the power sputtered out and the sump pumps that had been pushing out the endless gallons of water shut off. Water quickly flooded the basement as if someone was filling a swimming pool. In no time at all it rose more than a foot high and wouldn't stop. I picked up a flashlight and carefully headed downstairs. As I splashed through the water all I could see was ruined possessions. The books and records on lower shelves were soaked. My office was downstairs and everything below desk-level was underwater, and I couldn't do a thing about it.

On a side note, no matter how illogical it might seem, I always worry that I'll get bit by a shark anytime I am in any body of water. Even as I tried to pry open the swollen closet door where passports and birth certificates were held in a safe that I would find out was NOT waterproof—thanks, unnamed safe company!—I was still slightly cautious not to step on a great white that maybe fell from one of the hurricane clouds into my basement.

I got the portable generator working and the sump pumps turned back on. It was only then that the true havoc revealed itself: My office was destroyed. Drawers and cabinets filled with papers and notebooks were soaked to oblivion. And in an ironic twist that Alanis Morissette herself would've rejected for being too on the nose, a box stuffed with letters and photographs upon which I had literally written "Nice Memories" was now a pile of soaking wet garbage. To paraphrase Borat, "is not nice."

I am torn about how upset one should be when it comes to ruined personal belongings. Part of me acknowledges that "it's just stuff" and that there are worse things that could've happened! But on the other hand, this was MY fucking stuff! Is your stuff all wet? No? Then please leave me be with my waterlogged Dan Clowes books.

I spent a week of twenty-hour days throwing everything out. I'm not exaggerating the length of those workdays; I would wake up with the sun and immediately start cleaning and throwing out stuff, continuing until deep into the night. I was able to dry some things on the backyard clothesline, but most anything that was below the two-foot mark had to be junked. One of the few "good" things that came out of this cleaning marathon was an opportunity to indulge my love of throwing shit into dumpsters that I don't have any right to use. It is my only true vice at this point in my life. Nothing gives me a bigger buzz than rolling into an office plaza, sneakily pulling up next to a dumpster, and heaving bag after bag of my own trash into it. Does this make me a bad person? Probably. Will I ever stop? NEVER. Sometimes I feel that throwing trash into dumpsters is why God put me on this earth. I love it and I am good at it; I still revel in the joy I felt the time I tossed a broken flat-screen television into a Best Buy dumpster, symbolically and literally "returning" to its maker the worthless TV that stopped working six hours after the warranty expired.

As I swept up the wet sludge in a damp corner of the basement, I noticed a stray piece of curved white plastic. Its edges were uneven, a fractured piece of something larger. Two rows of red lettering were printed on its face. I picked it up and felt the second hurricane roll in. This one was only between my ears but it unleashed a flood as strong as Hurricane Irene upon my brain. And unlike the hundreds of comic books and albums I had thrown out, there was no way to chuck this memory into a local trash bin.

The piece of plastic was an artifact preserving one of my true low points. It was a portion of a cheap plastic visor I had been handed as a consolation prize decades earlier.

The text on the visor read "I survived the NEW MONKEES audition."

It was all too true. I auditioned for the New Monkees back in the summer of 1986. Now, I know what you're saying. "Who or what the fuck is 'the New Monkees'?" And to that I say how can you not remember Dino, Marty, Jared, and Larry? Have you also forgotten your mother's first name by any chance? We all know that the New Monkees were a quartet of young men selected to pick up the mantle the original Monkees set down fifteen years earlier.

The New Monkees weren't created to scratch any sort of artistic itch. Far from it; this was a calculated business decision aimed at cashing in on the resurgence that the original Monkees had undergone at the time. By 1986 the "Pre-Fab Four" as they were disparagingly called had mounted an improbable comeback thanks to MTV running episodes of the old show from the mid-1960s. I guess someone in a boardroom looked at a chart that had arrows trending upward and decided the world needed four new young guys to sing and jump around and be silly so he could buy a second yacht. And he wasn't wrong; it's important to have a backup yacht. You never know what's gonna happen to the first one!

I'm not putting down the New Monkees for being corporate. The original Monkees were as corporate as it gets, created for the sole purpose of siphoning some of that sweet Beatles loot into the pockets of producers Bob Rafelson and Bert Schneider. And that is exactly what happened: The Monkees dutifully sang the songs and made funny faces on their TV series and within months "Last Train to Clarksville" was topping the charts.

But thanks to whatever cosmic convergence was both in the air and in the era, the Monkees somehow morphed into one of the best bands of the '60s. An unexpected weirdness crept in. They demanded to write the songs and to play the instruments. They followed up the pop perfection of "I'm a Believer" with an album called *Headquarters*, on which they proudly played every instrument. It didn't matter that only two of them were actual musicians and that Micky Dolenz drummed as if he was blindfolded. That record has a DIY spirit that more than makes up for any technical shortcomings. I certainly admire people who can play their instruments, but I'd rather listen to someone whose ideas outweigh their proficiency than the other way round. Who would you rather listen to, the mile-a-minute technical snoozery of Yngwie Malmsteen or the passionate and primitive chunking of Lou Reed?

The Monkees had a national platform and they used every bit of it. It wasn't long before Mike Nesmith, Micky Dolenz, Davy Jones, and Peter Tork were slipping pot jokes onto national television, introducing some legit psychedelia into their music, and showcasing people like Frank Zappa and Tim Buckley on their show. Within a few years the whole thing came crashing down, leaving behind some of my favorite music ever. I wasn't alone in loving their music either. The songs—and to a lesser degree the series—were fantastic enough to convince a generation of '80s kids who loved the Thompson Twins to get obsessed with a band that hadn't been active in almost twenty years.

My attachment to the Monkees was actually quite personal. I had just gotten out of the hospital as the show started running on MTV. At that point I was completely isolated from everyone in my life after the electroshock therapy. Nobody could relate to what I had been through and ultimately I didn't want anyone to relate to it. I just wanted to be normal. I wanted to go to college and I wanted a girlfriend. At the point where everyone is working overtime to stand out from the pack, all I wanted was to anonymously blend in. I hated who I was, and the embarrassment and shame surrounding what I had gone through just kept growing. I had to swallow it because that was the only way to survive. The last thing I wanted was for anyone to know what had happened to me. This might seem strange in our present day, a time of people rightfully owning the circumstances of whatever they are dealing with in their lives, but things were very different as a teen in the 1980s. You just didn't talk about the things that made you different.

The Monkees arrived precisely when I needed them to. The show was like an ice pack for my head: great music, funny characters, and dopey comedy with a winking sense of awareness. It provided real comfort, so I grabbed the band and show with both hands. I would watch the series on a constant loop and I started buying up every used Monkees album I could find. Mike, Micky, Peter, and Davy were my guys. My friends.

One of the first memories I can recall after my hospitalization was going to the Garden State Arts Center that summer to see the Monkees. Micky, Davy, and Peter—no Mike—were headlining a nostalgia tour alongside bands like the Grass Roots and Gary Puckett & the Union Gap. The Garden State Arts Center is one of those summertime open-air venues that has kept Mike Love swimming in sailor's caps for the last forty years. I don't think I had been to the venue since I was a little kid at a cheapo staging of *Peter Pan*. Even as a child I could tell the production was suffering from budgetary restraints. Tinker Bell was literally a badminton shuttlecock attached to a string that some PA sitting in the rafters bobbed up and down every once in a while. There is a part in *Peter Pan* when everyone in the audience has to clap to bring Tinker Bell back to life, so every kid in the building went bonkers, making as much noise as they could. But Tinker Bell never returned! Maybe the kid on "Tink duty" decided to take a mid-show smoke break? Whatever the cause, our clapping wasn't enough to save the life of the magical fairy that day and we all went home with a little less of our childhood intact.

Even back then I knew this iteration of the Monkees was pretty corny. For starters there was no Mike, inarguably the coolest Monkee. The band also indulged the best fashions that 1986 had to offer, making them look like extras in a *Miami Vice* porn parody. Micky played a truly ridiculous set of electronic drum pads standing up, Peter's shiny angular guitar would've made sense if he had been jamming with Ratt, and they all strutted around the stage wearing wireless headsets as if they were doing warm-up for Tony Robbins.

But I didn't care. That was just window dressing, because the music was perfect and the guys that sang the songs were now singing them right in front of me. It made me feel great, the first thing in a long time that made me feel great.

My love for the band grew over the years. It was strong enough to withstand a Hall of Fame–level snub from Micky Dolenz. We're talking about 2006 or so. I was a few seasons into writing on *Monk*, and since the USA Network aired the United States Open tennis tournament, the writers got free tickets. I'm not a big tennis fan but it's legitimately fun to watch from amazing box seats while shoveling free food into your mouth. I could and would watch someone do their laundry if I had a comfortable chair and a pile of shrimp skewers but that's beside the point.

On this particular evening there was a pre-match reception as part of the opening festivities. Sometimes you watch tennis on television and celebrities like Martha Stewart or Alec Baldwin are peppered throughout the stands, but the star power on this night was running at a lower wattage. The biggest names in attendance were Tim Blake Nelson from *O Brother, Where Art Thou?*, lovable New York Knicks benchwarmer Herb Williams, and OH MY GOD THAT'S MICKY DOLENZ STANDING IN FRONT OF ONE OF THE SNACK STATIONS.

Micky was rocking his then-standard Panama hat and sunglasses combo and was firmly planted next to a table covered in cubed cheese and crackers. The guy from the band that helped heal my tired electrocuted brain was standing right in front of me! I walked over to say hi. I wasn't going to bug him or outstay my welcome, just a quick hello and thank-you.

I spoke to Micky. "Hi, I just wanted to say that your music has been so important to me and that *Head* is maybe my favorite movie ever."

I wasn't lying about *Head*. After their television show ended, the Monkees made a film called *Head*. Co-written by Jack Nicholson and directed by Bob Rafelson just before he made *Five Easy Pieces* and *King of Marvin Gardens*, the movie is a giant middle finger to the plight of being in a prefabricated band. It is one of the darkest and most beautiful movies ever, featuring perhaps the best original soundtrack in rock movie history. *Head* is a straight-up masterpiece and you should see it immediately.

One thing that I couldn't see immediately was Micky's eyes. They were obscured behind his sunglasses. I couldn't get a read on the guy but it didn't matter, because our conversation was destined to land on the short side of things. And when I say "short," I mean he didn't say a single word to me. What he did was kind of make a sound *at* me.

"Myyyah."

The syllable dropped out of his mouth as if he was attempting a Nyquil-fueled version of his famous James Cagney impression from the show. I wasn't sure what he meant: "Yeah"? "Nah"? It didn't matter much because he turned his head away, more interested in the stacks of cubed cheese than another annoying fan. I slowly found my way back to the stadium box and jammed spanakopita triangles into my mouth all night, wondering why the guy who sang "Pleasant Valley Sunday" hated me so much.

There's a positive end to this story. I have since met Micky Dolenz a couple of times, once backstage at a Monkees show and once on the set of *Difficult People*. The creator of the show, Julie Klausner—a great friend and another Monkees obsessive—wrote an entire episode around Dolenz, so I got an opportunity to reintroduce myself twice. He is a legitimately nice guy. He used actual words and didn't lob a single grunt my way either time. Micky, you helped me when I needed it, so you've got a lifetime pass with me.

Myyyah.

I HAVE BEEN the type of person who goes all in on whatever excites me. If I fall in love with a band or filmmaker or author, I have to know everything about them. Outtakes, obscurities, rarities—I want it all! As I look back, I realize that my love of the Monkees apparently ran so deep that I needed to see if I could actually *become* a member of the New Monkees. The ultimate collectible is to look in the mirror and realize that *you are literally the thing you love*. I'm not entirely sure how I heard about the auditions. I have since pieced together that MTV was running announcements on a loop, so I must've seen the commercial and said, "A chance to be a member of the New Monkees? Sign me up!" This is one of the only stretches in my life where I can honestly say my psychiatrist should've given me more electroshock therapy because my brain has retained too many elements of this story.

Now I have never been known for my love of performing in front of others. If there is one common thread running through my creative journeys, it is that NOBODY WATCHES ME DO THEM. I write in solitude. I host *The Best Show* alone in a studio. Even when I direct, I am not the focal point. So when I ask myself, "What the fuck was I thinking auditioning for a television rock band?" I truly do not have an answer. I had literally zero stage experience. I was at best a passable bedroom bass guitar player. And while I can hold my own when it comes to singing, I had never actually sung in front of anyone. My personal style was a disaster: My hair was a mop of unkempt curls with a short wavy drape hanging down the back of my neck, like Tom Hanks when he played the alcoholic uncle on *Family Ties* who drank vanilla extract to get loaded.

Where was my brain on this one? Did I think that when I stepped into that audition I would suddenly wow the producers with a brassy version of "Papa Don't Preach" while laying down a bit of soft shoe? Did I think I would suddenly transform into the second coming of Sammy Davis Jr.? I had no idea what I was thinking. I really wish I did.

I picked up my very heavy bass guitar and boarded a train into NYC. An hour later, I dragged myself in the August heat to SIR Studios in Midtown Manhattan. The audition line snaked around the block with thousands of young dreamers hoping that they just might be anointed the next Peter Tork. I headed to the back of the queue and waited. And waited. The line was endless.

When I realized I had to include this story in the book, I sat down at my Dell and typed "New Monkees" into Bing. There is a dearth of footage (shocker!), but the two clips I did find chilled me to the bone. As I watched video documenting the long line of hopefuls, I prayed that I had not been filmed that day. *Please please please don't let there be a stray shot of me anywhere on this,* I begged. Thankfully I was nowhere to be seen (NOBODY GO AND LOOK!), but what I did witness was pretty horrifying on its own. Hundreds of maniacs gleefully making spectacles of themselves in the hope that the producers would mistake "self-humiliation" for "talent." These buffoons would stick their tongues out and make "funny" faces whenever the lens swung in their direction. Some people lifted up their shirts, others danced and jumped around and sang—anything to break away from the pack. One guy jammed a whole banana into his mouth, not realizing that the Monkees had nothing to do with actual monkeys.

After a few hours I was finally guided to a table in a large rehearsal room. Someone sat across from me and asked me a few questions. I might've taken my very heavy bass out of its case and played something. Probably "Day Tripper." I'm honestly not sure what I did or didn't do, but the "audition" was over within literally a minute—almost as long as it would take Micky Dolenz to ice me out many years later. The person behind the table thanked me for coming in, handed me a white plastic visor, and promptly bounced me back onto the streets of Manhattan. I never considered asking when I might hear from them because even in the moment I knew it was not meant to be.

The YouTube clips of the New Monkees auditions are kinda nauseating. The smugness of the producers is palpable; yes, I know a lot of it is clearly staged for the camera but there is no way to mask the true contempt the interviewers held for this sea of delusional suckers. Looking back I can say with confidence that I am glad I did not live up to their idea of what constituted "New Monkee material." I would've been doing something very very wrong if I had been able to make those Hawaiian shirt–wearing jerkoffs happy. And who would want to impress these guys? THEY CREATED THE FUCK-ING NEW MONKEES. And unlike the original Monkees, the New Monkees sucked shit. The show was awful and the music was terrible and the whole endeavor was over within a year.

I have no idea what I was trying to accomplish by showing up at those auditions. It's bizarre and disheartening but if I tap the brakes on the self-abuse train for a second I see a confused young guy who is trying. He's making mistakes, but he is working very hard to not be the kid in the hospital anymore. He is just trying to clean up after the hurricane.

It was hard to watch my friends pass me by as their lives and careers blossomed while I was still stalled on the runway. But I'll take it! I realize that I am a late bloomer career-wise. Things didn't start breaking my way until I was well into adulthood, and in so many aspects it still feels like I'm just getting started. I am steadily and thankfully moving upward while some of my peers who were killing it back in their twenties are now out of the race. All things considered I'm exactly where I should be.

I'm not a New Monkee. I'm not a "new" anything. I'm Good Old(er) Tom Scharpling and it's fine. That said, I will be conducting auditions to become the New(er) Tom Scharpling. Just show up at SIR Studios in Midtown Manhattan—the only requirement is that you must be able to nervously sweat while playing "Day Tripper" on an extremely heavy bass guitar.

Since I didn't become a New Monkee, that meant I had to figure out what my future would look like. It was time to enter the world of higher education, so I put away my bass guitar and took out a pencil and began the fantastic adventure that is community college.

CHAPTER EIGHT

HIGHER EDUCATION

I HAVE ALWAYS loved the town of Princeton, New Jersey. It is truly and objectively beautiful, home to waves of lush greenery, dignified old houses, great bookstores, and the Princeton Record Exchange, one of the better record stores on the planet. There's an understated majesty to the town, the kind of place where you could follow up a Cornel West lecture by eating a gallon of ice cream at Thomas Sweet's, a business that was at the forefront of the blending of toppings into ice cream. You could get Kit Kat bars or M&M's—or even gummy worms for weirdos who are into that sort of crap—crushed into a cup of the best ice cream ever. Princeton is a place that promises the opportunity to live a well-rounded life, and the primary appeal to me was Princeton University.

For as long as I had been alive (give or take "the baby years"), Princeton University was supposed to be my future. I'm not sure if it was deliberate or even true, but the school always seemed to maintain a respect for the pursuit of intelligence while establishing an equivalent appreciation for the working-class slobs who lived right outside of its egghead bubble. I planned on striking that balance with my own life, developing into a cultured brainiac who also knew the power in working for a living.

I know I'm laying it on so thick that someone from the Princeton Board of Tourism would be like, "For the love of Christ, it's just a town, Tom. Tap the brakes." But I cannot convey the hold that this school had—and still kinda has—on me. Whenever I would feel confused or in need of some mental or spiritual rejuvenation I would get in my car and drive down to Princeton for a few hours. I would hit the Record Exchange, eat at the (admittedly subpar) pizza place or the (obviously subpar) Panera Bread for a (always subpar) lunch, then I'd walk the campus and listen to Lana Del Rey or John Coltrane on my headphones while staring longingly at the buildings, quietly imagining that I was a part of the school's fabric. (And for the record, I NEVER once stared into any dorm-room windows. I also deny any connection to "the Princeton Creeper," no matter how much those police sketches look like me!) Walking around the school grounds would invigorate me. I felt a connection to the place even though I never actually attended a single class there. In those moments, even though the pesky facts said otherwise, I was a student of Princeton University.

I took my Princeton mythologizing so seriously that I would refuse to pass through the gated entranceway on Nassau Street because a deep superstition surrounds FitzRandolph Gate: Legend has it that any student who would dare to walk through these gates would never graduate. Sure, I wasn't a student, but who knew what the future might hold? Maybe I would pull a *Back to School* and attend Princeton later in life, bringing a dose of that good old-fashioned Rodney Dangerfield–esque slob know-how to the otherwise stuffy lecture halls? Hey, stranger things have happened!

But alas I never got my opportunity to become the Thornton Melon of the New Jersey Ivy League because I chose to attend Middlesex County College, a community college located a mere nineteen miles away. MCC—as the locals refer to it—doesn't have its own FitzRandolph Gate, but if you take a left too early at the main entranceway you'll end up in the parking lot of a strip mall that has a Subway and a nail salon. It's a tricky turn to be fair, so don't be too hard on yourself.

The decision to attend Middlesex County College was a surprisingly easy one, propelled primarily by my inability to get into literally any other school on the planet. The notion of applying to Princeton was impossible; for starters I had been struggling to not kill myself back when the application paperwork was due. And on top of that my grades were terrible—it's funny what mental illness can do to your GPA! No self-respecting school would let me within a mile of their classrooms. I also didn't have the money for a top-notch education. My family was still recovering from the staggering medical bills from my hospitalizations. Young Tom was damaged goods, and I probably had better odds of being accepted by the space program than Princeton. And for the record I would've been pretty good at being in space. I know I could've drummed up some pretty sweet comedy in zero gravity. None of that "oooh, watch this pen float by" shit either; I would've dropped some real game changers on the space comedy community.

So with my only remaining options being community college or taking out a classified ad in *Soldier of Fortune* magazine offering my services as a mercenary for hire, I lugged myself to the campus and picked out some classes, and before I knew it I was a College Man! Look at me!

I can't remember what the minimum requirements were to attend Middlesex County College. A pencil? An envelope filled with unmarked twenties? Whatever they were, I fit the bill, so come September I was off to school just like everyone else. Sure, I didn't have the classic experience of getting dropped off by my parents, carrying boxes filled with my things up to my dorm room, meeting my roommate, the two of us bonding over the cool stop sign that I just hung over my bed. "You are a unique person," my roommate would declare. "Yeah," I'd reply with confidence. "I'm *not exactly* like everyone else. I'm *preeeetty* interesting." Then my roommate would insert me into their social circles and before you know it I'm hanging backstage with the bassist from Crowded House at the Ritz.

No, my adventures in higher learning started with me driving the half hour from my parents' house in my shitbox Nissan, parking in the student lot, locating my first classroom, and meekly taking a seat in the back. It felt more like jury duty than college, being dropped in the middle of a sea—more like a pond, actually—of New Jerseyans with literally nothing in common outside of their dream of earning an associate's degree. After a while I created a game I'd play every time a new person entered the classroom. The game was called "ADULT STUDENT, SUBSTITUTE TEACHER, or JANITOR?" I would take a good hard look at this new arrival and try to determine whether this fresh face was an adult student, a replacement teacher stepping in to take over the class (assuming that our regular professor was found strangled in a Route 1 motel room), or a custodian at the college.

The game was resolved when one of the following happened:

- If they walk toward the back of the classroom and sit down at an empty desk, then start asking too many questions that are not actually questions but a chance to talk about their children or former spouse, they are an adult student.
- If they set their stuff down on the desk at the front of the room with a defeated sigh, they are a substitute teacher.
- If they grab the garbage can and empty it into a larger garbage can in the hallway, they are a custodian.

Now it probably sounds like I'm besmirching Middlesex County College. That's not the case. (For the most part.) Do I wish I attended a fancier school? Are you kidding? Absolutely! MCC felt rinky-dink even by lowly community college standards. The student center—the hub of all activity on campus—consisted of a pizzeria that stopped making pizza around 4:00 P.M., an arcade with a handful of janky video games, and one of those old projection TVs that weighed four tons and was forever playing a safe-for-everyone movie like *Look Who's Talking*. I would be forced to burn any downtime between class here, eating whatever food the vending machines were coughing out. Probably Pop-Tarts. My memories are fuzzy about so many things from this period of my life but I distinctly recall eating a fair amount of untoasted Pop-Tarts. I would select a table directly below one of the speakers mounted into the ceiling so I could listen to WMCC while flipping through the latest issue of whatever music fanzine I was obsessively poring over.

WMCC was Middlesex County College's radio station. It wasn't actually a radio station at all. WMCC was little more than a small studio located on the upper floor of the student center, with a turntable and a CD player. It was as much of a radio station as a child selling lemonade in their driveway is the owner of a Jamba Juice. The disc jockey would play music that was pumped through the speakers mounted throughout the building and nowhere else.

The WMCC listenership comprised anyone who was able to pay attention to the music as it competed with the sounds of John Travolta arguing with a baby that sounds a lot like Bruce Willis. There were plenty of days where the only people listening to WMCC were me and the DJ. Sometimes I would sit in the student center only to realize that someone had switched off WMCC in favor of a Top 40 radio station like Z100, which meant that either the studio was empty or the poor disc jockey was playing records for an audience of one.

Nevertheless, I wanted a piece of the action. I loved radio so much and I was dying to be a part of it in any way. So many of my remaining earliest memories are related to radio: I can remember sitting in my parents' Datsun B210, listening to WABC back before it was a right-wing hate outlet. I remember being transfixed by the song "Dream Weaver," which makes sense because it's a pretty amazing song, a prog-lite jam for youngsters looking to expand their consciousness with only Dr Pepper and Snickers bars at their disposal.

I also recall hearing "Octopus's Garden" by the Beatles as my mother and I waited in the parking lot of a sporting goods store for my father to buy something dumb like a baseball glove or a baseball. I couldn't have been older than five at this point, which put me about two years past the cutoff for unironically liking "Octopus's Garden," one of those "Ringo specials" that stunk up every Beatles album.

Radio helped me develop those two passions in my creative life that will forever define me: comedy and music. I would obsessively keep track of which songs I liked on the radio and save up to buy singles by Electric Light Orchestra and Olivia Newton-John (just imagine what happened to my young brain when they teamed up for the *Xanadu* soundtrack!). Before long I was making note of the people who played the music on the radio. I became obsessed with disc jockeys.

I started listening to Don Imus before middle school, running a cassette before leaving to catch the bus, which would buy me an extra hour of listening pleasure when I got home. For those who don't know, Don Imus was one of the first "shock jocks," broadcasters who did more than just enthusiastically announce the next song. He would perform comedy routines and incorporate his personality into the mix. I knew his show was objectively terrible even as a child, but there wasn't anything better available at the time. The bits were corny and I always hated the performative hooting and hollering in the background, a forced party atmosphere that made my skin crawl. But there was something to the concept of a disembodied voice providing entertainment and companionship that really resonated with me. I appreciated the world building he was doing, even if I didn't want to live in that particular world. This version of *Imus in the Morning* wasn't yet a right-leaning hate fest;

it was disposable and pretty toothless. The show featured dumb bits like Moby Worm (literally the serialized adventures of a giant worm attacking New York City) and the Reverend Billy Sol Hargus (a holy roller preacher) that I knew were corny garbage even at the tender age of eleven. But it was better than nothing.

All bets were off when I discovered Howard Stern. He was an afternoon DJ on WNBC at that point and his show wasn't that much better than Imus's. But he did one thing that Imus didn't: He complained. I was at my friend Bill's house after school one day and his mother had left the radio on in their kitchen. I heard this guy talking on the air, moaning about everything under the sun. I was hooked! Hearing this guy on the radio gripe about not being treated fairly by life and not getting recognized for his inherent greatness struck a chord in me. When the show moved to K-Rock and became more edgy and outrageous, I went deeper into the tank. Sure, I didn't love him mocking people for their sexuality or mental capacity and I still don't understand the appeal of hearing a naked lady on the radio, but the comedy and the attitude spoke to me. I immediately handed him the figurative keys to my car: I bought the dumb videotapes he sold; I watched his shoddy pay-per-view specials; I even skipped school to attend his "FCC Freedom Rally," an early-morning protest of the Federal Communications Commission for levying fines against Stern's "indecent" broadcast content. The highlight of this event was watching Al Lewis—best known as Grandpa Munster on *The Munsters*—go rogue, screaming "FUCK THE FCC! FUCK 'EM!" from the stage and over the airwaves. One of the more magical moments I have ever witnessed.

My love of Stern would carry on for years, up until he transformed his radio show into a nonstop infomercial for his movie *Private Parts*. Every minute of every show consisted of Stern braying about how enormous the film was going to be. I bought into all of it, believing that *Private Parts* was going to be one of the biggest movies in history. Stern warned the audience that every screening at every theater was going to be packed, so I went into high panic mode. I frantically drove to a local theater on the opening Friday, praying that Lady Fortune would grace me with a ticket.

I arrived at the box office and asked if they had any seats for the 1:00 P.M. showing and was met with a snort from the guy working the ticket booth. I wasn't sure what was so funny, but I bought a ticket and ran into the theater, only to discover the room was mostly empty save for a scattering of degenerates lightly peppered throughout. It looked more like a porn theater with the "customers" maintaining a respectful jacking distance than a blockbuster film on its opening afternoon.

I took my seat and watched the movie. Even though I enjoyed *Private Parts*, I felt the enthusiasm I held for Stern slowly leaking from my brain. I felt like a sucker for having allowed myself to get roped into some old-fashioned carny-style hucksterism.

This turn of events also revealed what lay beneath so many of my rooting interests. I side with the underdog time after time, and for years Stern had been the underdog. He was the talented guy who hadn't gotten a fair shake from the entertainment biz. He was gunning for those stronger and more successful than him, people who maybe didn't deserve their ranking in the industry. But once his movie came out, he was now the Man. And I just can't root for the Man. I will always select the scrappier option even if they aren't the best. I prefer John Starks over Michael Jordan even though Jordan was the living embodiment of perfection and Starks was a ham-and-egger who clawed his way into the NBA and hung on for as long as he could. Jordan's success was destiny, but Starks going from grocery clerk to NBA All-Star was never a part of the script. It's so much more satisfying to watch someone punch above their weight, because when they win, all of us slobs win.

Maybe I'm drawn to music so enthusiastically because being the best has almost never meant being the most popular (see: "Matthews, Dave" or "Chili Peppers, The Red Hot"). On any given day, a band self-releasing an EP can literally be the best band on the planet.

Statistics make it hard to justify that a guy averaging twelve points a game is better than someone putting up twenty-eight points a game, but in the arts, everybody can potentially be the Greatest. It isn't hard to see why I am always comfortable embracing the role of the outsider, forever "the aggrieved" as John Hodgman once labeled me with cold (but fair!) accuracy.

I became more obsessed with what people called "indie rock" or "college rock" around this time. The only way to hear this exciting new music that was barely if ever on MTV was to (1) work at a record store, (2) have cool friends, or (3) listen to college radio. I was working at a sheet music store, so #1 was off the table, and I *definitely* didn't have any cool friends, so it was all about college radio for me. New Jersey had so many great college radio stations and I would obsessively listen to all of them, writing down the names of bands and songs that I liked before heading to cool record stores like Pier Platters in Hoboken to track them down.

Pier Platters was the greatest record store ever. Tucked into a tiny storefront a few blocks from the Hoboken train station, it was a dream for any fan of obscure music. You could find yourself shopping alongside members of Sonic Youth or Pussy Galore, trying to play it cool and give them "the nod" as if we were all on the same team. ("The nod" is an affected upward bend of the neck executed in a tossed-off manner, a nonverbal way of expressing a disinterested "hey." Maybe there's a slight sneer or smirk but that depends on the individual.) I would throw "the nod" to Thurston Moore and hopefully get a reciprocal nod sent back my way, all the while struggling to refrain from saying something dumb, like "SO WAS IT FUN RECORDING *DAYDREAM NATION*?"

I would stare at the wall of collectible singles, strategizing my purchases like a busted gambler at the track, figuring out what I could afford. I didn't want to be the sucker who overpaid for a limited edition colored vinyl pressing of a record because collecting colored vinyl was for saps. I was in it for the music, not for the collectibility. But that said, if the option was there to snag something you knew would go up in value, you grabbed that record with both hands. Who knew what you'd be able to trade a pink vinyl Cows 7" for down the road? This all sounds slightly stupid to recall, but I loved it. Every week there were five new bands putting out debut singles, and the thrill of slapping a hot-off-the-presses record on my turntable and having my head explode with the greatness of the first releases by Love Child or Pavement or Unrest felt like becoming the musical equivalent of Indiana Jones: These perfect jewels are hidden from the regular world, but *I* know how and where to find them!

Pier Platters was also notorious for being staffed by the most intimidating employees on earth. When the "Soup Nazi" episode of *Seinfeld* aired, my friends and I were unfazed, reacting with a familiar "Oh, it's like Pier Platters but with soup instead of records." The employees were absolutely terrifying, starting with Bill, the owner. He was older than the rest of the characters who made up the scene, a grizzled dude whose past was a mystery to me. I didn't know two things about his life but I knew he owned the coolest record store on earth and I didn't want him to think I sucked.

It was a straight-up terror bringing your selections to the counter. The feeling of horror is still palpable. Susanne was one of the other employees who struck fear into me. She was one of the coolest people I had—and have—ever met, infinitely stylish with a long wave of shocking red hair. I wasn't good with people who knew how to play things close to the vest, and I've come to learn that—duh!—most of the time these people are busy dealing with their own lives. But when you're an overly nervous suburban kid who couldn't feel less cool, someone like Susanne can easily assume some all-powerful status. It felt like an ordeal to ask the employees to lift themselves from the stool behind the counter to ring up the purchases. I'd set my records down, praying that my choices would pass muster. You would never catch me dropping something overly dumb or commercial on the counter! (I am just now realizing that I shouldn't have worried about being judged for buying an "uncool" record because THEY WERE THE ONES WHO STOCKED IT! IF THEY HAD SUCH A PROBLEM WITH IT THEY SHOULDN'T HAVE IT IN THEIR OWN STORE!) It was dumb, but getting the occasional "This is a good record" from the employees meant that I lived to fight another day. I know it sounds like I'm overdramatizing this, and I kinda am. But the intimidation and attitude was not a figment of my imagination. I have friends who still bear the scars of being on the wrong side of the Pier Platters staff. One friend—let's call him Jeff—can mentally transport back to 1991 with one mention of Pier Platters. "Fuck those assholes," he will say. "I spent hundreds of dollars there and they always treated me like shit."

For some reason I managed to get myself in the good graces of the staff by assuming the role of a clown, making jokes while handing them every nickel I possessed for an import single by the Clean. I brought down the house with my tight five minutes on the news that Das Damen had signed to Twin/Tone Records. They would laugh and I would feel a part of the circle. My dual loves of music and comedy aligned and served me well.

I wanted to be involved in the NYC indie music scene as much as possible but I was dealing with a couple of disadvantages right off the top. For starters, there was literally no way in hell that I could make music. The idea of playing in a band felt like the dumbest thing ever. I simply don't possess the gene that would allow me to unironically rock out onstage. The comedian in me ran too deep for me to ever feel like being a cool musician was an option. If I was in a band I would've tried to be funny and next thing you know I'm the wacky guy in the band, the one making everyone laugh while my bandmates are off looking cool. It might've worked for Rick Nielsen from Cheap Trick but I couldn't pull off any version of that.

Then there is that towering lack of interest in performing I have always possessed. I am much more suited to moving in the shadows. It's no coincidence that the two things I am best at—talking into a microphone and writing—are generally done in solitude. I wasn't gonna shed that fear anytime soon. Drop a good helping of "I just got out of a mental hospital" into the mix and you've got a kid who makes the Crumb brother who drew smaller and smaller illustrations look like Mariah Carey.

So I started a fanzine. For the uninitiated, fanzines were the lifeblood of the music scene in the pre-Internet age. The music world moved so differently back then. Without a social media profile to define your worth, you had to figure out something that would do the talking for you. If you didn't have a talent that could be listened to or read or watched, you were relegated to life on the other side of the line. You were a fan, just another consumer. Which is fine, but I knew I was capable of *something*—I just had no idea what that was. I liked being funny and I enjoyed writing and I loved talking about good music, so doing a fanzine seemed like the way to go.

There was a sizable culture of independent publications from all across the country dedicated to celebrating obscure bands, and every fanzine became a de facto catalogue of which records to buy. (And you had to actually BUY them! There wasn't really any way of sampling stuff the way there is now. I was driven to call college stations and ask the disc jockey to play certain records that I had read about in zines like *Forced Exposure* or *Conflict* or *Chemical Imbalance,* only to receive a withering "Naaaah, I'm not gonna play that" on the other end of the phone.)

Publishing a fanzine made perfect sense: I could write about the music I liked in a way that allowed me to also flash some of the comedy chops that had yet to find an avenue of expression. I launched *EIGHTEEN WHEELER* with money that I saved up at one of my many jobs. The fanzine was music-based but the writing was funny, heavily influenced by legends like Gerard Cosloy, the editor of *Conflict*. Gerard was equal parts hilarious and insightful when it came to the music he loved, and his fanzine showed that it was possible to do something that straddled that line. He was also the head of two influential indie record labels—Homestead and then Matador—that changed the face of music more than once. I was able to strike up a friendship with him from a weird request he made in an issue of *Conflict*.

Gerard mentioned in his fanzine that he was looking for a VHS copy of the episode of *Diff'rent Strokes* in which Gordon Jump played a child molester. Being the complete mutant that I am, I had recently taped this episode off television, thrilled to have captured one of the white whales of ironic garbage culture. If you're not familiar, Gordon Jump—best known as the actor who played the Maytag repairman or the program director on *WKRP in Cincinnati*—portrayed a child molester in a "very special episode" of *Diff'rent Strokes*. In the two-parter, he runs the local bicycle repair shop and lures young Arnold and his friend Dudley into the back room to drink wine and watch dirty movies. It is truly skin crawling.

I wrote Gerard to tell him that I had the episode on tape. We arranged a handoff in lower Manhattan. This took place in the late 1980s, a time when New York City was ravaged by drugs and sleaze, a never-ending sea of scum flowing down its streets to a degree that would make Travis Bickle scream "Uncle!" With all that in mind, I am certain that the apple-cheeked New Jersey boy slipping a VHS tape of the *Diff'rent Strokes* child molester episode to the indie record mogul was the sleaziest thing that happened in New York City that year.

Events like this weren't too far out of the ordinary. It is stunning to look back and realize how much work went into establishing and maintaining contact with your friends and associates. If you were interested in saying something to someone in a band that you admired, you sent them a letter. Hopefully you'd get a letter back within the next four months. Maybe you'd exchange phone numbers and start calling each other late at night. The phone proposition was problematic because I was still living at home and nothing terrified me more than the notion of Lou Barlow having an extended conversation with my mother.

I jumped into writing *EIGHTEEN WHEELER* with a redemptive sense of purpose. This was a chance for me to literally rewrite my ticket. I had something I could pour all my enthusiasm into and show everybody on the music scene that I had something to offer. It was a blast, writing record reviews, interviewing bands that I loved, and probably being too mean toward bands that I didn't like.

Being funny really is like a superpower because you can control situations with an offhand comment or wisecrack that kind of just falls from your brainpan without much effort. But like Spider-Man so often says, "With great power comes great responsibility," and when you've got this "talent" that allows you to break down a person or event to their core essence in a way that can make everyone else dissolve into peals of laughter, you carry a huge responsibility.

It generally takes burgeoning comedians a while to learn the difference between being funny and just being mean and shitty. There is a learning curve and it's an important one. If you can be naturally hilarious you are the possessor of a skill set that in the larger sense is not much different from stacking cups or juggling. It's a parlor trick, like math nerds who can multiply huge numbers within seconds, but not nearly as useful. Maybe you can work to get better at it, but the odds are the chemicals running through your body shook out in a specific configuration that allows your mind to assemble thoughts in a pattern that can make people laugh. If you're completely honest you don't have a whole lot to do with the genesis of the initial skill. So if you're one of the people who can do this, appreciate the magic of your gift and *don't use it to make people feel worse about things.*

This is easier said than done. It is an unfortunate rite of passage for funny people to struggle with control of their talent at first. Using comedy to be mean is very easy and it is unfortunately very satisfying sometimes. But meanness is just one tool in the toolbox, and it should be broken out only when the right target demands it.

And I have no problem with meanness in comedy. I love being mean sometimes! People tell me that the clip of me making fun of Billy Crystal on *The Best Show* for his cringey "Jazz Man" performance during one of the Comic Relief shows is their favorite thing

I've ever done, and I might agree. But I felt it was completely justified for a few reasons, the first being IT WAS FUCKING AWFUL.

If you're not sure what I'm talking about, years ago Billy Crystal performed a segment during a televised charity show as a "jazz cat" (person of color). He shuffled around the stage and used phrases like "terlet" (toilet) and "licorice stick" (clarinet) in an attempt to capture the voice of this particular character. I'm sure he meant well with it—I don't recall Billy swinging a tiki torch around in Charlottesville, Virginia—but he missed the mark. Actually, he more than missed the mark. The mark caught the bus out of town before Billy tried to hit it. So I goofed on him throughout an extended clip, breaking down each moment of his routine. Famous comedians and talk show hosts have told me that they reveled in every moment of that bit, and those compliments made me feel good because they understood I was taking shots at a hypocritical blowhard.

Being catty or deliberately shitty with your comedy is a fun place to visit when you're focusing on a deserving target, but don't make a habit out of it, because before long you won't be able to differentiate between a righteous takedown and merely punching down for cheap thrills. I know this might sound preachy but all I'm trying to say is realize that when you've got a bat in your hands, you're holding a potential weapon. I know that in my past I made fun of people or bands that didn't deserve it, and I apologize for any of the mean shit I wrote. If I gave your band a bad review in *EIGHTEEN WHEELER*, I hope I wasn't too crummy about it. And if I was, produce a copy of the review and prove that you were the slighted party and I will make it up to you. I'm serious—I'll buy you a street pretzel or something.

I was pretty angry back then because I was the textbook definition of a loser. If you had looked up the definition of "loser" in the dictionary, it would've said, "Please use this dictionary to beat Tom Scharpling over his loser head." I focused on my studies as much as I could but it was hard. I was living at home, relatively friendless and completely girlfriend-less. I was embarrassed at who I had become. Most of my friends were off enjoying their traditional college experiences at state schools, but I was at a joke of a community college, feeling incredibly small and lost and rudderless. I would fall apart every day, crying in my car before and after class. I was still reliant on a pile of pills that kept me foggy and dead-eyed. All I had were my enthusiasms.

My days consisted of attending community college and praying that the wheels wouldn't come off my newfound recovery, a constant and unrelenting fear. I was working at a music store and starting to cobble together some version of a normal existence. The fanzine was just a pile of pages, yet to be assembled or shown to the world, a dreamy notion that I had yet to complete.

My life had been destroyed by my mental illness. I was terrified to meet new people because the fear of them learning that I had just gotten out of a mental hospital was too much to handle. The life I had inherited was ruined, and my future was still off somewhere in the distance. I needed a way out, an escape hatch to the next chapter. I deserved a future of some kind—I didn't think I was special by any stretch, but I knew I was entitled to something. I deserved a chance to pursue my future.

So I did the only logical thing. I created a new identity.

CHAPTER NINE

THE BIRTH OF SCHARPLING

A NEW IDENTITY!? WHAAAAAT?!!?

When I set out to write this book I knew there were a few stories that I would dread sharing. The mental hospital stuff is obvious. Auditioning for the New Monkees is way up there. But this next stretch is as difficult as any for me to write. But since you paid sixty-five dollars for this book I gotta give you some bang for your buck. So now I will tell the story of the Birth of Scharpling.

What does that mean? It means that Tom Scharpling is not my legal name. It is not my family name either. I made it up when I was eighteen or nineteen. But I never told anybody the story. Over the years, I would find myself trapped in various situations involving the name on my driver's license, renting a car or a hotel room in front of a friend, and I would say something like, "Oh, Scharpling is my mother's name—I've been using it since I was eighteen," and my friend would invariably go, "Oh, okay." I'd continue to stammer out some sort of explanation about how "Scharpling" sounded better anyway and blah blah blah but their eyes would glaze over with indifference and I would shift the conversation to my favorite candy bar or least favorite pizza topping and life would go on.

To all those friends, allow me to issue a collective and all-encompassing apology. I'm sorry for lying. It was a mistruth that grew from necessity. The decision was shame-based: I simply haven't been ready to address how all this madness started, so I chose to fib my way through a portion of my life. It was a lie that allowed me the ability to move forward, but one lie is still a lie and it's not cool to lie to your friends. So I once again say that I am sorry. You can get in line behind the people I wrote shitty reviews of in my fanzine and claim your soft pretzel. I'll throw in a small soda since we are friends.

Without further ado, here is how I became Tom Scharpling.

For starters my legal surname is Giuliano. Tom Giuliano. That's the name I was born with. It's also my father's name, which actually made my full name Thomas Giuliano II. Gotta love the fancy "II," as if I'm heir to a fortune or something.

Tom Giuliano was a fine name for a long time, maybe two or three vowels more than necessary, sure. The order of the "i" and "u" has always been a nuisance; nobody ever spells it correctly. The pronunciation is a whole other bag of fish; the proper way to say it is "JOOL-ee-AH-no" but all I heard as a youth was "GHOUL-ee-ah-no," which sounds like a name more suited to a Neapolitan horror movie host than a nine-year-old boy whose lone goal in life was to someday meet R2-D2.

Then along came Rudy Giuliani. By the time I had started community college, Rudy was the attorney general of New York City, best known for prosecuting mafia dudes and Wall Street trash. He sucked shit but he wasn't yet one of the worst people on the planet, just another tough guy who increasingly looked like a balding chipmunk. The nightmare that Future Rudy would become eventually made this whole name-changing thing a total blessing. I dodged a bullet by not being tied to that dipshit in any form. At that point in time the biggest problem Rudy created involved people hearing my name and asking, "Ah, like the guy from New York City?" and I'd have to say no, his name ends with an "i" and mine ends with an "o," but close enough.

I had gotten deeper into my music fandom, now adding collecting and trading tapes of live concerts to my obsession. I would buy a record-collecting magazine like *Goldmine* and scan the classifieds for people selling bootleg tapes of my favorite bands. I'd ask for a list of available shows and if they had anything I needed, I would send them a money order. After a while I had acquired enough shows that I could trade tapes with other collectors instead of having to pay for them. It was exciting to open the mailbox to find an envelope that clearly had cassettes in it, like a kid on Christmas rattling a package that they know the contents of.

This created a bit of a situation since my father and I shared the same name. Was I worried that I would walk in on my dad blasting a soundboard tape of the Butthole Surfers' July 4, 1986, show at the Ritz in Austin, Texas? No, but I guess I wanted some territory of my own. I settled on a name to use with my tape-trading cohorts: Mel Sharples. You might recognize that name from the sitcom *Alice*: He was the surly short-order cook played by Vic Tayback (which is actually a better name than "Sharples" or "Scharpling" for that matter. I should've gone with Tom Tayback!). And things were fine for a stretch. Envelopes and packages showed up at the house and there was no confusion about who they were meant for.

The Mel Sharples Era came to an end when one of the tape traders asked if we could speak on the phone. I said yes and gave him my number. One night my mother told me to pick up the phone because some guy on the other end of the line wanted to talk to "Mel." We chatted for a while about stuff like the merits of late-1960s Beach Boys outtakes. The guy insisted on constantly referring to me by my first name throughout our conversation, as if I were at risk of forgetting my own name, which wasn't my own name.

"Mel, if I can get my hands on any more 'Smile' bootlegs I'll definitely let you know."

"I'm telling you, Mel. There are a lot of Dinosaur Jr. tapes that are just not soundboard quality."

"So Mel, what did you think of the tape of that Big Star radio session?"

Hearing the name "Mel" thrown at me over and over made me feel really fucking dumb. I wasn't a "Mel," for starters. Mels run parking garages and repair air conditioners; they don't trade live Sonic Youth cassettes. (My apologies to any Mels who love Sonic Youth.) With that in mind I immediately reverted to "Tom" as my first name but stuck with "Sharples," until another tape trader literally said to me, "So you got the same last name as the guy from *Alice*," which made me feel even dumber.

I wasn't going back to Giuliano, because by now I had tasted the freedom that came with having a new last name. I wasn't the nineteen-year-old who had been in the hospital anymore. That was Tom Giuliano. But this new guy? He carried zero baggage, outside of an unnatural predilection for giving out his parents' home phone number to shady tape traders. Something about the switch felt promising. I decided the solution was to fine-tune the surname, leaning on some of the biggest influences in my life at that point for inspiration.

And those two towers of power were none other than Al Sharpton and Garry Shandling.

I was a big fan of Al Sharpton at the time: He was a major league NYC shit-stirrer, putting the entire city on trial for being undeniably racist and corrupt. Was he a hustler? Yeah, of course! Look, I don't know what really happened with Tawana Brawley, but a city that was as racially tilted against people of color as New York City was (is!) needed a champion who wasn't afraid to occasionally play dirty, just as the entrenched scumbags had for centuries.

Garry Shandling was a massive comedic influence on my life. This predates *The Larry Sanders Show* and it most definitely predates Garry himself being a dick to me on Twitter a handful of years before his death. That's right, your guy got into an old-fashioned

Twitter beef with Garry Shandling! The short version of that story is as follows: I tweeted a *Larry Sanders* question to Garry, asking him if he thought Artie, the producer, was actually a fan of Larry's comedy or merely a good soldier who would defend his star whether or not he found him funny. Garry somehow took offense to this question as if I was implying *he himself* wasn't funny. He let me have it and that was the end of that. I promptly threw my *Larry Sanders* box set in the street.

It's fine—Shandling was a hero. So what if he was ultimately the Don McLean of comedy, someone who put out one game-changing song that keeps him on the map ("American Pie"), had another solid hit ("Vincent"), then promptly crawled into an artistic toilet for the next three decades. Shandling was not a nice guy, and this isn't based on my momentary encounter; I know a few people who worked with him over the years and he treated them like absolute trash. And I've always found his assuming the mantle of "comedy guru" to be something of a cop-out. You're funny? Then keep being funny! We have enough Eckhart Tolle in stock! I guess it comes down to my lack of empathy for people who live for their legacy rather than for the act of making stuff. I'll always gravitate to those who just keep producing, unafraid of tainting their reputation. The greats keep going and don't get too hung up on playing to the future. Whatever. The guy did more than most, so RIP Garry. Just be nicer in your next life! And my apologies to the bicyclist who ran over my *Larry Sanders* box. I'll gladly pay for your tire.

Whether or not Shandling treated me like garbage, he and Sharpton were legit influences, so what better way to honor them than to combine their names? If I framed it as a math equation it would look something like this:

$$(\text{Sharpton} - \text{ton}) + (\text{Shandling} - \text{Shand}) = \text{Sharpling}$$

I threw in a "c" to add some panache and voilà! Tom Scharpling was born. The name fit. I was comfortable speaking to tape traders as Tom Scharpling. Keeping Tom as my first name was an important part of all this; I have always liked being a "Tom." The name is perfect in its middle-of-the-pack-ness, not as common as David or Michael or John or William, which freed me from having to deal with differentiating from other Toms with hazardous attachments like "Big Tom" or "Less Smart Tom."

The name was also generic enough to make me not stand out from the crowd, which in retrospect has been my life's sole driving purpose. The name Tom has served me well, partly because I knew enough to shy away from "Tommy," which evokes a stunted man-child (Lee, Stinson, Wiseau, Chong) or, strangely enough, a tormented soul drenched in endless reservoirs of anger (Lee Jones, Lasorda). If "Tommy" felt juvenile, then "Thomas" was waaaay too formal (Jefferson, Pynchon, Edison, the Apostle). "Tom" was just right, and there are some pretty sweet Toms sharing my handle. Hanks. Cruise. Petty. Wopat. Jones. Skerritt. Baker. Wopat. Holland. Hollander. Arnold. Green. Wopat. (And if any of these Toms turns out to be a creep after this book is published, I request they switch to "Thom," a variant that only Thom Yorke has managed to successfully pull off.)

As far as the last name went, I was good to go. There weren't any Scharplings clogging up the scene and nobody would ever again confuse me with the bridge troll who would soon become mayor of New York City. One unexpected perk to this new identity was that a fair number of people assumed "Tom Scharpling" was Jewish. I don't think anything thrilled me as much as being mistaken for a member of the tribe.

Understand this: I am not looking to be the next Rachel Dolezal. I have never once identified as anything other than the lapsed Catholic boy that I was raised to be. I never denied that I had been confirmed. (A fun story: When I had to select my confirmation name, I picked "Paul" because my middle name was "John" and it paid tribute to my love of the Beatles! I can remember the groan my mother made when she pieced together the nonreligious logic behind my decision.) But so many of my favorite comedians and musicians were Jewish—along with the aforementioned Howard Stern there was a pre-scum Woody Allen, Lou Reed, Rodney Dangerfield, Albert Brooks, Joan Rivers, Bugs Bunny, and Bob Dylan just to name a few. There was a connective thread running through all of them that I had never really put words to, but I felt it deeply. They were never the cool kids. They were always some version of the Other, accepted for their talent but never truly allowed into the inner circle. There was always going to be something or someone that denied them unconditional inclusion, and that worldview was infused in their art. The lifetimes of true pain made the comedy funnier and the lyrics richer. And while I didn't know much about actual Judaism, I felt a kinship with the cultural side of it, even more so after having undergone all my problems. I had never felt more like an outsider, so to be mistaken for a member of an amazing people who were forever on the outside looking in was a gift.

Years later I was at the home of Andy Breckman, the man who gave me my first television job writing on *Monk*. It was Hanukkah and Andy asked me if I would read something for the holiday. I was confused for a moment, until it dawned on me: *OH MY GOD HE THINKS I'M JEWISH!* I had to confess to him that I wasn't one of the chosen people, and he seemed a little surprised. His confusion was my heroin; I felt invigorated by this misunderstanding. (Heroin makes you feel invigorated, right?) I recused myself, leaving Andy and his family to celebrate without a dirty Catholic interloper. The significance was deep: A Jewish comedian thought that I, a fellow comedian, was also Jewish. While I certainly wasn't trying to "pass" as Jewish, it was validation that I carried myself as someone who had transmuted his own pain in the same way as my heroes.

Anything was better than identifying as Italian, especially as a kid growing up in the tri-state area. This might seem like I'm being anti-Italian, but I'm not. So many of my favorite artists were also Italians, like Martin Scorsese, Bruce Springsteen, Francis Ford Coppola, Robert De Niro, Captain Lou Albano, Bugs Bunny, and Madonna. And I've always been a fan of pizza and raviolis and those oval cookies that have a diagonal streak of chocolate and sprinkles on them. I also love those cookies with the dot of red goop in the middle, so if we're ever eating cookies together you know which ones are off-limits.

I wasn't surrounded by great filmmakers and musicians as a young man in New Jersey, but I was knee-deep in bullying meat-heads who expressed their "Italian pride" in the form of being shitty to anyone weaker than them. They were guys who reveled in acting deliberately dumb, upholding their connection to monstrous characters like Don Corleone and Tony Manero as a point of pride. It was a bad scene and I didn't want to be associated with any of it, but I had the wrong last name for a kid who was more at home memorizing box office grosses than strutting around like Vinnie Barbarino (another unfortunate spiritual forebearer).

I have come to terms with most aspects of my Italian roots, mainly because it became apparent that I wasn't actually raised to celebrate any portion of Italian culture. What connection did I have beyond my last name? My grandparents were all born in America and literally none of them spoke Italian. You can throw a rock and hit great Italian food in New Jersey, but for some reason they were perfectly happy eating at the worst Italian restaurants that the Garden State had to offer. If you've ever driven around and passed an Italian restaurant that didn't have a single car in the parking lot and you asked yourself, "How on earth do they stay in business?" I can answer your query. They are staying in business because my grandparents wanted to eat there. Maybe they enjoyed the predictability of these places. You could always count on the butter pats being frozen and you could take it to the bank that the pasta would be boiled into oblivion. The other thing you could rely on was my family eating all of it and coming back for more.

When the idea to publish a fanzine crept into my mind, I knew I would do it as Tom Scharpling. I was terrified that anybody I met post-hospitalization would know anything about who I actually was. So I simply became Tom Scharpling for good.

I assembled the first issue of my fanzine (entitled *EIGHTEEN WHEELER* because from the moment I started driving I carried a fear of my car getting crushed by a tractor trailer on the New Jersey Turnpike). I handled every part of the process, from writing the content and laying out the pages to learning how to get the fanzine into stores. It was a one-person operation, pretty basic, just a few interviews with some bands I liked along with a bunch of record reviews. But its mere existence meant the world to me. I made something and people responded to it to some degree. People started to know me as the guy who put out *EIGHTEEN WHEELER*.

The fanzine didn't exactly set the world on fire, but it garnered some attention within the local scene, and that was enough for me. Even though things were still cloudy, I started to believe that there might be a future waiting for me beyond all the hospital stuff. Well, it was waiting for Tom Scharpling, but close enough.

With this slight burst of confidence under my belt, I decided to take a step toward something I had always dreamed of. One day between classes I walked to the second floor of the student center and located the offices of WMCC. The disc jockey was a guy in his midtwenties, lazily leaning backward in an office chair. A vinyl copy of *Brain Salad Surgery* by Emerson, Lake & Palmer spun on the record player. He looked up with an indifferent glare at the young guy in the doorway.

"Hello," I nervously declared. "I'm a student at Middlesex County College and I'd like to find out about getting a show on WMCC. I'm a big music fan and I—"

"We're all booked up. Maybe next semester."

"Oh. Okay," I stammered. "Thank you."

He turned away. I was stunned. I walked away, the sounds of "Karn Evil 9: 1st Impression, Part 1" mocking me as I headed toward the parking lot. With one swift strike my dream of becoming a disc jockey had been murdered. For the rest of my days I would never have the chance to host a radio show.

Actually, I would get a chance to host a radio show, just not on that dumb station.

CHAPTER TEN

A BOY AND HIS MICROPHONE

It was the early 1990s and magic was in the air. We all wore "Wayne's World" ball caps and flannel "grunge" shirts. Our nights were spent dancing to the sounds of Color Me Badd and Jesus Jones. President Bill Clinton got caught having sex with the Berlin Wall, and we just couldn't get enough of those amazing characters in the movie *Backdraft*. Is this the truth? I don't know because we couldn't handle the truth!

I think that's what was happening. I wasn't paying too much attention to the mainstream to be honest; I was deep in my love of all things outside of the popular culture. I wanted nothing to do with Hollywood movies, so I didn't see films like *Jurassic Park* or *Terminator 2* until years later. I was too busy renting grey market VHS tapes of movies by John Woo and Richard Kern from weird video stores hidden in strip malls and flea markets across New Jersey.

When it came to music, I was all about the indie scene. No room for the mainstream. I wasn't the type to shout, "Sellout!" at cool bands that signed major-label deals. Quite the opposite, actually; I wanted to know that I was right, that the bands I loved were actually the best in the world. I had no problem with them grabbing their cash as long as they stayed true to their original calling. It was validating to watch Nirvana—whose first album and single I loved to death—explode globally. Sure, I thought that *Nevermind* sucked the first time I heard it, especially compared to the beautiful stupidity of their first album. But it was still nice to see a band that I saw play Maxwell's alter the musical landscape. (And I forever hold firm on my "Nirvana wasn't that great" stand. I saw them play with Tad, their mountainous Sub Pop labelmate, and Tad handed them their lunch that night. And *Nevermind* can be reduced to "Foghat being mopey" when you get down to it.)

I was beginning to cobble together some semblance of a post-ECT life. I started working at a sheet music store and continued attending community college. I had made a few friends on the scene. It was a good time, except for one thing. I was so lonely. The closest thing I had to a girlfriend was another patient from the first hospital I had been committed in. Romantic, I know! She was cool and we would hang out once in a while after we had both been discharged, but it wasn't what I was looking for. I wanted to be in love.

I had been listening to a ton of shows on WFMU around this time, and my favorite was a program hosted by a disc jockey who called herself Terre T. Her show was a revelation: She would assemble music like nobody else, combining the most amazing "what the fuck was *that*!?" punk and psychedelic gems from the '60s and '70s with amazing songs by new groups that nobody had heard of yet. I would find myself reaching for a pen whenever I listened to her show, writing down as many band names and song titles as I could when she back-announced her previous playlist. And her on-air presence was equally captivating. She had a pronounced and incredibly charming Staten Island accent and was seriously funny when she plugged upcoming shows or hyped new records. I was smitten. I started calling in to ask questions about certain records and before long I was making her laugh. My gift of laffs came in handy. It's the closest thing I'll ever have to a superpower.

Every week or so I would listen to Terre's show and give her a call whenever she played a long song. The conversation was easy and comfortable. We made plans to meet up at a Laughing Hyenas show in New Brunswick. She was beautiful and cool and I felt severely overmatched, but somehow I hung in there long enough to establish a connection. I realized that she liked me as much as I liked her, so I asked her if she wanted to see a band called Suckdog at Maxwell's the following weekend. I know what you're thinking: a Suckdog show? The romance never stops with Tom! We went to the show and had an amazing time.

We had our second date at a restaurant in New Jersey. I was nervous because I felt like I was living a lie. She didn't know my real name, and she didn't know about my mental history. So I did what any cool dude on a second date would do: I told her everything. I poured my guts out about my hospitalization and the creation of Scharpling, all of it. Terre was the first person I had entrusted with any of this. I prayed she wouldn't be scared off by who I really was, but she listened and told me everything was fine.

I remember being so impressed by her strength. If there was any kind of conflict or situation, Terre would stick up for herself like it was the most natural thing in the world. It's embarrassing to realize how uncomfortable I was with the concept of defending myself, but years of people-pleasing combined with all the medical trauma left me feeling inherently wrong about just about everything. One time early in our relationship I was a guest at a college rock music festival. The panel had something to do with independent media and I was invited to talk about my fanzine. I was extremely nervous and I'm sure it showed, but ultimately I felt okay about how the panel went.

A few bands were playing afterward, so Terre and I stuck around. A couple of young women who had watched the panel were also there. They had probably been drinking and when they saw the nervous kid from the panel earlier in the day, they approached me under the guise of asking me questions, but it was pretty clear they were goofing on me. I just took the abuse, unsure of how to respond to the teasing. Again, every action was filtered through the lens of having been hospitalized. I was trying to pass as "normal"—whatever that meant—and I didn't want to rock the boat. So I just took it. Terre clocked what was happening and tore the women a new one. "What the fuck is wrong with you?" she said. "Why would you make fun of him? Seriously, who do you think you are?" The women apologized before slinking away, and I felt protected for the first time in a long time.

BEFORE LONG I started hanging out with Terre during her radio show. I watched her put together sets of music, still in awe of the artistry she demonstrated. I wanted to be a part of WFMU but it was a very intimidating place. The station wasn't a typical college radio affair populated by students; the staff was composed of adults, all of them punishingly knowledgeable about their particular musical area of expertise. Most of the disc jockeys had worked at other stations before joining WFMU, so I didn't see any way a garden-variety indie kid with no prior radio experience could offer anything of value to this legendary station. Nevertheless I volunteered at the station, gladly stuffing envelopes and packing mail orders, just happy to help the cause. I would've traded a year of my life to do an overnight fill-in. I wasn't sure I would be any good at it but I certainly wanted to try.

After a year or two of hanging around WFMU, Terre convinced the music director to let me try out for the station. I was approved after some time and took the mandatory training classes along with a handful of other prospective DJs. After learning how to run the board, management said I could make a demo that replicated what an hour of my "show" might sound like. I went to town assembling a set that showcased the range of my musical interests. I probably cast a wider net than I was comfortable with, jamming Stockhausen and Borbetomagus alongside Volcano Suns and Galaxie 500, but sometimes you gotta play to the house. My mic checks were pretty flat, just me announcing the songs with a crumb of personality here and there. I submitted the tape and promptly heard nothing for months. Finally, I received a phone call: Could I do an overnight fill-in for a DJ who was out of town? I said yes and immediately started plotting out my music sets. I was gonna be a disc jockey on my favorite radio station and I didn't even have to trade a year of my life for the opportunity!

An overnight show meant broadcasting from 2:00 until 6:00 A.M., which is actually a pretty amazing time slot, because whoever is out there listening *really* appreciates you being there. They need someone to help them pass the night, to make them feel a little less alone. Radio is a powerful medium, forging immediate connections between the broadcaster and the listener. When it works, you feel like you're hanging out with a fun friend with an insane record collection. I understood the power of all this. For years I wanted to be the host instead of the listener. And now I was getting my shot.

I HAD PLANNED TO play it safe on the air, to let the music do the talking. I wasn't going to worry about being Mr. Entertainment on the mic. This whole endeavor was intimidating enough and I didn't want to fuck it all up with too much blabber, so I kicked things off with a long set of music. But something happened the first time I potted up my mic.

Have you ever heard performers talk about the first time they got onstage? They describe it in the most reverent of terms, saying that they found the place they had been looking for their entire life. They were finally *home*.

That is precisely how I felt the moment I started talking into that microphone. I knew this was exactly where I belonged. Even though I hadn't planned for it, by the second mic break I started making jokes. It all felt incredibly natural, like I was born to do this. If my story was a movie, *this* is the scene in which the protagonist discovers their true power. This is Happy Gilmore driving a golf ball for the first time or the kid from *Rookie of the Year* surprising everyone—including himself!—with his dangerous fastball. A curtain pulled back to reveal my purpose in life. I know this might sound hokey but it's completely true: When I talked into that mic and said whatever I was thinking, the universe literally handed me my voice. I might've taken on the name Tom Scharpling a couple of years earlier, but this was the moment that I truly *became* Tom Scharpling.

Again, I know this is corny! I just wrote a paragraph that my fellow sarcastic comedian friends are gonna secretly share behind my back to mock my pretentiousness. But fuck it, the experience was real and true. And to those comedian friends all I can say is that I will be mocking your vulnerable moments as well. It is the line of work that we have chosen and this is what we do to one another.

By the end of the shift, I was sorry that I had to stop. I had been bitten by the radio bug and I wanted more. I immediately made myself available for any and all fill-ins, and every time I got back on the air I felt myself getting stronger. I had a passion and a purpose, and the scraps of feedback I received from the listeners validated those feelings. Sure, I wasn't doing a talk show yet. But the mic breaks got longer and longer, and soon I began taking phone calls from the listeners. The pieces were coming together.

A year or so later I was the proud owner of the 2:00 to 6:00 A.M. time slot on Sunday nights. This is probably the least desirable slot on the schedule but I didn't care. I had a chance to do a radio show every single week! I loved it to death and I improved with each passing episode. When I was promoted to a cushy 11:00 P.M. to 2:00 A.M. slot the following year I felt ready to crack things open a little bit. I was ready to take a legitimate stab at doing some comedy on the show. But I would need a partner to truly realize this goal.

I MET JON WURSTER a couple of years before the weekly radio show. I was at the Ritz in NYC checking out a triple bill of My Bloody Valentine, Superchunk, and Pavement. I had become friendly with Superchunk, an amazing indie band from Chapel

Hill, North Carolina, with some of the most anthemic choruses in the biz. By this point I had seen them around a dozen times and interviewed them for *EIGHTEEN WHEELER*. I talked to their front man, Mac, on the phone a few days before the show and he told me that they had replaced their original drummer, Chuck. This was a bit of a curveball; Chuck was an amazing drummer. I was bummed but Mac assured me that the new guy was even better.

Mac was right. Chuck was great but Jon took Superchunk to the next level; with Wurster on the traps Superchunk became a powerhouse. (And for the record, Pavement was great that night. My Bloody Valentine was okay. They were always kinda overrated. If they weren't British, the world would've slotted them in between the Lilys and Velocity Girl, two solid American indie-noise bands. Trust me on this!) I was introduced to Jon after the show and we hit it off, discovering that we were both fans of the legendarily under-appreciated Chris Elliott sitcom *Get a Life*. Superchunk had loaded their equipment into the van and we all headed to a nearby bar. Jon and I kept talking as we all walked through lower Manhattan.

At a point in the conversation, one of us asked the other—I can't remember which—about an MTV veejay named "Smash." Now, if you don't remember Smash, you clearly did something right with your youth. Smash was grizzled and mulleted, giving off a decidedly "assistant manager of an AutoZone who got fired for stealing brake pads" vibe. His crowning achievement was encouraging a young Guns N' Roses to trash the MTV studios, which they did with all the limp vigor that only a perennially wasted band can muster. Smash got clonked on the head by part of the wreckage, which only added to his "substitute gym teacher gone to seed" luster.

If you happened to catch him on MTV, you would either work overtime to block him from your brain or you'd become forever obsessed. Every time I asked anyone if they remembered Smash I was greeted with a dumb stare. Jon was the first person who also remembered him, and it turns out he was in the same boat, just another soul hoping that someone remembered Smash. That night we became friends. I had no idea that five years later we would become comedy partners.

FAST-FORWARD TO 1997. My radio show now airs on Wednesday nights in a more manageable nine to midnight slot. By this point Jon and I are the best of friends even though I'm living in New Jersey and he is in Chapel Hill. We talk on the phone all the time about comedy and movies and TV and music, filling in the blanks for each other on various cultural obscurities ("Did you see *Real Life* by Albert Brooks?" "No, I'll check it out. But have you seen *The Dresser*?") Superchunk was a big deal by this point, playing shows all around the world and releasing a series of legitimately masterful albums. By comparison I was working at a music store and trying to figure out my future. I wrote comedy sketches and short film ideas but I didn't show them to anyone. To paraphrase the Raspberries, I didn't know what I wanted but I wanted it now.

I have no clue which of us came up with the idea of Jon calling in to the radio show as a fake character but it made complete sense. We promptly worked up a premise for a call that made us laugh hysterically. Jon would pose as Ronald Thomas Clontle, the author of a new book called *Rock, Rot & Rule* in which he determined—based on "research" that consisted of him asking friends at his local coffee shop—whether a musical act rocks, rots, or rules. The rankings were deliberately stupid and designed to infuriate: For example, Puff Daddy and Bruce Hornsby ruled while the Beatles only rocked, because according to Clontle they had "a lot of bad songs." It was totally insane and we'd get on the phone and laugh at the possibilities of bringing this character to life.

It was strangely risky to leave my comfort zone to this degree. We were about to do a comedy bit on a radio station that didn't exactly encourage laughter. Even Terre was concerned, asking if I knew what I was doing. She wasn't asking from a position of doubting my laff chops, but she knew the WFMU audience generally had a stick up their ass when it came to having a good time. Sure, they would chuckle knowingly at a Jacques Tati film and they'd yuk it up over the beauty of a wildly incompetent (but brilliant) outsider band like the Shaggs. But when it came to actual comedy, you'd best look somewhere else. Jon and I persevered with our plan, knowing that the character and the concept were both funny. If we bombed, then so be it.

The call started unassumingly enough, with Clontle telling me that the book wouldn't be released in time for Christmas because "that's not a big book buying time." Jon played it perfectly, building the reality of this subtly insane character. I locked in as the straight man, acting surprised and shocked by the increasingly outrageous claims that Clontle made. This was the night that my partnership with Jon was cemented. We performed the dumbest thing ever, live, without a net, and it was magical. One of the funnier exchanges was when Clontle discussed David Bowie and Neil Young:

> TOM: Who do you and your—for lack of a better term—
> buddies think "rot"?
> CLONTLE: Hanson, No Doubt, Hootie, LeAnn Rimes,
> Kansas, Mary J. Blige, Bowie, Jewel.
> TOM: David Bowie?
> CLONTLE: Yeah.
> TOM: So, he rots?
> CLONTLE: Yeah.
> TOM: So, what makes him not "rock" or "rule"?
> CLONTLE: Too many changes.
> TOM [*laughing*]: Too many . . . ?!
> CLONTLE: He's always changing and, for the same
> reason, I put Neil Young in there.
> TOM: So, you consider that Neil Young rots?
> CLONTLE: Yeah. *Old Ways, Trans, Landing on Water* . . .
> TOM: So, those albums . . . have you ever heard any of the
> stuff he did in the seventies?
> CLONTLE: No.

TOM: Like . . . you ever hear *Rust Never Sleeps*?

CLONTLE: No.

TOM: *After the Gold Rush*?

CLONTLE: No. I did hear the *American Dream* album that he did with Crosby, Stills & Nash, though. Came out in about '89 or so. I hated that record.

TOM: Yeah, but I think you're not getting a good enough sampling of what Neil Young is about.

CLONTLE: Well, that's like five records right there.

TOM: I mean, I think the guy's put out like fifty [albums]. I think, actually, of his whole catalogue, you picked the most misrepresentative five records.

CLONTLE: That's your opinion. That's the beauty of America: differences of opinions that put us where we are today.

TOM: I guess it's also your book . . . like you said . . . what was that phrase you used?

CLONTLE: "The Ultimate Argument Settler."

TOM: But how is it that we're having an argument now over it?

CLONTLE: That's up to you—the ball's in your court.

The bit only got funnier once we started taking calls from increasingly irritated listeners. The WFMU audience couldn't believe that a brash idiot like Clontle was acting like such an authority while making numerous mistakes. Jon took it to the next level when the callers started venting their outrage. He made an offhand but very deliberate claim that the '80s band Madness invented ska, which sent the know-it-all WFMU audience into a tailspin.

The joy I got from performing Actual Comedy that I co-wrote with Jon that night was like winning an Academy Award. I finally saw a chance to create funny content and I finally had someone to make it with. We tapped into something truly special on our first try.

I felt ten feet tall after that performance and we immediately started writing concepts for our next call.

But reality likes to intervene. I was doing the radio show in addition to my full-time job and the writing I would do at night. There simply weren't enough hours in the day and something had to go. As happy as the radio show made me it just wasn't putting food on the table. I needed to channel my focus into getting my writing career off the ground, so I reluctantly quit WFMU. My burgeoning partnership with Jon was over before it had really started. Would we ever make comedy together? Yes. The answer is yes. We would make a whole lot of it—I told you about it a couple of times already. But for the sake of ending a chapter with a real cliffhanger, let's just pretend we don't know.

CHAPTER ELEVEN

AN AFTERNOON WITH PAPA ROACH

WITH MY RADIO show now a distant memory, I channeled my energies into launching my career. I wanted to write but I also needed to save money so Terre and I could get married and buy a house. So I pinched every penny by still living at home and working at a music store in suburban New Jersey.

Now when I say I was working at a music store, I'm not talking about a record store. This wasn't me living out some sort of *High Fidelity* fantasy, recommending obscure records to people desperately chasing indie cred. It wasn't my opportunity to dole out empiric thumbs up/thumbs down verdicts over the potential purchases some sweaty kid would nervously bring to the register.

No, I was working at a sheet music store—a *huge* difference.

The store was called World of Music in Summit, New Jersey. If you're unfamiliar with Summit, it is a midsize suburban town filled with rich people from around the world who want to live in a house while remaining a short train ride from Wall Street.

If Summit had a flag it would depict an ascot-wearing rich guy getting mad at a gas station attendant for taking too long. Summit was flush with money, so providing an artistic foundation for these young Richie Riches was a given. I know it's hard to believe, but there was literally nothing cool about this job. I spent half my day catering to defeated eighty-year-old piano teachers in the market for entry-level instruction books and the other half renting starter violins to children who had absolutely no interest in music.

There's a special kind of magic in the air when you're working at a place where everybody kinda knows the whole endeavor is a crock. The students aren't remotely interested in learning trombone; they go through the motions only because their parents will buy them a new helicopter if they graduate seventh grade. The teachers know that 98 percent of their students will quit after a few lessons, yet they plow forward, courageously biting their cheek so as not to fall asleep while their charges stumble through a seasick rendition of "Heart and Soul."

The parents were in the same boat. Renting a clarinet was the same as buying a lottery ticket; maybe your kid was a secret prodigy just waiting to bloom, and maybe they would land a music scholarship at a good college so you can hold on to even more of your dirty ill-gotten Wall Street money.

We would rent instruments in September, with the contract coming due nine months later. Just like a little talent baby! Most of my June was spent phoning renters to remind them that the rental period on their instrument had expired. I would get back a confused "Flute? We don't—oh, that's right! I think it's still in the trunk of the car." A couple of days later they would pull up in front of the store and hand back the unplayed flute, looking away not unlike a pervert returning a defective Fleshlight to their local porn establishment.

Aside from witnessing the never-ending death of unborn dreams, the job was pretty great. The owner of the store was Jim, a funny and likable guy who could best be described as an "Italian Kenny Rogers–type." Maybe it was the years of dealing with pseudo-talents at the store while disguising his talent as a seriously great piano player. Jim carried a hatred for the rich blowhards who frequented the store and he refused to subscribe to the maxim that "the customer is always right." He ran the store with a philosophy more along the lines of *"The customer isn't always right. The customer is actually wrong most of the time. The customer is a mutant. Smile at the customer, take the money from the customer, and make fun of the customer the second they leave the store."*

I remember Jim getting pushed to the brink of sanity by a particularly cheap guitar teacher. This guy would float around the store for hours staring at songbooks but never spending any money. (This was right before the Internet completely demolished everything. At this point in history you actually had to go to a store to learn how to play a song!) The guy was clearly burning an empty afternoon and his constant presence was driving Jim crazy.

Jim would plant himself behind the counter and just stare at the guy as he attempted to memorize the chord changes to a Jimmy Buffett song, burning holes into the back of his unknowing head. This went on forever. Then finally the guitar teacher stopped staring at sheet music and headed to the front register so he could stare at the guitar picks. After a few minutes he fished two picks from the display and set them on the counter.

Jim looked down at the picks, then looked up at the guitar teacher. "This is all you're gonna buy today?" he asked.

The teacher snidely said, "Yup."

Working retail is hard. I come from generations of counter jockeys. I've done it for huge stretches of my life and I assume I will wear a vest at some chain store before I die. Working retail feels like rolling a boulder up a hill over and over, except the boulder can talk and is complaining about why the sheet music for "My Heart Will Go On" is so expensive. The boulder sometimes asks you if they can just take the sheet music to the library and photocopy it. You reach a point where you just can't take it anymore, and it's always the little things that break you. These two measly guitar picks were the straws that broke Jim's back.

"You know what? You're a cheapskate," Jim said, staring him directly in the face. The teacher was taken aback but quickly matched Jim's tone.

"This is all I need today. Something wrong with that?" he said indignantly.

Jim just looked at him. "You come in here for hours and *this* is all you buy? Just take the fucking picks and get out."

"You know you're not the only place that sells sheet music," the teacher said as he threw a dollar bill on the counter and headed toward the door.

Jim said, "You've got short arms and deep pockets!" (one of the classic old-timey insults that still has some juice in my opinion) as the teacher walked away. Jim gathered himself and yelled, "NOW GET! THE! FUCK! OUUUUT!" to the teacher's back as he left, never to return.

Jim assumed the role of a wizened uncle in my life, and dispensed tons of practical advice to me throughout our time together. There were two things Jim said to me during my years of working for him that I have never forgotten. At the end of one workday we were unpacking boxes of instructional books and Jim asked how my writing was going.

I told him about how I had six ideas for six different projects and I was struggling with having too many amazing ideas. I just didn't know what to do with the burden of my massive talent. At this point in my life I was working round the clock. My goal was to be some kind of writer, but I needed the safety net of the retail job to pay bills and to save up for a house. This meant that I would work full-time at the store, then head home and eat dinner, only to sit back down around 10:00 P.M. to write until I fell asleep.

Jim interrupted me and said, "Ideas are cheap, and if you just talk about what you're gonna do, you'll never do it. The only thing that matters are the things you finish, so just pick one thing and finish it." This advice has resonated with me through so many parts of my life and has kept me on a productive artistic path. He revealed the difference between the talkers and the doers. When you talk over and over about whatever creative endeavor you're going to accomplish to anyone who will listen, your brain processes this as if you have actually accomplished your goal. And once your brain is satisfied, you lose the passion and drive to actually do what you wanted to, because you already felt the satisfaction of accomplishment by flapping your gums about it. (How do I know all this brain stuff to be true? I studied brain stuff at the community college!) You can't talk about the thing—you gotta do the thing. Simple but true.

The other piece of wisdom Jim imparted to me took place a day before Christmas. We had been working together a handful of years by this point and would exchange presents on Christmas Eve. December 24 was always a magical day at the store, because every single customer *had* to buy something. The last-minute shoppers were hours away from Christmas morning, which meant they had zero leverage. Half the customers were panicked deadbeat dads buying drum sets at full price because the store was gonna close in two hours. It was paradise. Jim always gave me a sizable bonus at the end of the day, so I wanted to reciprocate his generosity. I asked him what he wanted for Christmas. I figured he would ask for a nice bottle of booze or something along those lines.

Jim thought for a few seconds and then said, "What I'd really like is a pile of porn magazines." I wasn't sure if he was serious. "Yeah, it's what I want, so get me that." So a yuletide tradition began that year: Every Christmas Eve I would walk over to the local newsstand and grab a copy of literally every stroke mag from the top shelf. After we locked up for the day I would drop a grocery bag in front of him. He would tear it open and flip through his Christmas bounty with a smile. It was a look of innocence, not unlike a child unwrapping a bicycle-shaped present underneath the tree. Except this was a grown man flipping through the latest issue of *Nugget*, staring at all the pretty naked ladies.

However much I enjoyed working for Jim, managing at a music store just wasn't the career I wanted. I wanted to write for a living. I knew I wasn't where I was supposed to be, but I was having a hard time making a move. I suppose it's in my upbringing; I come from a pretty cautious family that lives as if everything could end tomorrow. So while my actions can be moronically risky in some ways, I can also box myself in from making transitions that are long overdue.

The final shove I needed came one night at an NYC comedy show. By this point I was hanging out with creative friends who had burgeoning writing and directing careers. Every Monday night, I would go to Luna Lounge in lower Manhattan to watch a comedy show called *Eating It*. This was a showcase for comedians like Dave Chappelle, Sarah Silverman, and Todd Barry to try out new material on an NYC audience that could roll with just about anything.

A pre-*WTF* Marc Maron was the de facto weekly anchor of the show. Sometimes he was hilarious; sometimes he was furious or despondent, which can also be hilarious; in its own way. But he was always exciting. Being in the audience was thrilling, one of the rare times that I knew I was witnessing something that wouldn't last forever. This was also the show where a comedian named Nick Di Paolo decided to make fun of me for sitting in the audience with a heavy winter jacket. "Look at that coat," he said derisively. Stupid me, wearing a coat in February! I guess I should've opted for the cheap leather jacket he was sporting, as if he was on his way back from an audition for a *Lords of Flatbush* reboot.

One Monday night I was sitting in the audience with my friend and occasional writing partner Joe Ventura. Joe is one of the funniest people I know and we worked well together, both of us striving to escape our suburban Jersey roots. He had just gotten a job writing promo commercials for MTV, which meant he was on set working with all sorts of talented people. He saw his ideas actually get filmed, which sounded thrilling. I was very happy for him, but I was also very unhappy for myself.

Maron was onstage recounting a story that happened to him earlier that day. In the course of his story—I can't remember what it was about—he tried to convey the gulf between one person he considered legitimate and another he marked as a no-talent fraud. To this day I still cannot believe it, but Marc literally said, "The difference between these two guys is like the difference between working at MTV and working at a music store." The audience laughed. I just shrunk into my seat like the loser I was. At that point Marc had no idea that I was drawing air on the planet, so it wasn't aimed at me specifically, but somehow he summed up my existence with one offhand joke. If he had been hired and coached to write a joke that would reduce me to a pile of defeated goo, he would've fallen short of this bullseye.

The sting of the joke was a blessing in disguise, because now I had something to prove. I was determined to become a writer. But like so many other things, you have to take the leap. I couldn't have a safety net. So in classic Tom fashion I did what I was supposed to do, but a couple of years later than I should've done it. I told Jim I was going to quit World of Music to become a full-time writer. He understood and even gave me a huge farewell bonus that helped sustain me for months after leaving the job. You're one of the all-time greats, Jim!

And with that I was officially a writer! I was also officially without a weekly paycheck, so it was time to bust some ass. I took literally any writing job I could get my mitts on. By this time I was a staff writer for *Slam*, a cool basketball magazine that I had loved from its debut issue. I wrote their editor an impassioned letter begging them to let me write for them. If I remember correctly I offered to come to the office and empty their garbage cans if it would help get me an assignment.

They countered by hiring me to write a 150-word article on Jim McIlvaine, an NBA journeyman who was famous for two things: He blocked Michael Jordan's shot once and signed a contract with the Seattle Sonics that was so ridiculously huge that Sonics All-Star

Shawn Kemp more or less refused to play for the team unless they overpaid him as well.

It didn't matter to me that McIlvaine was a stiff. I had my shot and I wasn't going to blow it. I don't think I ever worked on something as hard as I worked on that McIlvaine article. I toiled for ages, making sure each of the 150 words was perfectly arranged. Swiss watchmakers don't craft their watches as delicately as I crafted this article. I handed it in and waited. After a few days Anna Gebbie—my point person at the magazine and one of the humans I will always be indebted to for keeping me employed for those lean years—was like, "Great job trying to make this stiff look compelling. How about giving us two hundred fifty words on Vitaly Potapenko?"

Before long they were tossing all sorts of assignments my way and I took them all. Anna paid me a compliment that I never forgot. I was talking to her about how hard I worked on each piece and she said something to the effect of "That's why we like you. You can write, but you're the most low-maintenance person we've got on staff." Low maintenance. I wore that compliment like Nick Di Paolo wore his cheap leather jacket that night he made fun of my winter coat. Seriously, what did he have against staying warm?!

Since I didn't have to work conventional office hours to write for the basketball magazine, I slowly adopted a schedule that could best be described as "troublesome." I would write deep into the night, stopping only when my brain literally shut me down, then sleeping until midmorning when I would start all over. My body clock had nothing in common with those of normal people. I did the work until the work was done, and little did I know that when you're a freelancer the work is NEVER done. My circumstances upgraded from "troublesome" to "severely disconcerting" when I began incorporating matinee screenings of literally any movie playing at the multiplex near my house into my routine.

The true low point of this era—actually any era, not just for me but for humanity as a whole—would be an otherwise unassuming June morning in 2001. I got up a hair before 10:00 A.M. I rubbed the sleep from my tired eyes, rolled out of bed, and quickly threw on some clothes. Within five minutes I was in my car driving to the movie theater.

I parked and sleepily wandered through the lobby. I stepped up to the counter and said these five fateful words:

"One for *The Animal*, please."

If you can't remember, *The Animal* was Rob Schneider's follow-up to *Deuce Bigalow: Male Gigolo*, a movie in which Rob received organ transplants from a variety of animals and found himself assuming different traits of the beasts. If the details elude you, it's probably because you didn't feel strangely compelled to see every comedy ever made in an effort to "know the marketplace" like I did at the time. I wanted to write movies and for some reason figured this was the way to get prepared for the day my number was called. But what could I have learned from *The Animal*? Don't include a scene in your screenplay that features Rob Schneider throwing his own feces? (I'm assuming that happened, either in the movie or just on the set between takes.)

Those truly were simpler times, the years before America had felt the horrors of 9/11, a time when hardworking folks would turn to Rob Schneider to blow off some steam after a long day in the salt mines. Rob's co-star for *The Animal* was Colleen Haskell, who is better known as Colleen from the first season of *Survivor*, and this movie more or less ended her thespian endeavors.

Did I buy something from the concession stand at 10:00 A.M.? The probability is high; most likely a Diet Coke and a bag of Peanut M&M's. While I might not recall the specifics, we can safely assume I ate some sort of garbage for breakfast at a movie theater concession stand. I entered the theater and sat down to watch the 10:15 showing of *The Animal*. Eighty-four minutes later I went back to my car, drove home, walked through my front door, and ONLY THEN DID I BRUSH MY FUCKING TEETH AND TAKE A SHOWER.

I told you it was a low point!

But my life wasn't all Peanut M&M's and morning movies; I was taking any job that came my way. If there was a potential writing assignment, the call generally went like this:

> EDITOR: Hey, Tom. I was wondering if you'd be
>   interested in writing about—
> TOM: Yes.
> EDITOR: I didn't say what I was—
> TOM: Fine, I'll take less money.
> EDITOR: I'm not sure you understand what—
> TOM: You need it written by tonight? Yeah, I can make
>   that happen.
> EDITOR: Tom, you can have a couple of weeks to write
>   the article, and—
> TOM [*rooting through wallet*]: Look, I can pay you a
>   hundred dollars. But not a penny more. [*Beat*] Okay,
>   one fifty is the highest I can go!

Joe moved on from MTV and I took over for him, writing promo spots for a variety of projects. Perhaps you've thrilled to the MTV Movie Awards campaign featuring Jimmy Fallon and Kirsten Dunst hosting a sleepover? That was ALL ME. Or maybe you've watched the commercials for an MTV-produced film called *200 Cigarettes* that starred the only actor associated with the movie who would do promos, a young man by the name of Dave Chappelle? Wait, you don't remember that?!

Meanwhile the editorial crew at *Slam* magazine defected from the self-proclaimed "In Your FACE Basketball Magazine" to run *Inside Stuff* and *Hoop,* a pair of NBA-sanctioned mags. The jobs became a little more whitewashed—the celebration of players the old guard considered "thugs" was kept to a league-ordained minimum and tattoos were often airbrushed into oblivion—but two magazines meant twice as much work. And I took everything they would shovel my way.

I covered all sorts of events, like the inaugural NBA Fashion Show, a completely normal and non-stupid event featuring NBA players walking the runway and celebrities like Tatyana Ali modeling a dress made entirely out of basketball cards. I was quite the investigative reporter back then, asking Carmen Electra questions like "Did you grow up a basketball fan?" or pressing Ice Cube to answer questions like "Did you grow up a basketball fan?" It was pretty dumb but also very fun, no complaints from me.

One time I flew to Orlando to cover the then-young duo of future Hall of Famer Paul Pierce and future slumlord Antoine Walker as they read to children at Universal Studios. I was supposed to ask them questions like "Do you like reading books?" and "What book are you reading right now?" (I made an executive decision not to ask them "Did you grow up a basketball fan?") The job was completely harmless stuff, a piece of cake waiting to be eaten.

The only hair on said cake was that the Celtics—the team Pierce and Walker played for—were on the verge of missing the playoffs. They were playing the Orlando Magic later that evening and more or less had to win to keep their postseason hopes alive. I arrived at the arena where the Celtics were participating in a midmorning practice session. I could hear their coach Rick Pitino screaming at the team through a very heavy steel door. I couldn't make out what he was saying but it was loud and extremely angry. Not exactly the kind of thing that sets a good mood for a fun interview.

Pierce and Walker eventually climbed into a limousine with me and an NBA publicity person. The tandem were in an incredibly sour mood, almost as if they had just been yelled at for an hour by their coach.

I made a great impression on them, sitting in the back of the limousine, sweat streaming down my face as if someone had poured a bucket of water over my head, shakily holding my mini-cassette recorder as I attempted to ask them about reading.

The two players ignored me completely, instead zeroing in on the NBA flack. "You put Dirk Nowitzki and Steve Nash on the cover of the magazines but you don't do anything with us," Pierce lashed out. The NBA rep countered with a brutally cold retort, telling them, "Maybe if you guys would make the playoffs, the league would promote you more."

Complete silence as the two players stared icily out the window, ignoring everyone in the car, most especially the dumb sweaty dude who wouldn't stop asking them about books. If I close my eyes I can recall the feeling in the back of that limousine: The punishingly bright Florida sun reducing my eyes to squinting slits combined with the tension in the car made me queasy. Eventually Walker quietly told me that he liked books about finance and Paul Pierce begrudgingly said he was reading a book about learning Spanish.

We arrived at Universal Studios and the two players were guided into a Dr. Seuss area where a bunch of kids were sitting in the broiling Orlando sun waiting to have a book read to them. Funny thing: When a bunch of people were watching and filming, Paul Pierce and Antoine Walker suddenly got nicer!

They cheerfully read from *The Sneetches* and the kids had a great time. Antoine Walker even put one of those insanely tall *Cat in the Hat* hats on his head. I watched them charm the pants off everyone as I tried to furtively wring the sweat out of my shirt. And to his credit, a still–Cat in the Hatted Antoine Walker thanked me for writing the article. So he's all right in my book. I take back the slumlord thing, Antoine! Paul Pierce and I never got square, so he's still on my shit list.

Another exciting moment was when I attended Knicks training camp to get some random quotes from players that would be peppered through the magazine. Barn burners like "We hope we can win it all this year" or "Ultimately it's a team game." There was a buzz in the air that Michael Jordan was planning to un-retire and return to the NBA, so Anna called me with an enticing proposition: I would be paid fifty dollars for every quote I could get about Michael Jordan possibly coming out of retirement. I saw dollar signs as I drove up to the town of Purchase, New York, ready to build my retirement fund one quote at a time.

The event was clogged with beat reporters from all the New York sports pages. They would surround any player who stepped off the court, throwing out question after question. The player would generally field a handful of queries before escaping to the locker room.

I was intimidated by this scene, and for whatever reason—most likely a combination of sheer terror and embarrassment—could not manage to shout out, "Howard Eisley, how do you feel about the news that Michael Jordan might be coming out of retirement?" I saw my golden parachute fading into the distance, but then I spotted my meal ticket sitting at the far end of the gymnasium. Leaning against the back wall was Spike Lee. He was alone. Not talking on the phone, not even reading a newspaper. He was literally just leaning on the wall and watching the players get interviewed.

This was what I had been waiting for: an opportunity to land a quote from a guy who literally directed Michael Jordan in his classic Nike commercials! Spike is a true legend. He is America's Jean-Luc Godard, a towering and versatile figure whose work remains underappreciated. I was a huge fan. I steeled myself and started walking toward him. The practice facility was composed of two basketball courts laid out next to each other. I cannot overstate how far away he was from me. And it was just me and Spike. Nobody else was around. And he watched me the entire time, never moving a muscle.

Finally I stepped up to him, five feet away as I opened my mouth. "Excuse me—"

Spike cut me off. "I'm not working today, man." And with that he turned and looked away from me.

I walked away, unsure of what had just happened. He had three solid minutes to tell me he wasn't working today, but he let me walk the entire length of two basketball courts before telling me. I stood stunned by the insanity of the moment and staggered out of the practice facility back to my car, my brain still spinning. A battery of questions sprouted in my mind: He wasn't working today? Yeah, I had figured he wasn't working since he wasn't directing a movie. And I know he was laughing to himself as soon as I started walking away. He had to have known what he did to me.

But any trace of anger fell away as I realized that Spike Lee had just pulled a major league troll job on me, one so meaninglessly and epically shitty that I actually respected it. If Andy Kaufman had done something like that while wearing a wrestling unitard, we'd all be celebrating his genius. So if Spike Lee ever reads this, I tip my hat to you, sir. I legitimately admire what you did to me that day. It was beautiful in its own bizarre way, and I am proud to have been a part of it. Oh, and in *BlacKkKlansman*, why didn't the main guy when he got on the phone with the Klansman just say he had a cold to explain why his voice sounded different? These details matter, Spike! But first things first: kudos on the top-notch burn.

One of the best parts of writing for basketball magazines was the thrill of going to games. The teams feed the writers beforehand, they sit in amazing seats to watch the game, they get a solid dessert spread during halftime, and at the end of the night they go into the locker room and talk to the athletes before knocking out their articles.

I gave serious consideration to pursuing a career in sportswriting. I felt like I was at a crossroads; if I wanted to make this my life, I had to make a full commitment. It could've been a sweet path to pursue but I got scared off the pursuit one night at a New Jersey Nets game. The contest I was covering was a real battle, the score going back and forth all night until it ended in a tie. I had a few minutes to run to the men's room before overtime began, and I ran into Fred Kerber, the beat guy for the *New York Post*. He was taking a leak at a urinal. I was the only other person in the bathroom. He turned to me and said, "Overtime, can you believe this shit?" in the most defeated tone, like we were workers at a urine-tasting factory being summoned back to our posts for an extra shift.

This guy was lucky enough to be paid to sit in great seats and write about the sport we all loved, and yet here he was, living in hell.

I loved basketball too much to risk becoming a younger version of him. (I saved all my illogical resentment and petty scorekeeping for television writing.)

I redoubled my focus on getting a non-sportswriting job, but I kept taking basketball assignments until the day I got hired to write on *Monk*. I'm glad I kept at it, because covering the NBA for the magazines I wrote for was fun and ridiculous. When I look back at my basketball writing days, I feel like Rutger Hauer at the end of *Blade Runner*: "I've seen things you people wouldn't believe. I interrupted coach Jack Ramsay's dinner by calling too early for an interview. I watched Stephon Marbury strip naked and take a bath with his son while I asked him about his sneaker line. All these moments will be lost in time, like tears in rain. Time to die."

The absolute highlight of this stretch of my life took place sometime in 2002 before I landed my first television writing job for the series *Monk*. Anna Gebbie called me and asked the greatest question I have and ever will get asked: "Would you be interested in writing about Papa Roach playing a basketball game against some people who won a contest?" These are the perverse moments in life where you know you're going to be a part of something so colossally dumb that a wave of giddiness washes over you. These are the special moments and if you feel one on the horizon, run toward it with every ounce of energy in your soul. And that is precisely what I did.

"Yes, I would like to write about Papa Roach playing basketball," I replied. "I would like that very much."

For anyone who doesn't remember, Papa Roach was a wildly popular nu metal–ish band circa 2001. Their biggest hit was "Last Resort"; it's one of those early millennium heavy rap-rock songs with a massive chorus. The video for the song is very much of the era, a style best described as "band plays in front of a swarm of excited kids and lots of people give the finger." Not exactly my cup of tea but it's not bad if you're into that kinda thing. Look, it's hard enough to find things you love in this miserable world and if you love Papa Roach I'm not going to take that away from you (says the person who attacks Billy Joel every chance he gets).

The event went as follows: The makers of Jim Beam—a bourbon that I had last drank from a bottle stolen from my friend's parents' liquor cabinet around the age of fourteen—held a contest in which the winner would bring three of their friends to New York City to play full-court basketball against the four dudes in Papa Roach. Now I know what you're asking yourself: "Tom, you said the contest winner could bring three friends. And there are four members of Papa Roach: Dave Buckner, Jerry Horton, Jacoby Shaddix, and Tobin Esperance. So how could they play a proper game of five-on-five basketball with only four players per side?!"

The promotions people at Jim Beam are waaaaay ahead of you, friend. Because they remedied the situation by adding a member of the Harlem Globetrotters to each team. Now you've got five-on-five roundball the way James Naismith envisioned it back in 1891: four out-of-shape winners of a bourbon contest squaring off against four out-of-shape nu metal dudes, with two members of America's leading comedy basketball troupe thrown in to balance everything out.

The festivities were held on the outdoor basketball courts at Chelsea Piers, a mammoth sports complex next to the Hudson River. I arrived and was immediately intercepted by a Jim Beam representative who excitedly slapped a laminated security pass that read "Throw Down the Rock" in my hand. I wasn't really sure why I needed the lammy, since nobody was attending this event outside of Jim Beam's media team. No spectators, no gawkers. It was actually quite an accomplishment, considering how popular Papa Roach was at the time; they had sold millions of albums and were fixtures on MTV. But for anyone who might've caught a glimpse of them at Chelsea Piers that day, they were just a quartet of bozos hooping it up in uniforms that read JIM BEAM in huge letters across their chests.

The media flack bombarded me with questions, almost all of them revolving around how many times I was going to mention Jim

Beam in my article. I had to bite my tongue because the cold reality of the situation was I would be plugging Jim Beam exactly zero times. I was writing this article for a children's basketball magazine; if I couldn't write about Allen Iverson's tattoos, there was no chance in hell I would be encouraging the youth of America to start drinking bourbon. But I returned vague answers and dopey nods her way as I slid the laminate over my head.

The game was the shitshow it was always destined to be. Both teams were abysmal and nobody could make a basket. The two Globetrotters did their best to set up their teammates, serving up passes for layups that missed the rim and kicking the ball out for jumpers that soared high over the backboard. I'm sure the Globetrotters wanted nothing more than to take over the game so we could all go home but they were obligated to feed bounce passes to the bassist in Papa Roach so he could brick yet another four-footer.

This went on forever, the slow creep of futility spreading over the event like a blanket. The common truth shared between everyone was the same: *I don't want to be here.* The guys in Papa Roach would most definitely rather have been acting like the rock stars they truly were at that point instead of running up and down a basketball court. The contest winners were probably wondering when they would be able to check out the M&M's store in Times Square and "get to visit 9/11" instead of playing a sport they had no business playing. And as far as the two Harlem Globetrotters went, this was far beneath the station of guys whose games involved buckets of confetti and basketballs attached to elastic strings.

At some point, the game ended. Who won? I don't have a fucking clue but now it was time for me to interview the guys from Papa Roach. I was led into a catering tent. There was food everywhere. I recall a surprising amount of shrimp. And there sat the four members of Papa Roach, completely exhausted from their basketball adventure, helping themselves to the spread. There is no better combination than sweat and shrimp, and Papa Roach was living proof.

I asked them some more of my trademark dumb questions and quickly realized they had zero interest in basketball. When I asked if he had played before, Dave Buckner rubbed his ample stomach and said, "Do I look like I could play basketball, man?" I asked Jacoby why they decided to participate in this event. He looked at me and said, "Jim Beam, dude!"

I had everything I needed for my article.

But the day was far from over. While the members of Papa Roach had fulfilled their contractual obligation and driven back to California in a tractor trailer filled with cash and Jim Beam, the contest winners weren't off the hook. We headed over to Madison Square Garden, where New York Knicks legend Walt "Clyde" Frazier would lead them through a series of basketball drills on the Knicks' home court.

Walt stood on the very floor on which he'd led the Knicks to a pair of NBA championships, but now he was attempting to dole out tips to a quartet of nonathletes who had already played a full game of basketball a couple of hours earlier before loading up on catered food and booze. They sluggishly attempted to dribble the ball between a row of cones and make simple layups but the seafood had taken its toll and the shots just weren't dropping.

One bright spot took place at the end of the day. After the drills concluded I went onto the court and dribbled a basketball around for a bit, then hoisted a three-pointer. I missed it badly because I also suck at basketball. I jacked up another shot and missed again. But I would not be denied. After about five shots, one finally ripped the net. I had shot a three-pointer on the court where some of my favorite players had also played! But there were no cheers. I looked around, but the stands were empty. Complete silence. A magical moment just for myself.

But if that building could've talked that day, our conversation would've gone something like this:

"Congratulations on making a three-pointer, Tom. You are now a part of the legend of Madison Square Garden."

"Thank you, Madison Square Garden."

"You can call me MSG. Oh, and remember when you saw the Scorpions here?"

"Yeah, that was a good show. Bon Jovi opened."

"I forgot about that! That was right before they blew up. Hey, that was the first time you ever saw anyone do coke, right?"

"It was! A couple of dudes one row in front of me. They just poured it out on a tour program. Why did you bring that up, MSG?"

"Because you are standing right where you stood that night. Think about that. Fifteen years ago you watched some metal dummies doing sloppy lines at a Scorpions show. And a couple of years earlier, this was where you stood when that security guard snuck you onto the floor for the Billy Joel show."

"Wow, that's right. I never made the connection until now."

"You were a spectator then but now you're draining three-pointers in the same spot. Who knows what will bring you back onto this floor fifteen years from now?"

"Who knows? Life is funny that way, MSG."

"It sure is, Tom. It sure is. Now get out of here before you barf your shrimp-filled stomach on me."

CHAPTER TWELVE

MONK AND *THE BEST SHOW*

WHEN PEOPLE ASK me how they can start writing for television, I never have an answer that makes any sense outside of "You just have to write a lot and keep writing and try to meet people and get your stuff out into the world even though you're probably not good at pitching a show because you're a writer." My path to a career in writing on TV shows was circuitous and unpredictable, and I'm still not sure how it happened.

I had been writing for basketball magazines for a few years but I knew in my heart that I wasn't meant to be a sportswriter as a career. My desire was always to be a Professional Funny Person and it was high time to make that a reality. But I was a shy young fella who didn't have a single connection to anyone in the entertainment industry. My best showbiz contact at that point would've been the magician my parents hired for my sixth birthday party. I remember being blown away when he made milk pour out of my shirtsleeve, but that doesn't mean he could've provided decent feedback on my *Just Shoot Me!* spec script. Although who knows? Maybe he was as masterful at punching up a script as he was at pulling a quarter from my ear.

A development around this period was one of the scariest things that ever happened to me: Terre was diagnosed with a very aggressive form of breast cancer a couple of years after we got married. It was one of the most brutal experiences of my life and I was merely a spectator. I cannot express how difficult it is to watch someone you love get sick. You simply aren't supposed to worry whether your wife is going to die from a disease when you're still in your twenties. But she dealt with it by displaying superhuman strength and determination, and after a year of surgeries and chemotherapy treatments she was declared cancer-free. This is ultimately Terre's story to tell and I hope she tells it, but what I will say is that she stood up to cancer and beat it and it was one of the most impressive feats of courage I have ever witnessed.

With Terre thankfully on the mend and my writing career finally starting to take shape I felt I could manage a return to WFMU (Terre would resume doing her show the following year). I just couldn't get rid of that radio bug no matter how hard I tried to move on! I knew that nothing made me happier than sitting behind the board and doing my show. But I also understood that I wasn't really a disc jockey. If I was going to do another radio show it would need to be more than just me playing music. I knew that Wurster and I had tapped into something in the few scripted calls we did, so the goal was now to create a radio show that would be the broadcasting equivalent of the New York City comedy scene I had fallen in love with.

By this period the Upright Citizens Brigade had begun to make serious waves in NYC. They'd opened their own theater a year or so prior, and every Sunday I would line up to see ASSSCAT, their weekly long-form improv show. This was and still is the best collection of talent I've ever seen on one stage. The show consisted of the four core UCB members—Amy Poehler, Matt Walsh, Ian

Roberts, and Matt Besser—along with a cast of regulars like Adam McKay, Tina Fey, Andy Richter, Jerry Minor, Rachel Dratch, Jon Glaser, Kevin Dorff, Horatio Sanz, Brian McCann, and many many more, joining together to perform improvised scene after improvised scene. They could take a premise and explore every angle of it before blowing the whole thing up and starting again. One time I remember Tina Fey and Rachel Dratch doing a scene in which they portrayed a mother and daughter having a revealing conversation about life. It was intimate and human and hilarious. Then McKay stepped in and declared that this scene was now taking place on the moon, and everything got exponentially funnier and weirder. I have been lucky in my life when it comes to seeing legendary performances. I have seen the best bands *and* the best comedians do their thing at the peak of their powers.

It might sound like hubris, but I knew that I had it in me to do something great. Or maybe I just wanted to try to do something great. I envisioned doing a radio show that brought the spirit of those ASSSCAT shows to whatever this new version of my program would be. Those performers were liberated onstage, doing and saying whatever they wanted as long as they were entertaining themselves. They took risks. Sometimes they failed but sometimes they made magic.

I called up Jon Wurster and ran this by him. It had been a few years since we had done Rock, Rot & Rule on the radio, and the legend of the call had grown throughout our absence. Jon made cassette dubs of the call and passed them out to fellow bands during his tours with Superchunk, which was how cool/weird things got around at the tail end of the pre-Internet era. It became a low-level proto-viral sensation among hipsters; every once in a while someone would come up to me at a show and throw RRR quotes at me. There were a few surprising celebrations of the call as well, like the time "ROCK ROT & RULE" appeared on a chalkboard in an episode of *Strangers with Candy*. It felt as if Jon and I had stumbled upon something truly special, something that got cut short before we had a chance to explore it further. Now was our chance.

> TOM: Jon, what if we did a version of Rock, Rot & Rule on the radio every week?
> JON: Hold on, I'm watching the latest episode of *Alias*. This Jennifer Garner has "it," trust me. She's gonna be a big star.
> TOM: Should I call back?
> JON: No, let me just watch this fight scene.
> [*Five minutes later*]
> JON: Whew, Alias won the fight. It was getting a little sticky there.
> TOM: Her character's name is Alias on the show *Alias*?
> JON: I'm not really sure. What is it you wanted again?
> TOM: I was wondering what you would think about doing what we did with Rock, Rot & Rule on the radio every week?
> JON: I'm in.

Jon is the funniest person I have ever met. Nobody has made me laugh more than he has, outside of the time Kelsey Grammer fell off the stage at Disney World. If the two of us dedicated ourselves to writing and performing comedy every week, then it would make at least two people—me and Jon—laugh. Anybody else would be gravy.

I pitched the show to Brian Turner, the program director at WFMU at the time. He gave me a time slot on the upcoming schedule. I was now the host of a show on Tuesday nights at 9:00 P.M. I wanted to make a real splash with the program. I wanted people to know we weren't here to waste anyone's time, so calling the show something limp like "The Tom Scharpling Show" wasn't gonna cut it. I needed a title that listeners would not forget.

I always love when people make oversized pronouncements. The key to their bluster is that they know that making a bold proclamation has nothing to do with the truth but has everything to do with creating a discussion. When Muhammad Ali called himself "the Greatest," he gave everyone permission to call him the Greatest. (And he was the greatest.) Or when the Clash declared themselves to be "the only band that matters," they redrew the parameters of that debate; rather than dispute whether the Clash was a good band, people were now debating whether they were the only band that matters. (They weren't "the only band that matters," by the way. Both the Ramones and Alvin and the Chipmunks mattered at least as much.) I needed to come up with my version of that.

The show titles came fast and furious. "Blabbermouth." "Tom Time." "Laugh It Up." One worse than the next.

Then it hit me.

"What if I declared my show to be *the best*?"

Terre countered, suggesting "The Best Show."

I wrote it out on a small piece of notebook paper:

THE BEST SHOW ON WFMU

It popped off the page just like in *Boogie Nights* when Dirk Diggler envisioned his own name exploding in lights. That was the title! Jon and I immediately started creating a variety of characters and scripting out calls. We were pumped, ready to take on the world.

The Best Show on WFMU debuted on October 10, 2000, to resounding silence. Nobody was debating whether the show was "the best" or not, because they were too busy telling me to shut up and play music. WFMU is primarily a music-based station, arguably the most renowned freeform station on earth. The listeners love music from all over the world and they absolutely love when the DJs play the weirdest and harshest and most polarizing sounds ever recorded. But like I said, most of them don't know anything about comedy. When it comes to the laffs they become as conservative as Chuck Woolery at a chili cook-off.

Over and over the listeners would call in to complain, telling me that the on-air bits with Wurster were endless and unfunny. They said I was embarrassing myself. The first episode of the show—which is not online anywhere and never will be—made my skin crawl when I listened to it more than a decade later. The audience talked to me as if I was one of those turn-of-the-century dummies you see in grainy footage trying to invent a workable airplane. They treated me like I was no different from the dope who strapped massive flapping wings to a bicycle only to watch the entire machine collapse in a pile of futility. At one point a WFMU disc jockey called in over the air and "politely" told me to just play a record and stop talking because what I was doing simply wasn't any good.

But it was fine, really. Beyond a very limited point none of this phased me because I knew that we were funny! I was laughing, Jon was laughing, and a handful of people whose taste we respected were laughing. I knew we were right.

It reminds me of the time I was strolling down the Seaside Heights boardwalk on a summer evening a few years ago. I stopped at an ice cream stand to get myself a soft vanilla cone, and within a minute some guy noticed my King Crimson T-shirt. Now, King Crimson is one of my all-time top bands, a progressive rock unit that has repeatedly changed and revolutionized music over the last five decades. They aren't for everyone but if they make sense to you, they are your favorite. He pointed at my shirt and said in a conspiratorial tone, "*We* get it." He then swept his free hand wide, pointing at the sea of oblivious people walking past, mockingly adding, "*They* don't." It is a powerful thing to not give a flying fuck about what others think when you're making something. Not the easiest mindset to achieve, I know, but if you can get there you'll feel invincible. (And for the record the guy then launched into a story about how he talked to Crimson guitarist Robert Fripp at Guitar Center and I promptly fell asleep in the middle of the boardwalk.)

For too many years of my life I was hesitant about putting myself out there. I never felt like I fit into any scene, primarily because I actually didn't fit into any scene. I always felt like an outsider, a kid with no country. Those feelings became turbocharged after my hospitalization. I never felt strong enough to express myself without fear of being shut down for being dumb or poor or mentally ill. But for whatever reason, when I started *The Best Show* I didn't worry for a second. Even though the audience didn't like it—and it would take a couple of years before people truly got on board—I kept pushing forward, knowing in my heart that this radio show was my ASSS-CAT, the purest and most liberating form for me to express myself and be funny and honest and human. If you're lucky enough to spot an opportunity like this in your own life, grab it with both hands and give it everything you've got. Because *you* get it. Who really gives a fuck if they don't?

THE BEST SHOW provided countless opportunities for me to demonstrate exactly how I was funny, but there was one glitch: WFMU is a listener-sponsored station, so I wasn't earning a nickel off it, yet my enthusiasm for making the show as amazing as it could possibly be turned it into a full-time job. This situation was simply not sustainable, so I needed to get some paying work and quick. I wasn't a part of any clique or fraternity that took care of their own like Harvard graduates or Amway salespeople. I felt confident in my talent, but to anyone handing out jobs I was still a former sheet music salesman with a sense of humor. I needed to find a way into the industry. I was desperate to get the ball rolling; I would've sat in a dunk tank if I knew that a supervising producer from *Veronica's Closet* would be whipping the balls at me.

I was hanging out at WFMU one night when I realized that a talk show host named Dorian Devins had an Actual Screenwriter on her program. And this was no fly-by-night Charlie either: David Newman was her guest, the co-writer of *Bonnie and Clyde* and the first *Superman* movie with Christopher Reeve. I listened intently to the show in the station kitchen, trying to glean any wisdom I could from the conversation. After the program ended I said hi to Dorian and introduced myself to Newman. It turned out that he needed a ride back to Manhattan. This was a good chance to talk to this legendary screenwriter, so I offered to drive him home, even though I didn't live anywhere near his Manhattan apartment.

We had a perfectly fine time talking about movies and radio while I drove into Manhattan. As we approached his apartment I finally gathered the courage to tell Newman that I was working to be a screenwriter and that I wrote every day and night. This exchange took up perhaps forty-five seconds of our trip, but he could not have shown less interest in me after I revealed this. I was a little disappointed but I also realized full well that he was in my car for a ride, not to host a screenwriting seminar. I dropped him off and said goodbye to someone I knew I would never see again.

I eventually learned what David Newman thought of our car ride a month or two later when I came across a piece he had written for the *New York Times*. Entitled "Learning to Talk Screenwriterese (And Other Tips)," the article discussed the early days of his career:

> When I first started out in this line of work, which was roughly somewhere between the end of silent films and the commencement of psychedelic drugs, the enduring myth among writers of my generation was that if you were a scribbler, working away at your advertising copy or writing newspaper captions, what you were really doing was working on the Great American Novel. You worked on that sometime between dessert and exhaustion, so you did about 10 minutes a night. And then you went to sleep.

I understood that loud and clear. We are on the same page, David! But Newman changed things up a little in his next paragraph.

Now, everybody is writing screenplays. You get in a cab and the driver hears you talking about the movie business and, before you get out, the driver asks you if you will read his screenplay. It's happened to me three times.

My heart plummeted into my stomach. Look, I know what it's like when someone tries to pick your brain and I most definitely wasn't doing that. I was just a dumb young guy trying to be less dumb. I had dedicated myself to the art of screenwriting with a monastic focus, desperately interested in knowing as much as I could about the medium. And it's not enough that I clearly bothered this guy with the one screenwriting question I asked during an hour-long car ride. He had to use me as a buffoonish prop to make his point, which I guess was "it's not like it used to be in the good old days when I was the only screenwriter I knew." Oh, and there is one key difference between me and a cab driver: A CAB DRIVER WOULD'VE GOTTEN PAID FOR GIVING YOU THAT FUCKING RIDE.

I felt humiliated but I handled it the only way I knew. I blew up the offending paragraphs on a photocopier and got the page laminated. I thumbtacked it to the wall directly in front of my desk. This article stared me in the face every time I sat down to work. And work I did, knowing that I now had to succeed if only to prove that pantload wrong.

On a more somber note, David Newman passed away in 2003. Rest in peace, sir. You mocked me and that drove me to defeat you. Thank you for the spark.

I HAD BECOME FRIENDS with Andy Breckman, another WFMU radio host who did the only other comedy program on the station. Andy had an insanely respectable pedigree as a comedy writer: He wrote for David Letterman during his early years, then jumped to *Saturday Night Live*, where he wrote sketches like the one where Eddie Murphy becomes a white guy for a day and realizes that the world suddenly becomes easier. Andy then transitioned out of television into feature films. He was doing what I had only dreamed of doing, and he was doing it while living in suburban New Jersey. Just like me!

Terre knew Andy a little bit and slipped him a copy of a screenplay that I had co-written with Joe Ventura called *Flyin V*, which still might be the funniest thing I've ever worked on. I would tell you what it's about but I still hold out hope that someday it will get made. All I will say is that it is chock-full of the cringey comedy America would soon fall in love with, so if you're a fancy showbiz producer and/or owner of a major Hollywood studio, drop me a line! A copy of the screenplay was in Andy's possession and I was dying to know what he thought of it, desperate for feedback. I didn't hear anything.

By this point I assumed that the script had ended up in a garbage can or a birdcage, but seven months later my phone rang. It was Andy! He had thrown the script in the backseat of his car, where it stayed for half a year, but he unearthed it during a recent cleaning. Andy said he received a lot of scripts and they were uniformly terrible but he thought *Flyin V* was really funny and he wanted to know what my deal was. We soon became friends, watching movies at his house and hanging out. Andy eventually asked me if I would work as his assistant a few days a week. The job didn't require me to fetch him lattes or redirect his calls. It was basically me sitting with him while he wrote, providing him a sounding board for ideas and jokes and pitches. I learned so much about writing and navigating the entertainment biz working for him. I am forever grateful for the experience and for the career kick start. If you're reading this, thank you, Andy. You're my hero!

The assistant job turned out to be a bit of an audition. I was able to be funny with Andy, and I could make him laugh, which always felt amazing. Andy was mostly a features guy at that point but he would occasionally mention a TV show that he had sold to ABC about a brilliant San Francisco–based detective afflicted with obsessive-compulsive disorder. The show was called *Monk* and unfortunately it looked like it was dead in the water, a place most TV shows in development end up. But an executive moving from ABC to the USA Network presented the *Monk* pilot script as the kind of programming they wanted to develop. The network responded by saying, "Instead of trying to create shows like this, why don't we literally make *this* show?" They wrested the rights from ABC and suddenly *Monk* was back in active development. Andy said that if *Monk* moved forward, I would be the first person he hired.

Fast-forward a year or so, the pilot for *Monk* had been filmed and it came out great. I helped come up with a few gags for it, so I felt a teeny sense of pride about the whole thing. The show got picked up to series and Andy hired me as a story editor, a bottom-of-the-ladder writing position that virtually all scribes must endure. I didn't care. I had taken my first step through the door and I was going to do everything within my power not to mess this up.

Monk remained on the air for eight years, growing from a weird curiosity on the USA Network—a channel whose previous calling card was *Walker, Texas Ranger* reruns—to a legitimate success. Tony Shalhoub won three Emmys for Outstanding Lead Actor in a Comedy Series. I was on board for the entire run of the show, helping to write and produce every episode. I believe I was the only writer besides Andy who was there from the beginning to the end. I received writing credit for twenty-five or so episodes, but I worked on every last one of them. Except the terrible ones.

There is a common misconception about how television shows are written. People think that if your name is on an episode, you were the one who figured out the story and the jokes. Sometimes that can be completely true, but on most shows the writers all sit in a room together and collectively kick around plotlines and ideas. At some point an episode takes shape, and once the room "breaks" the story, one of the writers goes off and actually writes it. There have been times that I came up with huge ideas or jokes for an episode, but since someone else was assigned to write that particular script I didn't get specific credit for those contributions.

I never cared about any of that because it ultimately cuts both ways: There have been countless times I was assigned a script that someone else in the room contributed to mightily without receiving a specific credit. It all works out in the end, and it's a good lesson in teamwork: People who get obsessed with receiving credit for every single notion they pitch out will always wind up unhappy. My philosophy is to simply do the best I can and assume that my talent will take care of me in the long run.

There is nothing more exciting for a writer on a TV show than the first moment you are on set and the entire production is bringing something you wrote to life. It is an amazing thing to witness: The jokes or storyline that you wrote while sporting a tattered HOMEWORK IS HAZARDOUS TO MY HEALTH T-shirt in your basement while eating stale Tostitos is now the focus of dozens of professionals, all working to execute your vision to the letter. I had already had MTV promo commercials filmed, so it wasn't entirely new to me, but when your words are going to be the basis of an actual television show, it's something else. I remember being absolutely devastated the first time I witnessed the filming of an episode I wrote: Willie Nelson was the guest star, portraying himself in a story that had him accused of murder. Willie was the coolest and absolutely crushed his performance. I got a little choked up seeing the Red Headed Stranger saying words that I wrote. Those are the moments that remind you that the struggle is sometimes worth it. The residual checks are a close second but watching my writing get filmed was the best.

Willie Nelson wasn't the only legend to guest on *Monk*. The show actually cast a young Jennifer Lawrence in an episode during the fifth season. The only thing was that she got the part of a mascot during a high school basketball game, which meant for 95 percent of her screen time she was hidden beneath a cougar costume. She certainly gave it her all, running up and down the sidelines and even jumping on Shalhoub's back without her enormous cougar mascot head falling off.

For one brief scene the mascot removes her head and yup, there is Jennifer Lawrence in all her glory, announcing to Monk's assistant that the game is all tied up. I'm sure J-Law is proud of her turn as "Mascot" and credits this performance with opening the gateway to her role in *Winter's Bone* a few years later. I could ask the universe why she wasn't cast as one of the basketball players, of which there was an entire team's worth in the episode. There were actually two teams. But I think it all worked out for Jennifer in the end.

WRITING ON *MONK* was rewarding in so many ways. Right out of the box, I have to say that when it comes to Nice People in Showbiz (As Well As in Real Life), Tony Shalhoub is the heavyweight champion for all eternity. I have never seen anyone more thoughtful or kind to their co-workers. The guy was in virtually every scene of every episode, which meant he pulled twelve-to-fourteen-hour days five times a week for eight years. (You might be like, "So what, he was getting paid a ton of money to do it!" And yeah, that is entirely true. But so many actors are asked to do much less and they treat everyone like piles of garbage, so his kindness is both definitely and unfortunately the exception.)

Here is one of the many examples of Tony being a good guy: About four seasons into *Monk* I was between contracts, and the network would not give me a raise that came close to matching the contributions I was making to the show. I started out with the title of story editor but quickly climbed the ranks, assuming the responsibilities of an executive producer long before I was given the title. The network based their raises on what I had received on my previous contract, but since I started off getting paid half of what anyone else in the same slot would've gotten, the pay bumps left me forever operating from a deficit. I tried to straighten this out but the network refused to budge.

Tony found out about this and called the president of the USA Network, telling him that he simply couldn't continue to do the show without me. He forced the network to blink, and they begrudgingly gave me a solid raise. The next time I ran into the president of the network he smiled and said, "You won." But the thing is that Tony *wanted* to help. He most certainly could've done the show without me, but he stepped up because he is, as Tina Turner said, "simply the best."

Shalhoub gave the writers the greatest gift that any actor can ever give. We would regularly put his character into all sorts of ridiculous situations and Tony would go along with all of them—Monk gets dropped in a vat of pudding! Monk gets splashed by a puddle! Monk gets a milkshake dumped over his head!—but he had just one small caveat. "All I need is an entry point," he explained. "I know you're trying to make it funny, and I am too. But as an actor I need some way into a scene from an actor's perspective. I just need enough so that I can *believe* it." This is honestly the bare minimum an actor can ask for from the writers. Shalhoub was incredibly dedicated and reliable, and it was an honor to write for him.

The rest of the cast was more of a mixed bag. Some were amazing, and others were more "complex." Lots of ups and downs over the course of eight years. And look, I get it. Eight years is a long time to spend making the same television show. It is nearly impossible to keep things funny and compelling over 125 episodes. By the time we finished I was so fried I felt like I needed a five-year nap. Weird things are bound to happen throughout the course of eight seasons. That said, nothing could've prepared any of us for the level of weirdness that would surface midway through season two of the show.

It all started when Shalhoub won his first Emmy for the show. Tony was up for Outstanding Lead Actor in a Comedy Series, pitting him against Larry David, Matt LeBlanc, Ray Romano, Bernie Mac, and Eric McCormack. In retrospect I shouldn't have been so shocked that Tony won, but at the time it was definitely an unexpected triumph. Tony dedicated the victory to his nephew, who had tragically passed away earlier that week. The nicest guy somehow got nicer! But success can sometimes create dissent, and a short time afterward some serious grumblings arose from the rest of the cast. I'm not going to name names because I wasn't physically on set during this dustup; I was back in the writers' room in New Jersey. But the ramifications of this unhappiness soon touched all of us.

A few of the main actors were unhappy about how much they were getting paid, so they wanted to renegotiate their contracts midseason. In their eyes the show had succeeded far beyond what anyone had foreseen and they wanted raises to balance things out. Which I get completely! But the network had a policy of not renegotiating during a season, which I also understand. So, the actors did the only thing they could to make their point: They staged an elaborate "sick out," which means they would call in sick before the day's filming began. There are hundreds of thousands of dollars on the line every shoot day, so a disruption on the scale of a lead actor being unavailable to shoot their scenes creates an enormous problem.

Three actors were doing it in tandem, coming down with a migraine or a case of lower back pain precisely on the days they were heavy on the schedule. Their goal was to break the backs of the production, forcing everything to shut down so the network would have no choice but to renegotiate. And again, I understand the intent behind their actions. Money should end up in the hands of talent rather than the coffers of whichever shitty multinational conglomerate is running things. In this line of work—or in any line of work, really—you need to grab the money while you can because they will pull it out of your hands the second they can. But *Monk* was not a big show the way *Friends* or *Everybody Loves Raymond* were. We were living on a network that made its bones airing Chuck Norris's sloppy seconds. It was a sticky mess from every angle. Everybody did what they thought was right, which is so often when people get hurt.

When the reality of our new circumstances hit us—Actor X can't film today because they woke up with lower back pain—we had to scramble. The cold reality of a show getting shut down is things might not get turned back on. If the network loses enough money, they can pull the plug forever. So the decision was made to make sure that something—anything!—would get filmed every single day, even if it wasn't our best stuff. Ultimately it's not about keeping the lights on for the actors and writers; there are more than a hundred people working on every show, crew members who are reliant on filming to pay their bills. So we worked to keep things going for the lighting people and the craft service crew. You know, the people who hate the writers more than anyone else. And trust me, they *hate* the writers.

We would find out who was gonna be AWOL that morning and rewrite everything to accommodate their absence. There were a lot of cheap fixes, characters saying stuff like "Oh, they're off parking the car. They'll be back in a minute" to justify a missing character. It was exciting to generate new pages on the fly so filming could continue without pause, and somehow it worked; the stories held together and the seams weren't too obvious.

The "sick out" eventually faltered. From what I heard the actors' inability to stop the filming spooked them, but an incident took place toward the end of the first week that sunk the rebellion once and for all. One of the actors returned to work on a day another actor was at home with a "migraine." When they entered their trailer, this actor was met by a surprise sitting on their kitchen tabletop: a paper plate with a pile of human shit on it.

Once again, I was not there. I did not see the shit with my own eyes, because I was back in New Jersey rewriting scenes with the rest of the staff. But my phone blew up with people on set calling to tell me, "DID YOU HEAR THAT SOMEONE ON THE CREW LEFT

A PLATE OF HUMAN SHIT IN [name redacted]'s TRAILER?!" The rumor was that a crew member, angry about the possibility of the show getting shut down because of this salary dispute, took matters into their own hands (and ass). The actor in question quickly apologized to the crew and said this sort of thing would never happen again. The other two actors acquiesced as well and production went back to the way it used to be.

THE PREMISE OF the show itself—a brilliant detective dealing with severe mental health issues—was always a risky proposition. The possibility of portraying the character of Adrian Monk as a clown or the butt of jokes about mental illness was a constant concern, and I did my best to correct things whenever I could. I tried to protect the character from being a laughingstock, in no small part because of my personal sympathy toward these issues. I never told anyone working on the show about my past because the embarrassment was so great. I was sitting in a room of sarcastic comedy writers. *I* was a sarcastic comedy writer! Sure, sometimes the conversations we had could hurt. There was lots of discussion about a character getting locked up in a "nuthouse" and dumb shit like that. It wasn't done with malice, I know that. I spent enough time with my co-workers to know they were decent people. But my embarrassment over my past made the shame grow and I kept my lips firmly zipped.

Some version of this has happened in pretty much every writers' room I've been in. At some point the pitches would gravitate to a plot involving mental health and before long everyone would be yukking it up over the comedic potential of having one of the characters get electroshock therapy. I would slap a plastic smile on my face and pray that the idea would run out of gas on its own lack of merit.

I know that we clearly missed the mark with some of the stuff on *Monk* in terms of the depiction of mental health and that will always bother me, partly because I do feel like I sold myself out a little bit by just keeping quiet. I don't know what else to say other than shame can be a real motherfucker sometimes.

AFTER EIGHT SEASONS it was time for the show to end. We had told every story that there was to tell and a few that probably shouldn't have been. I think Monk might've ended up stuck in a fireplace six times and hypnotized on at least three different occasions. As much as I like to goof on the show—during a live performance I said there were two kinds of *Monk* fans: senior citizens and little kids whose favorite character in Star Wars is C-3PO—I loved it. The intention was sweet and Tony's performance was next-level amazing. Monk is an iconic character that will outlive us all. In many ways it is the best job I will ever have.

A huge box arrived on my doorstep a few weeks after the show had wrapped and the contents within this mysterious package taught me more about how show business works than any master class could ever teach you. I tore open the box to reveal a director's chair. The network had sent a series wrap gift to the staff of *Monk* as a gesture of gratitude. A director's chair might not be the way I would say "Thank you for keeping this network alive for eight years" but to each their own.

I unfolded the chair and slid the cloth backrest into place. One side of the backrest featured a monogrammed MONK logo and the other had my name stitched into the fabric, as if I was the star of the show and this was my chair. The only hitch was that my name was misspelled. It read "Sharpling" instead of "Scharpling." Eight years of work and they didn't even spell my fucking name right. It didn't matter how hard I worked on the job or how many episodes I wrote. The simple truth is that at the end of it all THEY JUST DON'T CARE. And that's okay. It's not their place to care! They pay you so they don't have to care!

And since they don't care, make sure you're doing the job for the right reasons. Try to have fun with the work if you're lucky enough to get it because the ride usually ends before you want it to. Get in the door by any means necessary, chase your happiness, do a great job, and grab your money.

Oh, and try not to be a dick, or one day you might find a plate covered with human shit in your trailer.

CHAPTER THIRTEEN

BEST SHOW CONFIDENTIAL

IN THE EARLY 1970s, Miles Davis was sitting on the steps of his Upper West Side apartment building when a fan approached. He was a longtime devotee of Davis, eagerly following him through all of his many genre-defying reinventions. But this fan had reached the end of his rope when Miles transformed his band into a monsoon of electric keyboards, wah-wah-infused trumpet, and low-end funk. He told Miles that he just couldn't get into the new material.

Miles responded by replying, "Should I wait for you, motherfucker?"

That is easily the coolest burn of all time. If I had been that guy I would've just handed Miles my wallet and maybe chopped off a finger out of respect for the scorching I had just received.

I'm not comparing myself to Miles Davis—don't get me wrong. (For starters, if I was gonna cover Cyndi Lauper, I would've gone with "She Bop" instead of "Time After Time.") But I do have a good idea what it's like to make something that you know is awesome only to find that your audience doesn't agree. That is what the first two years of *The Best Show on WFMU* felt like. Jon Wurster and I were producing fully realized long-form comedy routines every single week and I was filling in the non–Scharpling & Wurster parts of the show with content that I was proud of. The silence was deafening, but sometime in 2002 it all clicked. We waited and they caught up.

The Best Show became the primary focus of my non-television-writing creativity. Every thought or concept or idea I had now had a home. I would walk into the WFMU studio and sit behind the board and I knew I was right where I belonged. I would simply slide up the fader on my mic and say whatever made sense to me and the listeners liked it. Access to the airwaves was a precious commodity in the pre-podcast era, so I wanted to squeeze everything I could from every minute I had been granted. The show was heard on conventional radio throughout the NYC area as well as on the brand-new WFMU web stream, which opened things up considerably. Now we weren't just another local radio show. We were worldwide, baby!

The 180 minutes of blank canvas was both a gift and an opportunity to keep mixing things up. We tried different things with the platform from show to show. It was fun to do stuff that simply sounded fun: I would leave the studio and call in to my own show from my cell, hosting from my car as I drove around Jersey City. I would call the payphone in the Palm Springs desert next to the dinosaurs that appeared in *Pee-wee's Big Adventure* and talk at length with anyone who picked up. If it was exciting or stupid or ridiculous, it was worth trying at least once!

Even on the episodes where events were meticulously planned out, something unexpected would happen and I would travel down some strange unknown path, just me and the audience seeing where we ended up at the same time. That is the beauty of live broadcasting. No edits, no hiding, no escape. When you eat shit, everyone knows it. It is often bizarre to be juggling so many elements—the callers, the producers, any guests, the music, sound cues—while trying to focus on keeping the whole thing interesting and entertaining. Guests who have come by to watch me do the show comment afterward that it is like watching a conductor holding together an orchestra, which is a huge compliment because you know how deep my love of conductors runs. If I had my druthers this book would've focused primarily on my favorite baton twirlers, but Abrams didn't think a book of that nature had "value," insisting that they "wouldn't sell a single copy." I keep a lot of plates spinning when I'm doing the show but whenever I can turn a moment into magic, there is nothing else like it.

It's strange to think of shows that make structure such a point of pride. *Saturday Night Live* has embraced a format that you could set your watch to: If "Weekend Update" is on your television, you know that it's 12:10 A.M. If you were given ninety minutes of network airtime and a shitload of resources to make your comedy program, why on earth would you slavishly devote yourself to such a strict formula?

I know that the obvious answer is something like "Hey, asshole, they've been on the air for almost fifty years—they must be doing *something* right." And to that I say three things: First, don't call me asshole. That wasn't nice and it hurt my feelings. Second, I would ask if we're sure they're doing something right. One of the only things that all Americans agree on is that *SNL* generally sucks shit. The cast and writers are wildly talented and generally go on to make great work, but the show itself is a mess. Is all the overstructuring doing them any favors? Just imagine how thrilling it would be to turn on *Saturday Night Live* and have absolutely no idea what was going to happen next. Yeah, that version of the show probably wouldn't have lasted half a century, but why does that concern me? I'm not a shareholder; I don't give a fuck how long it stays on the air! It's too bad *SNL* didn't croak years ago to let another show that had a reason to exist fill that awesome time slot. But I'd be lying if I said I stopped watching the show, so I guess I'm a part of the problem. Physician, heal thyself!

The final thing I would say is that *The Best Show* has been cranking for almost two decades precisely because we know when it's time to retire an idea or a segment. You like formula? Well, guess what? FORMULA IS FOR BABIES. Now *that* is a burn! Imagine me dropping that zinger on Lorne Michaels in his opulent office before getting dragged into the streets of Midtown Manhattan by his Broadway Video security goons with their one-size-too-tight *Hot Rod* T-shirts.

The only restrictions that always hovered over *The Best Show* are the standard FCC limitations with "bad language." My opinion of dirty words should be clear from the healthy sprinkling throughout the book. I think cursing can be extremely funny; is there anything that makes you crack up more than a dad yelling, "GODDAMN MOTHERFUCKING SUNNOVABITCH!" from the garage after hitting his thumb?

But whoever is running the Federal Communications Commission never had a frustrated dad because they don't see the humor in cussing. That said, developing a work-around for swear words has always been a delightful challenge. The only thing funnier than an angry curse is the "clean" substitute for it. Don't believe me? I'm going to list a couple of radio-unfriendly terms and the acceptable alternatives we generated for the airwaves.

And if you are a child, I beg you to PLEASE skip this next part! Which is funnier:

"Dick" or "pant faucet"?

"Cumming" or "white walling your hand"?

(Before I continue let me congratulate the children who ignored my request to skip ahead. I knew you'd read it as soon as you noticed that "PLEASE" was in all caps. You just picked up a few cool toilet phrases you can use when you're hanging out with your pals at the panini shop or wherever it is the youth of today like to congregate.)

It's not even close: The second options are infinitely funnier than the standard-issue filth! And the cherry on top is that the "clean" substitutes are actually dirtier! It's a good creative life lesson: Limitations can be a good thing. They force your brain to generate options based on the restrictions you're dealing with. Wurster and I have had so much fun over the years swapping out swear words whenever one of the show's characters would need to curse that I am forced to thank the Federal Communications Commission for their dumb fucking rulebook.

The creative relationship I share with Jon Wurster is second to none. We have written and performed so much comedy over the years, stuff that still makes me giddy with excitement. We created a ton of characters, like Timmy von Trimble (a two-inch-tall racist), Matthew Tompkins (the head of the fictional Shout! Network, a channel that aired reality shows like *Buried Alive* and *Celebrity Buried Alive*), Barry Dworkin (the talentless leader of a band called the Gas Station Dogs, named because "there's nothing scarier than a gas station dog"), and Roland "the Gorch" Gorchnick. Jon would also appear as real-life characters like Gene Simmons or Marky Ramone, who called in to promote *Lady Wainsworth's Desires*, his book of historical erotic fiction.

The one constant with the characters was that if they made us laugh—even if the subject matter made sense to only me and Jon—we did it. Sometimes the concepts were *so* inside baseball, like the time Jon portrayed Bob Bogle Jr., the son of a founding member of the surf-rock legends the Ventures. Bob was promoting a reconstituted version of the band, whose stage show now revolved around promoting and selling water filtration systems. I remember thinking it was the funniest thing I had ever heard because it was maybe the most deliberately minor concept imaginable. I also remember the audience not being particularly into it; I was ready for the listeners to fall in love with Bob Bogle Jr., but he never found his audience. Hey, it made me laugh.

Over time *The Best Show* developed a pretty solid fan base among young kids, primarily because the show wasn't particularly dirty (outside of the sneaky filth references I mentioned earlier). Parents could feel safe listening to the show with their kids because I never strayed into sex talk or had naked ladies playing foosball or whatever it is shock jocks would do to titillate their audience. I also tried to be cool with kids whenever they called in, treating them with respect. There is nothing more fun than joking around with a kid, and they absolutely love when an adult acknowledges their reality and frustrations.

There have been many amazing child callers over the years. Liam was always one of my favorites, a kid who called up to talk about his invisible friend Bobby Joe, a pal of his who drove a toilet car that had one hundred tires on it. Then there was the force of nature known as Petey, a kid who regularly dialed in during the show's early years. Petey would tell insane stories and play songs that he wrote over the phone. Even as a youngster he understood we were building a world and he gladly joined in. But my all-time favorite might be Mac.

Mac started calling around the age of ten. He was a funny and engaging kid and he got the spirit of the show. Mac would often talk about how his favorite things in life were cars, drums, and Aerosmith. One night in 2005 Mac called in to discuss Aerosmith, reading from a book of rock facts. It started off simple enough, with Mac talking about the origins of the band and me pretending that I thought the lead singer's name was Aero Smith, not Steven Tyler. He also described the "kielbasa-thick lines of cocaine" that Tyler snorted in the band's heyday, a phrase that will forever be hilarious coming from a child.

Wurster was listening at home and saw an opportunity, so he called in as Jimmy Crespo, who replaced legendary Aerosmith guitarist Joe Perry for a few years during one of the band's fallow stretches. The fireworks between Mac and "Jimmy" started immediately.

> TOM: This is actually Jimmy Crespo from Aerosmith?
> JIMMY: Yeah.
> MAC [*shocked*]: What?!
> JIMMY: Who's this little chump?

TOM: He's doing a book report on Aerosmith.

JIMMY: Did I hear him say that we were doing cocaine? I wasn't. Maybe this kid's on cocaine.

MAC: I'm not on cocaine, I'm a thirteen-year-old. This isn't Jimmy Crespo.

After some convincing, Mac prepared a question to prove whether or not this was the real Jimmy Crespo:

MAC: Okay, okay. You should know this, obviously, if you're really Jimmy Crespo. How many units did Aerosmith sell?

JIMMY: "Units"? Who are you, Clive Davis?

MAC: How many CDs or records and stuff like that? How many albums did Aerosmith sell?

JIMMY: Of which album?

MAC: All of them. Like—

JIMMY: Oh, jeez. Sixty-two million.

MAC [*stunned*]: Holy crap.

It turned out that somehow Jon came shockingly close to guessing the total albums that Aerosmith sold throughout their career. Jon would later declare he took a shot in the dark, having absolutely no idea what the number actually was. Mac sounded truly shocked and it was pure magic.

TOM: So is he right?

MAC [*still stunned*]: Yeah, just about. It's 63.5 million.

Mac was a fan of the show and he knew that the goal was to make comedy. But he sounded truly surprised by this. This is all Jon needed and he was off to the races. I can listen to this a million times and I will always become delirious with happiness.

JIMMY: See? Who's laughing now, schmuck. How many
  pull-ups can you do?
MAC: What?
JIMMY: When I was thirteen I could do seventy-four
  pull-ups.
MAC: What are you talking about? What, were you doing
  crystal meth in those days?

That's a pretty funny line for a kid.

JIMMY: Maybe. Why?

And an equally funny reply from Jon.

JIMMY: So what's your favorite record I played on, son?
MAC: I don't know, I didn't pay attention.
JIMMY: There was an article in the *New York Times* this
  past Sunday about how kids are too lippy these days.
  You're a perfect example of that. So what kind of stuff
  are you into?
MAC: I don't know. Mostly metal.
JIMMY: Like what?
MAC: I don't know, Slayer.
JIMMY: Slayer?! That stuff's terrible! That's just noise!
  You need to put down the metal and get into some real
  hardcore stuff like MDC, Black Flag, Circle Jerks . . .

Now Jon decided to make the temp guitarist in Aerosmith a fan of
early-'80s hardcore, which makes absolutely no sense.

MAC: Rob Zombie?
JIMMY: Terrible.
MAC: Soundgarden. The Scorpions.

> JIMMY: Bad metal. Hey, Mac.
>
> MAC: What?
>
> JIMMY: Before I answer any more questions you got for me, I want you to put a necktie on.
>
> MAC: What?!
>
> JIMMY: A necktie. And a suit jacket. I want you to slick your hair back in respect to me.

The call went on, with "Jimmy" claiming that the band Deep Purple gave him "the worst wedgie I've ever gotten" among other things. I had to do everything within my power to not laugh during all this. This was just one of many unforgettable moments on the show, and stands as one of the countless examples of Jon Wurster being a comedic genius.

THE SHOW BECAME a magnet for oddballs, listeners who had zero interest in alternative comedy but saw an opportunity to get some primo airtime on a call-in show that let the listeners actually talk.

One caller who identified himself as "Captain Jack" would dial in regularly during the early days of *The Best Show*, talking in bizarre seafaring lingo, pretending he was calling the program after coming into port. He was just weird enough to be interesting, so I'd do my best to engage him. Things were fun with Captain Jack until they weren't: The party ended when he dropped off a cooler with a dead fish at the studio while I was doing the show. This spooked the shit out of me because I'm generally not in the habit of receiving dead fish as gifts. I interpreted this in the traditional mob definition: Someone gave me a fish because they wanted me to "sleep with the fishes" like in a mafia movie. Captain Jack called to explain that yes, he dropped off the fish, but he meant it as a tribute: It was a monkfish and I worked on the show *Monk*. But fuck that! It is terrifying enough to be alone in the station at night without someone dropping a gross dead fish in front of the door.

One caller would mutter phrases and non sequiturs into the phone, asking me "Where's Debbie?" before hanging up. The mystery of this unidentified listener piqued my curiosity, so I made it a goal to try to lure him out of his shell whenever he called by squeezing in as many questions as I could before he hung up. Eventually this caller identified himself as "Spike" and a magnificent relationship was born.

Our conversations were stunted and strange. They always started with Spike saying "Heeeeeeeeeeello, Tom" in a voice that sounded like Droopy dog on the losing end of a syrup-eating contest. Spike would unleash a troubling laugh before catching me up on what had been bugging him that week. He maintained a disdain for pop culture figures, awarding them mocking *Mad Magazine*–style nicknames. His favorite targets were "Baked Ziti Jones" (Catherine Zeta-Jones), "Jenny from the Bedroom" (Jennifer Lopez), and "Séance" (Beyoncé). Spike would also broadcast the things that he didn't "do," as in "I don't do . . ."

You're probably wondering what a guy who regularly referred to P. Diddy as "P. Dimwit" would consider beneath his station. Well, Spike didn't "do" Staten Island or shopping malls or coffee, for example. But fear not! Spike was a man of many passions, incredibly enthusiastic about horror movies and doo-wop music. He held a particular soft spot in his heart for Chucky from the *Child's Play* movies. He was also quite the fan of an actor named John Wesley Shipp, best known for portraying the DC superhero The Flash on TV. As funny as I thought I could be, there was no way in hell I could ever write a character one-tenth as unique as Spike.

I wasn't above winding up Spike when he would call. For all of the withering sarcasm he dumped on everyone and everything, he could be surprisingly gullible. He called in to review the movie *Little Miss Sunshine* one week and I saw a window to have some fun. I decided to use one of the big plays from my playbook: act dumber than I actually am. It works like a charm, especially on guys like Spike. This exchange should give you a solid example of our

"Abbott & Costello on Bath Salts" routine. And please keep in mind that Carroll O'Connor had been dead for five years at the time of this conversation:

> TOM: Now let's move on to your review of *Little Miss Sunshine*.
>
> SPIKE: Oh, it was a nice little cute movie. The little girl was very good. And, let's see, who was . . . Alan Arkin played the little girl's grandfather.
>
> TOM: I haven't seen a lot of him since *M*A*S*H*. It's so good to see him back on the screen.
>
> SPIKE: I think you mean Alan Alda.
>
> TOM: What's that?
>
> SPIKE: I think you mean Alan Alda.
>
> TOM [*"confused"*]: Alan Aldo . . .
>
> SPIKE: *M*A*S*H*. *M*A*S*H* was Alan Alda.
>
> TOM: Yes.
>
> SPIKE: No, Alan Arkin.
>
> TOM: Alan Arkin? Who's that?
>
> SPIKE: You don't know who Alan Arkin is? You never saw *The Russians Are Coming, the Russians Are Coming*?
>
> TOM: Alan Narkin? What is that?
>
> SPIKE: Arkin. Arkin. A-R-K-I-N.
>
> TOM: Oh, that's the guy who's in *Little Miss Sunshine*!
>
> SPIKE: Yes.
>
> TOM: Yes, yes. He's good.
>
> SPIKE: Yeah, that's the grandfather. I mean, he's been around a long time. I mean, he was once a member of a group in the fifties called the Tarriers—
>
> TOM [*cutting him off*]: The Platters, yes.
>
> SPIKE: No, the Tarriers.
>
> TOM: And what doo-wop song did they sing?
>
> SPIKE: It wasn't exactly doo-wop but they did "Black Denim Trousers and Motorcycle Boots."

TOM: So, it was a clothing company.

SPIKE: No, it's a song.

TOM: Okay, I'm—you lost me. Let's just move on. Who else did you like in *Little Miss Sunshine*?

SPIKE: Uh, the mother. Uh, Jeanie . . . what's her name? Jeanie Collette?

TOM: Toni Collette.

SPIKE: Toni Collette. Yes, I'm sorry.

TOM: Yes, that's all right. I'll let you slide on that one. So who *didn't* you like?

SPIKE: Actually, they're all quite good.

TOM: You liked everyone?

SPIKE: Yeah, Greg Kinnear . . . the guy from *The Office*. I forget his name.

TOM: Ricky Jervis. [I SAID THIS WRONG INTENTIONALLY.]

SPIKE: No, the American version of it.

TOM: Okay, that guy is . . .

SPIKE: *The 40-Year-Old Virgin*. That guy.

TOM: Yeah, Stephen Colbert.

SPIKE: No, his name is Steve but I don't—that's not his last name.

TOM: Steve—

SPIKE: *The 40-Year-Old Virgin*. But you know who I mean.

TOM: Oh, Steve Richards.

SPIKE: No, Carol . . . Carrel . . .

TOM: Carroll Stevens?

SPIKE: No, not Cat Stevens.

TOM: I didn't say Cat Stevens. I said Carroll Stevens.

SPIKE: I never heard of her.

TOM: *Him.* Like Carroll O'Connor.

SPIKE: I've heard of Carroll O'Connor but I never—

TOM: He was *not* in *Little Miss Sunshine*, Spike. You are
    mistaken. Carroll O'Connor is in very poor health and,
    I'm sure, could not have done that movie.
SPIKE: Carroll O'Connor's deceased.
TOM: Wait, hold on. What?!
SPIKE: Carroll O'Connor has been deceased for a number
    of years now.
TOM: Oh, good heavens! I didn't realize. I send my
    condolences out to the rest of the O'Connor family.
    Here at *The Best Show*, we just want the O'Connor
    family, in this moment of sadness, to realize that we are
    there for them.
SPIKE: Uh-huh.

I love you forever, Spike. Thanks for all the calls.

IN RECENT YEARS an incredibly polarizing caller named Avalanche Bob entered the pantheon of weirdos. He was an old dude, probably around the age of eighty, but that didn't slow down Bob's enthusiasm. Avalanche Bob called himself a pioneer of "rockabilly yodeling punk," and he would belt out a song every time he called in. The sound was indescribable, but the closest I can come to capturing it is to ask you to imagine a guy in his late seventies scream-yodeling at the top of his lungs about snowboarding. That's right, most of Bob's songs were about snowboarding. I could never tell if he was a fan of the sport or if writing songs about something as relatively contemporary as snowboarding was a calculated marketing move. The songs always went something like "BREKA-FLEKA-BEKA-MEKA-FLEKA-MEKA-NEKA WHOOOOOOOOO!" followed by lyrics written by a senior citizen about a sport I assume he never tried.

I always had a soft spot for Avalanche Bob. Some listeners considered him the worst part of the show and would shut off their speakers the second he called in. And yes, I know he wasn't "good" by most metrics. For starters he didn't actually listen to *The Best Show*; I could usually hear a TV blaring in the background during his calls. So he never had any idea what we were doing on the program. All he did was promote his music, mentioning an album that was in the works or a live show that he hoped would happen. After a while I just couldn't hang up on Bob because the airtime clearly meant so much to him. Eventually I learned that Bob had started making music nearly sixty years earlier; his debut single, "Rockabilly Yodel," was released in 1958 under the name Bob Cribbie. Bob passed away in late 2019, but his yodel will live on forever.

I generally try to be nice to the callers, even the ones who might be considered weird or strange. First of all, I knew what it was like to get treated like shit on a call to a radio station. So many WFMU disc jockeys were incredibly rude to me back when I was a listener. I'd call up to ask a question about music or maybe request a song and I would get belittled by the host. It made me feel terrible, so I tried my best to show my callers the respect that other DJs didn't show me. Besides, isn't it more interesting to talk to the weirdos? We oddballs gotta stick together, baby!

One of the most memorable nights on the show started off with zero fanfare. I was talking to a caller early in the program when I felt a sharp pain in my side. It was unlike anything I've ever felt, as if a leprechaun was stabbing me with a knife from the inside. Sweat poured from my brow and I stretched out in the chair in an attempt to find any physical position that would grant me some relief. After a few minutes I couldn't find an ounce of comfort, so I put on a Miles Davis album called *Pangaea,* which I kept in the studio in case I ever had an (toilet and/or non-toilet-based) emergency that required me to play a lonnnnng song. That moment had finally arrived, so I dropped *Pangaea* into the compact disc tray and played the forty-one-minute opening track, "Zimbabwe." The music started and I slumped back into the chair, praying for the pain to stop. I couldn't leave the studio because I was the only disc jockey in the building at the time and it was a violation of both station and FCC rules to leave the building if you were the licensed broadcaster, kind of like those dudes with the giant hair hats outside that palace in England.

After a half hour or so the pain diminished enough for me to resume the show. I described the pain I was experiencing to the listeners and the phones lit up. More than one caller said that I had just passed a kidney stone on the air. All I knew was that it still hurt like a motherfucker. I finished the show and promptly ran to my car, driving straight to my local emergency room. An MRI confirmed that I had a large kidney stone swirling around my intestines. It was severe enough to put me in the hospital for almost a week. Can you name another radio host who passed a kidney stone on the air? You can't, although Casey Kasem came close when he underwent triple bypass surgery during an episode of *American Top Forty*.

A few years into doing *The Best Show* I reached a point where I could feel a significant drop-off in the quality of the program when Jon and I weren't doing one of our calls. I wanted the show to be great from start to finish, not just a showcase for Scharpling & Wurster calls. My nightmare was imagining a listener merely tolerating everything that wasn't S&W, clicking off the show once we were done with our bit. I wanted every minute of the show to feel essential, all killer and no filler! This meant I had to step it up creatively and work to guarantee that all three hours of the show were mandatory listening.

To achieve that I needed to trust my voice. I was definitely comfortable talking on mic—don't get me wrong. That initial surge of power that I felt when I started my show hadn't dissipated: Every time I sat in the studio, I was attuned to the power of saying something that a couple hundred thousand people would hear. But it wasn't the act of talking that I had to deal with; it was *what* I was talking about. I was still doing a fair amount of hiding. It was easy to go on the show and be funny, but it was infinitely harder to open up on mic and talk about my actual life. *That* was the chasm I needed to bridge, so I ignored the comedy safeguard of maintaining an ironic detachment from everything, instead leaning into talking about aspects of my life I normally shied away from. If I was feeling depressed or sad, I brought it to the airwaves. If something was bothering me I would try to talk about it.

It wasn't easy because I was still carrying a mountain of fear over my past. There was hardly a day that would pass without the voice in my head saying the absolute worst stuff to me. I'm assuming we all have some version of a voice in our head, even if it is merely the conversation you conduct with yourself when you say things like "Okay, now I need to pick up the dry cleaning." My voice was a little more aggressive than that, forever telling me that I am a failure and a disappointment to everyone in my life. That I am unlovable, unworthy of anything good. At least it wasn't commanding me to eat another bottle of aspirin, but it's still a nightmare to have your brain work overtime to make you feel like you don't deserve to exist.

I have since come to understand that I have spent a lifetime constantly trying to "fix" everything. It started with a sick mother at the age of seven or eight. I saw my mother suffering, so I tried to help. The truth of the matter is that it is impossible for a child to address adult problems, but that didn't stop me. I was forever chasing the goal of fixing everything for everyone. If I could simply make everything better, life would get easier for the people around me, and maybe the fucking voice in my head would finally shut up for once. Things only got more extreme after adding all the hospital sadness to the mix. I was living the life of a high-functioning depressive, trying to keep saving the world while tamping down my shame.

Living my life as Tom Scharpling helped. It gave me a sense of distance from the damaged kid that I always knew was lurking right below the surface. I wasn't particularly nice to that kid, regularly ignoring his needs. The appeal of being a new person who could just deny the existence of all that baggage was too great. I could lean into being Tom Scharpling, the funny crabby guy whose story was maybe a little vague in spots. It was a survival technique that allowed me to move forward. The "there but for the grace of God (and electroshock therapy) go I" version of my reality was always hovering in the shadows. I had been in the hospital because of my broken brain for months already and who could say I wouldn't end up there again? Everything that I had built up felt like it was held together with masking tape. And not a good roll of masking tape— more like the kind that's a little too narrow and doesn't seem nearly as sticky as it should be.

I didn't specifically talk about my hospitalization on air but I did manage to open up. Some nights I fell apart to the point where I'd beg the listeners to cheer me up. Other nights I would despondently sing along to Elton John or Aimee Mann songs. It was liberating to own these emotions in front of the audience, even if I wasn't being specific about *why* I was feeling a certain way. And this was the moment I felt the show take a huge step forward. Wurster and I had our comedy locked down, but the rest of the show suddenly became more resonant. Based on the feedback I got, the listeners now felt like they *knew* me. Sharing your life with people you've never actually met is a unique and powerful thing. It's not always easy but it's ultimately a gift and I consider myself lucky to be of service to so many people.

The only problem was that underneath the surface, there was a hurt little kid named Tom Giuliano. His voice got ignored because Tom Scharpling was desperate to run as far away from him as possible. But like the movie says, "We may be through with the past but the past is never through with us."

The name of that movie? *Kung Fu Panda 3*.

OVER THE YEARS, people have asked me some version of "What is a week in *The Best Show* like?" I guess they're curious about what goes into assembling an episode of the show. Some of the details have changed over the years but there's a general consistency to the schedule, so this is what the week is like:

WEDNESDAY, 12:01 A.M.

ANOTHER EPISODE OF *The Best Show* is in the can! I gather up my laptop and slide whistle and squirrel puppet and lug all my crap out of the studio. After cleaning up and putting my things away I say goodbye to the producers and get in my car. If the show went badly I think about what I could've done better, often wishing I could get back in the studio right then and there for an immediate do-over. If it was a good show, I think about it for a few minutes, then move on. Former NBA coach George Karl said something like "The losses stay with me all week and the wins don't even get me to the parking lot anymore," and I get it. The self-punishing part of me hears that quote and is like, "Oooh, let's see if we can be a little meaner to ourselves!" but thankfully I'm able to enjoy all the shows to some degree, even the disastrous ones. (They end up being the favorites of a shocking number of listeners: "My favorite *Best Show* was the time you started bawling your eyes out and said you wanted to die because the phones weren't working!" Okay, ghoul, whatever.)

On the way home I will usually stop at a Wawa or a diner and get some "victory food," because I am not a "healthy person." There was a stretch where I would spend my drive listening to an overnight show on NJ 101.5, a radio station that boasted in their promos they were "NOT New York" and "NOT Philadelphia," instead declaring themselves "PROUD to be New Jersey," which is like saying you're NOT Coca-Cola and you're NOT Pepsi-Cola but you are PROUD to be RC COLA!

The overnight slot was hosted by a guy named Tommy G. Yes, I know that I am technically a "Tommy G" as well, and befitting of this irony, the other Tommy G did a bizarro version of my show. He took calls and ranted about subjects in the news, although he talked about more Jersey-based topics like residents of a shore town complaining about an air siren that would go off a few times a day. I know, real gripping stuff.

Most nights I would just be content to listen and use his show as a "how NOT to" guide. But there were far too many evenings that I would call in and join the discussion. I know, I had just done three hours of nonstop talking and somehow I needed to keep scratching the itch. Look up two paragraphs earlier where I said I was not a "healthy person." I wasn't joking!

I would call up and play the role of a disgruntled New Jerseyan, ranting about a variety of fictional issues that were bothering me. The goal was to see if Tommy G would eventually call me on my obvious bullshit, but he never did. I complained about how that air siren was so annoying that my beachside neighbor Robert Vaughn— the star of the '60s show *Man from U.N.C.L.E.*—went temporarily insane and shoved a fireman in the middle of the street. I moaned about how angry I was that the driver of my child's school bus would regularly park the bus in a strip club parking lot while he went inside for lap dances. None of my ridiculous premises would set off Tommy G's crap detector; all I would get in response was some right-leaning "common sense" horseshit that always boiled down to some version of "just keep it out of my backyard." Thank you for the memories, Tommy G. You helped fill some empty hours in the life of a fellow attention hound.

THE REST OF WEDNESDAY

I WAKE UP and fight the urge to ignore the Internet but ultimately find myself poking around social media and message boards to see what people thought of the previous night's show. When it comes to that stuff, I care but I kinda only care a little bit. The listeners are completely entitled to their opinions, especially when it comes to a radio show that is me giving my opinions, but THEY ARE TALKING ABOUT ME AND I NEED TO KNOW WHAT THEY THINK. After taking the temperature of things, it is already time to start assembling next week's show.

THURSDAY

THURSDAY IS TOM'S DAY. None of your business what happens on Thursdays.*

FRIDAY–MONDAY

JON AND I plan out a call for the upcoming week. We usually start with a general arena or character type and the next five days consist of me and Jon talking, texting, and emailing each other with jokes and concepts. We try not to repeat ourselves, so we often ask *Best Show* archivist Rob Meisch whether a certain topic or theme has already been touched upon. Rob is the master of reminding us of the status of a recurring character, alerting us that the last time we did a bit with the Gorch he was driving a Rascal scooter across the country to fight me but stalled out somewhere in the Midwest.

So much of what goes into building a successful Scharpling & Wurster call is making sure there is some sort of twist or surprise that will reveal itself midway through the bit. It wasn't enough for us to have Timmy von Trimble reveal he's two inches tall because his dad created him in his laboratory. We also needed to make him a racist, contrasting the ugliness of a hate monger with the undeniable cuteness of a two-inch person using a thimble for a chair.

*Nothing happens on Thursdays.

When we feel like we've gotten it hammered out to some degree, Jon goes off and writes up the call. Sometimes the notes consist of loose guidelines, tracking where we need to go and which cues move things forward, and other times Jon writes out a literal script that we both perform from. The material and the premise always determine how deep the scripting needs to go.

During this stretch I work on the other parts of the show, lining up guests and callers and figuring out topics and taking care of administrative work and emails.

TUESDAY

TUESDAYS ARE SHOW DAYS and I have grown to love them. I start my day working at whichever job I'm doing at the time, but then "The Shift" happens midway through the day. Co-workers over the years have noticed it and pointed it out to me. "The Shift" is the steady attitudinal ramping up that takes place as I get closer to showtime. Around lunchtime I begin to crack a little wiser than I normally would. I am more likely to hurl a zinger your way and the notion of me holding court makes more sense with every passing minute. This is basically me getting ready to take the steering wheel. Most of the week I am relatively soft-spoken and hardly ever look to be the center of attention. But hosting *The Best Show* requires me to be fully present and engaged, eyes on the prize. I gotta be locked in by the start of the program. Think of it like a basketball player pacing the arena corridor before the game. They jump up and down because the switch got thrown and the energy is coursing through them. That's kind of what it feels like: I can't wait to start the show!

After the workday ends, I get in my car and drive to the studio in Jersey City. Both WFMU and my current setup are in JC, so I've been able to maintain a similar routine:

1) I stop at a convenience store and get a soda, or I stop at a Starbucks and get an iced latte.

2) I listen to music that gets me fired up. For years I would play *The Blueprint* by Jay-Z or any Led Zeppelin. By the time I got out of my car I was ready to beat someone to death with a tire iron.

3) I sit down at a restaurant with my show notebook and write out last-minute notes while eating a light meal that won't make me reach for the Miles Davis CD midway through the show.

4) Wurster and I make sure we are square for the show. By now Jon has sent the script through and we review it.

5) I get to the studio and start prepping about an hour before the show starts. I get the music set and pull together any last-minute elements. By now the producers have arrived, so I joke around with AP Mike and Jason Gore and Pat Byrne. I review the overall flow of the show with them and goof around a little bit. I shove a few Peanut M&M's into my mouth as I head into the studio, and then it is showtime, baby!

Now just repeat this for twenty years and you too can have your own *Best Show*!

PEOPLE ARE OFTEN confused when they discover we did *The Best Show on WFMU* for free for thirteen years. It really was a matter of the show growing far beyond what any of us thought it would become. If I'd known that *The Best Show* would turn into such a big deal I might've acted differently, but it really was a case of the frog in the boiling water: Every year the show got slightly bigger until one day you turn around and you're getting served on a plate with sour cream and applesauce* at a twenty-four-hour diner.

*I'm a pierogi!

The show did indeed become a full-time endeavor, which was okay with me for most of its existence. I loved doing it more than anything else and I believed wholeheartedly in the importance of WFMU. The station was steadfastly freeform, which meant that dumb stuff like ratings or audience testing never defined what a "successful" show was. If management thought a show had merit, it got on the air. And once you got on the air, the time slot was yours to do whatever you wanted. Those three hours of broadcasting were a gift, and there is no better way to hone your voice than to make stuff without a boss hovering behind you.

The show kept growing in popularity with each year until it was clear we were tapping into something that had nothing in common with any other show on the station. We brought in a wide-ranging group of listeners, from music nerds to comedy obsessives to talk radio fans. The show's reach far exceeded that of the standard WFMU program, which was a boon for the station during the fundraising marathon.

Ah, the fundraising marathon. I just felt my stomach clench up as I typed those three words, even though it has been years since I've hosted one. The marathon is the anchor of WFMU's financial existence, two weeks of programming aimed at getting the listenership to raise money for the station's operating budget.

I will forever love WFMU. When I discovered the station as a teenager I immediately felt less alone. It spoke to every weird bone in my body. I listened obsessively over the years and was legitimately starstruck when I met a lot of the on-air personalities. I have donated thousands of dollars to the station and I lent them a huge amount of money during one of their financial crises. I would not be where I am or who I am if it wasn't for that station.

That said, the WFMU fundraising marathon is the primary reason that I had to stop doing *The Best Show on WFMU*. They took so much out of me on every level—mentally, physically, creatively, financially—that I simply could not do them anymore. Were there other reasons? Yes, absolutely. I wanted to get paid for writing and producing the show, and I wanted the same for Wurster and everyone else lending their talents to the program. And I'd be lying if I said there weren't some personality issues between me and management over the years.

The Best Show meant enough to me that for years I was able to hold my nose and press on, remembering that not unlike the United States of America, the defining value of the organization supersedes whatever I might think of whoever is currently in charge of the joint. WFMU is a beautiful concept that deserves to exist and I was glad to host a show that helped keep the station afloat.

The marathon took place for two weeks in March but I would begin preparing in January. I started lining up guests who would perform on-air during the fundraising shows and I needed to figure out a "premium" that listeners who donated a certain amount of money would receive, kind of like the classic NPR tote bag but not shitty.

I went all out for my premiums, begging my talented friends to donate a song or video to the cause. One year I compiled a tribute album featuring artists like Death Cab for Cutie and Aimee Mann interpreting the Paul and Linda McCartney classic album *Ram*. Another year we produced a DVD that featured contributions from Patton Oswalt and Paul F. Tompkins. These were real productions and they took forever to put together. Some disc jockeys would make an effort with their premiums, but many were content to compile a CD filled with rare songs. But not me! I had to go all out because that's what I do.

I thought that the audience deserved as much as they could get for their contribution dollar, so I gave everything I could. The station would cover the cost of manufacturing these premiums to a very basic point, but me being me, I would go into my pocket to cover the rest of the costs. I would regularly invest a few thousand dollars of my own. I considered it a donation to the cause.

The fundraising shows themselves were amazing. The broadcast studio was divided into two rooms: a narrow engineer booth where I would broadcast from and a performance room filled with telephones. Volunteers would answer the phones and take the pertinent information from everyone who called in to pledge. The phone room was quiet as my show began, the previous program's pledges reduced to a trickle as they wrapped things up.

I would step in front of the mic, pot up the channel, and yell to my audience that it was time to start dialing. A few moments of pregnant silence would pass as we waited for the seven-second delay to catch up. Then—BOOM. The phones started to ring, and they would never stop for the next three hours. The rush of watching a dozen phones explode was amazing, people from around the world dialing in to give money to the station that kept their favorite show on the air.

We kept things entertaining while raising money. One year we browbeat Senator Cory Booker into calling up to compete in Star Trek trivia with Patton Oswalt and John Hodgman. We had musicians like Carl Newman, Coco Hames, Ted Leo, Aimee Mann, and more perform. We were putting together our own PBS-style fundraiser variety show but with 100 percent less doo-wop.

The listeners came through like champs, year after year. By the 2012 marathon we raised more than two hundred grand in six hours of broadcasting. Most shows on the station brought in a few thousand per fundraising shift, and as someone who did a conventional music show for a few years before *The Best Show* took off, I know how hard it is to squeeze three or four grand from the listeners. It is VERY HARD. We were in rare air with our totals. My Tuesday night show accounted for a legitimate percentage of the WFMU fundraising target. No other show was bringing in numbers like *The Best Show*, and like Ma$e said, all that money brought with it a fair amount of pressure.

A lot of that pressure was self-generated. If you couldn't tell by now, I'm pretty good at turning the screws on myself. If there's an opportunity to constantly move my own goalposts, I'll do it—any chance to keep myself chasing some unachievable prize. Here is another one of the best examples of how screwy Tom can be: A few years ago I read a book called *The Complex*, written by John Duignan, a former member of the Church of Scientology. The author recounts the horror show of being trapped in a cult that moved him around the world and separated him from his family. It's a harrowing story and worth reading. Partway through the book, Duignan mentions that it took him twelve or so years to ascend to the ranking of OT VIII, which is apparently one of the highest levels within the church. What was my takeaway from reading this? "Twelve years? I would've reached OT VIII in ten years tops."

Let that sink in for a second. A guy got debased by a cult for more than a decade of his life and my immediate reaction was that I would've moved through the ranks of that cult faster than he did. I know, I know. Remember, they zapped my brain with electricity!

I have forever been competitive and I have also been a caretaker for my entire life. I handed my existence over to always trying to be the hero at an early age and I never stopped. The patterns may change but the dynamic stays the same: If there's a problem, Tom will try to fix it. So imagine the perfect storm of me joining a listener-sponsored radio station that is forever struggling to stay afloat. My codependent tendencies were in paradise—this radio station is always falling apart, so I can always try to fix it!

That brand of thinking is solely my responsibility. I would never blame anyone but myself for my playing into these patterns. But it was a two-way street: Someone in WFMU's management came up to me after a particularly grueling fundraiser and said, "Thank you for giving me a job for another year." My heart sunk when I heard that. I didn't join WFMU to save people's jobs! I joined for the same reason the rest of the staff did: to create radio you couldn't hear anywhere else! But now management pinned the responsibility of earning the budget on me, a DJ who didn't make a cent on the show that had become a full-time job? The pressure was all too real from that point onward. I knew it couldn't last.

I remember the moment I knew that I was going to leave WFMU. I had just finished my second and final show of the 2012 marathon. Everybody was high-fiving and celebrating the show breaking $200,000. I felt ecstatic for a minute or two but out of nowhere a wave of despair washed over me, accompanied by a single thought: I had only eight short months before I had to start working on the 2013 marathon. I didn't tell anyone, but my future was clear. I would end *The Best Show on WFMU*—the home for all my comedy and all my identity, the one thing that helped me feel like a whole person again—in December 2013. The countdown clock had begun.

CHAPTER FOURTEEN

A STORY OF UNQUALIFIED TRIUMPH #2

AN UNQUALIFIED TRIUMPH might mean something very different to me than it means to you. Sometimes it can be as simple as generating an idea and putting it out into the world and watching it sink or soar. On some level it feels the same to watch a joke succeed or fail. The trick is bringing the dumb idea to life; whatever happens after that is really none of your concern. People either get it or they don't, and it's kind of satisfying to watch something that you find incredibly entertaining merely create low-level confusion instead of laughter. The first two years of *The Best Show* were a parade of people not understanding something that made perfect sense to me. As frustrating as it can be to have people tell you that you suck, it's not so bad if you know that you don't suck.

Deliberate stupidity is a thing of beauty and it can be its own reward. Perhaps I should call those moments when you propose something that makes you laugh but merely confuses everyone else "Paul Simon moments," because that is what happened when I was asked to pitch concepts for a Paul Simon music video.

I figured that since Paul Simon was a funny guy—he had been funny on *SNL* over the years—he might be up for a comedic concept for a video. "What would be a funny thing that Paul Simon could do in a music video?" I asked myself. And the answer appeared like a beacon cutting through the night sky:

It would be funny to watch Paul Simon get seriously hurt.

The idea poured out of me. Paul Simon would be the star of an OK Go–style video but it wouldn't go well. If you don't remember, OK Go was a solid power pop band that made their bones with elaborate stunty videos that were legitimately impressive. My favorite of the bunch was their video for "This Too Shall Pass," which featured the band members as small cogs in a massive Rube Goldberg–type setup. So what would be better than putting Rhymin' Simon in the middle of his own OK Go video, albeit one that would go horribly wrong?

Here's the concept I presented:

> The video for OK Go's song "This Too Shall Pass" has gotten about twenty million hits.
>
> This would be a one-take video and would start with Paul Simon standing in a warehouse waiting for a similar stunt-style video to begin. He looks nervous, like he doesn't want to be there. The song starts and the first of the stunts gets underway and Paul is immediately hurt—an oil drum rolls into his leg and hits him hard. It does serious damage.
>
> The camera follows Paul as he doubles to the ground in pain. For a moment people aren't sure what is going on as he lies there writhing in agony. After a few moments the crew rushes in and tries to help him, still in the same take. Paul is in a lot of pain (and the song is still playing).
>
> Eventually the on-set medical crew arrives. They help Paul to his feet as best as they can and get him onto a stretcher, where he is strapped into place. The stretcher is

wheeled into the back of a nearby ambulance. The camera stays with Paul as he is taken to the hospital. The EMTs try to help Paul out as the song continues to play until its conclusion.

I never heard back.

All I hope is that the idea made it to Paul's manager, who stared at it with confusion, unsure why someone would pitch an idea as pointlessly stupid as seriously injuring Paul Simon in his own music video. What if it got all the way to Paul himself? I'm vibrating with joy just imagining this. Would he call Lorne Michaels for guidance, asking him if this was the dumbest thing ever? Would Lorne agree? If this happened, I'm gonna walk into the ocean because my life is complete.

If you're thinking I'm just some sort of crank pitching potentially life-threatening videos to musical legends, you are wrong. Well, you're completely right. But I guess I'm trying to say that I am a legitimate director of music videos. I have written and directed clips for artists like Aimee Mann, Ted Leo and the Pharmacists, and Real Estate, among others. Some of them have blown up, like my video for the New Pornographers' "Moves," which topped a million and a half views. And trust me—you don't break a million on YouTube unless you're *seriously* talented.

The budgets for the videos have been pretty low, which has its benefits. We made two Aimee Mann videos for a total of ten thousand bucks during a New York City heat wave, including my crowning achievement: a shot-for-shot remake of the legendary Til Tuesday video "Voices Carry" for Aimee's song "Labrador." When I first pitched it to her she thought I was joking, so I laughed as if I was. But then I shored myself up to pitch it for real, knowing that it would take a true commitment from Aimee to do it. She would be making herself incredibly vulnerable to fully realize the concept, but I assured her that I had her back and that she would never be on the wrong side of the joke.

I could never have pulled this video off without the generosity of a crew that was willing to get paid peanuts and accept that lunch would be eating pizza while standing on a Brooklyn street. At the top of the list are Puloma Basu and Rob Hatch-Miller, my producing partners for most everything I've directed. They are brilliant filmmakers in their own right and they managed to make our no-budget videos look impressive.

I've had a pretty high batting average in terms of landing video jobs, but they don't all go my way. The Paul Simon pitch wasn't the only one that bombed. I get a thrill out of pitching insane video ideas to artists. Other concepts I've floated over the years include:

- Kesha reads a list of the top artists of the year and realizes she came in eleventh. So she goes around and beats up everyone ahead of her on the list.
- An all-male remake of the MC Hammer video "Pumps and a Bump," featuring nothing but hot half-naked guys gyrating poolside and grinding on the band. I have pitched this idea to every indie band I have worked with or tried to work with.
- The Shins get chased by a parade of people who hate them.
- A Destroyer video that depicts the funeral of Dan Bejar. He would lie in his casket while actual friends mourned his death. Come to think of it I've pitched this one to a few people. Weird that nobody wanted to do it!

It's clear in retrospect that I have a fair amount of hostility toward musical artists. I'm going to need to talk to my therapist about this.

Sometimes aggressive stupidity goes south and the pile of burning tires left in its wake is the reward. But there are those moments when it goes very right, and the people rise up to say YES, WE LIKE THIS KIND OF DOPEY! This is what I call a *"Grown Ups 3* moment."

In 2019 I wrote a screenplay for *Grown Ups 3*. Literally nobody on the planet wanted this to exist, but I wrote it because it was a funny idea that I laughed about with my director friend Jason Woliner every once in a while. The idea was simple: The cast of *Grown Ups 1* and *2* are filming *Grown Ups 3* in the woods of New Hampshire when they get attacked by a masked maniac who kills them one by one. A funny idea that would've remained a stray notion until I sat down and wrote it. And why did I write it? Two reasons: because the existence of the actual script would make it exponentially funnier than merely laughing about it on the phone with Jason, and it was a great way to avoid writing this book.

The world didn't need this script. Or maybe the world merely thought it didn't need this script, because when I eventually dropped it online the response was overwhelming. I got legit praise from people like Patton Oswalt and Adam McKay and Peyton Reed. There were staged table reads for charity featuring an insane range of talented people. Sometimes doing a dumb thing that makes you laugh will lead to untold rewards. If people had hated me for writing something so aggressively pointless, it would've stung a little bit. But it would've still been kinda funny to watch them get twisted about it.

There is no high and low, really. I don't believe in "the good stuff" and "the bad stuff" if the end result is the needle bouncing into the red. If it makes you laugh, it's funny. It might not be funny to everyone else, but the world doesn't step forward without bold moves. And there is a boldness to being so dumb. Triumph!

CHAPTER FIFTEEN

MY LIFE AS A PLAYER

"You think this is a game?" —A character in the movie *Fight Club*, according to the internet.

"You think this is a game?" —A character in the movie *Ender's Game*, which I didn't see because it didn't look so good.

"Oh, you . . . you think it's a game?" —Someone in *Gone in Sixty Seconds*, which I also didn't see.

"You think this is a game?" —One of the bugs in *A Bug's Life*, which I saw once and didn't particularly care for.

"Soldier, you think this is a game?" —One of the ants in *Antz*, which I didn't see because it looked even worse than *A Bug's Life*.

"Think this is a game?" —A character in *Babylon A.D.*, a Vin Diesel movie that I didn't see.

"You think this is a game?" —Someone in *The Pacifier*, another Vin Diesel movie that I didn't see.

"You think this is a game?" —One of the annoying characters in *Funny People*, which I saw twice and liked even less the second time I saw it.

"You think this is a motherfuckin' game?" —Someone in *Get Hard*, a Kevin Hart/Will Ferrell movie that I have seen most of on cable and thought was something of a misfire for both stars.

"Oh, you think it's a game?" —Someone in *Ride Along*, another Kevin Hart movie that I didn't see even though it seems better than *Get Hard*.

"You think this is a fuckin' game?" —Someone in *The Hangover Part III*, which bears the distinction of not being as bad as *The Hangover Part II*.

"Do you think this is a fucking game?" —Someone in the remake of *Carrie*, a movie I didn't see because I like the original too much.

"You think we're playing games here?" —Someone in *Transporter 3*, a movie I skipped after not particularly enjoying *Transporter 2*.

"Would you like to play a game?" —The computer robot from the movie *WarGames*, which I did see and enjoyed as a child; no idea whether I'd be into it now.

FOR AS LONG as I can remember, I have been interested in games. Board games were most likely my earliest exposure to the form, and I took them very seriously. But truth be told I wasn't in it for the playing of the game. I wanted to win. The conceit that "it doesn't matter if you win or lose; it's how you play the game" felt like a cop-out in every possible way. Why would you play a game to lose? I loved games but it was the winning that always mattered.

It's no mystery where I got all those competitive instincts. My mother is without a doubt the most driven person in my life. She is relentlessly competitive; if she's gonna do it she expects to do it right. My mom makes Michael Jordan look like a kindly hippy working part-time at a granola depot, pleasantly dispensing scoops of sprouted oat cinnamon flax with a gentle "It's all good, man." (There is no such thing as a granola depot but you get the point.) My mother is so compelled to win that my sister had to discourage her from playing board games with her children. Marinate on that for a second: My mother was banned from playing Candyland with her own grandchildren because she would get legitimately pissed off if she got stuck on a licorice space while her five-year-old grand-daughter slid her yellow gingerbread board piece past hers on her way to Peanut Acres.

With that demented worldview comprising a large amount of my DNA, the idea of playing a game for the mere fun of it felt like a foreign concept. I developed a taste for winning and while I've been able to rein it in, it will always be a too-huge part of me. Case in point: A few years ago I was at an arcade playing pinball against a friend. (I'm not naming the arcade because I have mentioned them on *The Best Show* approximately eight thousand times and have brought countless customers through their door but they never gave me as much as a slice of their cheap heat-lamp pizza in return.) It was a friendly match, no money or pride on the line in any form. I watched her play, swatting the ball around before it inevitably rolled down past the flippers. She looked me in the eye before I could body up to the machine, asking me, "Tom, did you really say, 'Miss it!' under your breath while I was playing?" I was stunned, mostly because I was definitely screaming, "MISS IT!" at the top of my lungs *in my mind* but had no idea that the words had crossed my lips. I felt like a dope. This isn't the kind of thing you do to a friend! But that said, I would've literally signed a blood pact with Satan himself to beat her.

Pinball has played a gigantic role throughout my life. By the time I was ten my parents were both running their T-shirt busi-ness, which meant my sister and I were pretty much left to our own devices until they got home. In the summer this meant long days of floating around town, attempting to stay entertained until dinner-time. I quickly settled on a routine that worked for me: I would ride my bike to a sub shop a mile or so away from home, order a tuna sub, and play pinball until my paper route money ran out. This sub shop also had a jukebox that I would pump coins into, because of course I needed a soundtrack for my p-ballin'.

There I was, playing pinball while listening to "Rock 'n' Roll Fantasy" by Bad Company, one of those moments where it all feels so *right* that you feel like you're living in a movie. (A fun movie, for the record! So much of my life I have felt like I'm in a movie but it's usually a cross between *My Dinner with Andre* and *Gummo*.) It was a magical moment that wouldn't last long. Within a few years the sub shop would go under, replaced by a local video store that had no problem renting porn movies to a fifteen-year-old Tom, just because he was kinda tall for his age. No fake ID, no facial hair, just a little extra height compared to other fifteen-year-olds. If I could go back in time, I would march into that sub shop and tell my ten-year-old self to savor every minute of this tiny paradise because it won't last forever. I would also tell the ten-year-old me that in five short years this sub shop would be a video store and the owner would have no problem renting porn tapes to him.

I eventually ditched the sub shop for an arcade a few blocks away called Eight on the Break, which is pool-playing lingo for something pool-related. (I don't care for pool.) Eight on the Break did have a few pool tables but pool always felt like an exercise in dirty futility. No, I was in it for the video games and the pinball. One of the more exciting features of this arcade was the BANNED FOR LIFE list mounted on a wall directly across from the snack bar. This constantly evolving document recorded the names of customers who were no longer allowed in the arcade because they got caught fighting or sneaking in alcohol or erupting in a blind rage because they got their ass kicked at Joust. I loved checking out the list to see if anyone from my school had made the grade, and

I always noticed that one classmate—an admittedly intimidating kid named Vinny—had achieved the vaunted "Banned for Life" status. I felt a sense of refracted glory seeing that one of us had made it.

Eight on the Break has been in business for most of my life and as of 2020 it is still trucking along. Most of the elements are the same as they were decades earlier . . . including the Banned for Life list! When I say the list is still up, I'm not saying there's a new list documenting a new crop of troublemakers. No, I'm saying that THE EXACT SAME LIST IS ON THE WALL! Someone even took the trouble to laminate the now-tattered sheet of paper to prevent the passage of time from inflicting further damage. But to be fair a lifetime ban from an arcade is something that needs to be taken seriously. What kind of message would it send if the owners allowed a fifty-three-year-old Vinny to just stroll on back into Eight on the Break and drop a quarter into the Guardians of the Galaxy pinball machine? I mean, it's been only thirty-seven years since he got caught taking pulls from a bottle of peppermint schnapps! I for one salute the owners as they pursue justice at all costs.

The arcade management didn't seem to care as much when it came to catching any of the bullies who regularly shook me down for money. The hoodlums who frequented Eight on the Break saw me coming from a mile away, a gawky stick figure of a preteen whose pockets jingled with the sound of shiny quarters earned from his paper route. (This description of me makes me want to take this kid's money!) I invariably headed over to a Q*bert machine to play a couple of games, which didn't take long because I was terrible at Q*bert. As I moved down the aisles in search of an open machine, some teenage tearaway would block my passage, "asking" if he could "borrow" some money. Truth be told, these kids weren't particularly terrifying when seen from the vantage of adulthood, but Young Tom didn't stand a chance. I would hand them a few quarters or a dollar bill and get to spend another day not getting my face smeared into the side of a Galaga machine.

This dynamic created a real sense of resentment toward Eight on the Break. Why couldn't they protect their paying customers? Sure, I wasn't going to run to the owner and whine that someone was picking on me, because even at that tender age I understood that snitches get stitches. My grandfather had a saying about snitches. It was:

"Twinkle twinkle, little bitch
Mind your own business, you fucking snitch."

Okay, my grandfather never said that—I just found it on Etsy five minutes ago. But you get the idea. It wasn't really an option for me to ask for help, unless I wanted to see what wearing a pool ball rack as a necklace felt like. So I got out all that rapidly accumulating anger in the only way I knew how. I would prank call the arcade. Generally the calls were some variation on this theme:

ARCADE OWNER: Eight on the Break.

YOUNG TOM [*doing an adult voice*]: Yeah, is Johnny there?

ARCADE OWNER: Johnny?

YOUNG TOM: Yeah, Johnny. My brother. You know him, the guy with the long hair who hangs out near the air hockey table? He's a real fucking scumbag.

ARCADE OWNER [*getting wary*]: I don't know him. What's up?

YOUNG TOM: I just need to talk to him. He came down there to sell some drugs and I wanted to see what time he was gonna come home.

ARCADE OWNER [*getting angry*]: Your brother better not be down here selling drugs.

YOUNG TOM: Aw, come on, man. He's only selling drugs out of your bathroom!

ARCADE OWNER: Listen you—

YOUNG TOM: Your arcade is a piece of shit!

[*Tom hangs up, laughing victoriously*]

Yes, I realize that most of my prank phone calls lean on the theme of "someone is selling drugs." If I ever return to the prank game I'll tighten that up. But how about those anger issues? They would only keep growing to the point where I would eventually get swallowed up by them, but back then I was a youngster having some phone-based laughs, nothing more!

One thing I noticed was that nobody picked on me whenever I went to the arcade with my father, a pretty major pinball fan himself and in retrospect the person who instilled a love of arcades in me. I know that in some people's eyes it's probably pathetic for a twelve-year-old to play pinball with his dad, but fuck them. It was the best. I loved it then and I'm grateful that I did it now. I have not been fortunate enough to have a child of my own, but if and when I procreate, I will take my kid to whatever an arcade looks like in the future. I will hand them my money scanner chip card and let them select whichever games suit their fancy. But I will be watching. And waiting. If any kind of cyber-goon comes up to my child "asking" them for an unauthorized currency transfer, I will step out from behind a seventy-year-old Dig Dug machine and cave in the goon's head. If that means I end up on the arcade's Banned for Life machine, so be it!

Upon closer analysis this futuristic reverie of mine is rooted in an incident that informed a shocking amount of my life. My family had a screen printing business in the town of Metuchen, New Jersey, referred to by locals as "the Brainy Borough" because of what I'm assuming is the relatively high percentage of residents who use the library? I logged a fair amount of time in Metuchen as a kid, helping my folks stuff shirts into boxes and power washing the emulsion off used screen printing frames. When the work was done I would end up floating around the streets of Metuchen looking for anything fun to do. Having fun in this town meant either going to Friendly's for some ice cream or logging some time at whatever video game was jammed into the back of the corner convenience store. Since my tiny ten-year-old body could only hold so much Fribble—the extremely troubling name Friendly's gave its milkshakes—I always ended up playing the video game.

My parents had pulled the trigger on my new winter coat, so I proudly wore my insanely puffy down jacket into the store and pumped some quarters into whatever machine was on hand. I remember a couple of bigger kids stood behind while I played. They were laughing and smoking but they didn't pay me much mind as they waited for me to finish up. After my game was over, I returned to my parents' screen printing shop. They immediately noticed something wrong with my jacket: There were burn marks up and down the back. My dad asked me if I had leaned against a radiator at any point and I said no. This was upsetting to me because at this point in my life I was deathly afraid of ever doing anything that would cause my parents an ounce of stress. My mother was beaten up by the blood disease that drained my family both financially and emotionally and the goal was to always be good. I knew I hadn't done anything stupid to cause the markings. My father analyzed the burns and asked me if anybody else was around while I played video games. I told him there were a couple of kids behind me. He had me put the coat back on and we all returned to the corner store.

My dad instructed me to head back inside and play another game as if nothing was wrong while they monitored everything through a solid glass door right next to the machine. I followed the plan to the letter. The bigger kids were still hovering behind me, laughing among themselves. After a moment I heard a commotion. I turned to see my father holding one of the kids by the collar of his jacket, lifting him high in the air. My mother ran in behind him and joined the fray, shouting at the kids. It turns out they were poking the back of my jacket with their cigarettes while I played, and my folks saw all of it through the glass door. Sure, you could make a case that maybe my parents should've reconsidered their plan of "let's have our son go back into the convenience store and see if some kids try to set fire to the jacket he's wearing a second time," but I was on board for all of it. When you're ten years old, what could be more thrilling than to be a part of a miniature sting operation?

The main kid denied everything. The police were summoned and before long the cops and the kid's father—who was a pastor in town!—were on hand. The hoodlum's father joined his son in denying any culpability in the matter, and a report was filed. My family refused to back down on this, because it was as clear-cut as can be: They literally saw this piece of garbage poke the back of my jacket with a lit cigarette! We all ended up in small-claims court, partly because our family didn't want to lay out the money for another jacket—winters were always tough in the T-shirt business—but mostly because this shitbag did something wrong and wouldn't own up to it. He was gonna get away with it unless my parents pursued legal action.

Long story short, we lost the case. I remember the existential unfairness of it landing like a punch to the gut. It didn't matter in life whether you did the right thing or the wrong thing, because there would always be pieces of trash that would simply lie their way out of their terrible actions. And they would get away with it and hold that shitty smirk on their face as if the world was designed to naturally go their way. Everything felt futile, like a video game version of *Chinatown*.

This was one of the first times I can recall feeling like life was truly stacked against my family. We were the nice people who never seemed to catch a break. Life was doling out defeats on the regular for the family that sported a giant "L" on their collective forehead. I formed the concept in my little head that my family was cursed to a life of failure. It sounds dumb but it really took hold and informed so much of my thinking throughout the rest of my life.

But my failed immolation didn't thwart my love of video games. I regularly headed to the arcade with my paper route money and poured it directly into whichever machine was unoccupied at whichever deli/pizzeria/gas station in town. I was destined to a life of shooting aliens one quarter at a time, but my mother had other plans. She had seen enough of my arcade-loving ways, so one summer she took some initiative.

"Tommy," she said one day. "I signed you up for track camp."

There are days when I will be sitting at a coffee shop or driving in my car, focusing on any one of a million things, when suddenly a phrase wanders from the back of my brain.

Fucking track camp.

I can't be too hard on my parents. I was a confusing child. I always carried at least one book wherever I went. I would hide in my room listening to music and watching television. My bedroom walls were covered with ads for movies I clipped from the newspaper. Sure, I don't know how they decided that a kid who appeared to be made out of pipe cleaners would love track camp. Perhaps they looked in vain for a camp that appealed to thirteen-year-olds who were really good at taping *SCTV*. Maybe there simply wasn't a summer camp catering to the memorization of box office grosses. But the decision was made and I found myself wearing a pair of running shorts that John Stockton would reject for being too snug and getting dropped off at the campus of Rutgers University one late June morning.

This was truly the last place I wanted to be. What was I gonna do at track camp? Run around all day and then take a break so we can all talk about running around all day? I wanted nothing to do with it. I thought about my potential fate and somehow drummed up the courage to step out of the registration line. I walked toward the opposite end of the parking lot and entered the campus student center.

I don't know what I was looking for when I stepped through those doors, but I certainly found it when I spied a decent-size arcade tucked into the back corner. Within seconds track camp was nothing more than a dead leaf blowing away on a summer breeze. I spent the day feeding the machines (how much money was I carrying?! Clearly enough to play games for six hours!) and eating pizza in the campus food court. My fellow campers were probably running suicides in the hot New Jersey sun while I chugged Dr Pepper and knocked off another round of Ms. Pac-Man.

The day flew by and before I knew it my mother had returned to pick me up. I gathered my stuff and hurried back out to the parking lot. She pulled up and I hopped in the car, trying to act as sweaty and exhausted as possible.

"So how was it?" she asked with a decided strain of hope in her voice.

"Oh. It was great," I stammered. "Can't talk, too tired. Can we listen to the radio?"

The next day was more of the same. I got dropped off, feigned signing in, then did the only actual running I would do all day as I bolted into the arcade. I knew it was wrong. I was clearly wasting whatever my mother spent on registering me for this godforsaken camp. And on top of that my mother was trying to instill a love of physical fitness in me. But that Defender machine was calling me and I had to answer. The end of the day arrived and once again I jumped into my mom's car, huffing and puffing as if I had just run a marathon.

"Are you enjoying the camp?" my mom inquired.

"Yeah yeah, so much running! Hey, let's stop talking and see what's on the radio!"

This went on for another day. But the jig was up come Wednesday night. I had retired to my bedroom to watch *TRON* for the seventieth time when there was a knock on my door. My mother stood in front of me, looking confused.

"I just got off the phone with the track camp."

Uh-oh.

"They said that you haven't ever shown up."

"Huh."

"Is that true?"

"Yes. That is true."

I have never seen her look as disappointed as she did in that moment. I had worked so hard to never be a problem and here I was, shattering her dreams of having birthed the next Prefontaine. That moment impacted me to such a degree that I strove to never let her down again.

Did I ever let her down again?

Yes. Yes I did.

MY MOTHER'S COMPETITIVE spirit rubbed off on me in other ways. She showed me what it was like to truly care about your work, how to not stop until you achieved your goal. One of the best examples of this involves my setting a high score on a pinball machine.

The Silverball Museum opened up in Asbury Park about ten years ago and from the second I walked through their doors I was hooked. (And, okay, I named the arcade I said I wouldn't name. It's fine, all they had to do was throw me a can of soda every now and again for all the business I brought them.) The Silverball had pinball machines from every era, each machine in solid playing condition. It wasn't long before this palace of diversionary entertainment got twisted into a prison for damned souls desperate for victory. All it took was for the arcade to start ranking the high scores for each machine. I looked at the names written on the laminated cards the owners placed on top of the machines and I longed to see my name alongside all the greats, like "Marc D." Or "Edward K." Or "Billy." There was now a goal to be the best, and I wanted in. I wanted to be "Billy."

I settled on a machine called Gold Strike, a simple but extremely fun game from the early 1970s. The game has a million targets on it and presents some legitimate challenges. I was hooked from the get-go. The high score on the machine seemed achievable, something like 170,000 points. One thing to keep in mind is that the older units kept score manually, with a physical counter that would roll over back to zero once you broke 100,000 points. You had to keep track of how many times you went past 100,000 to tally up your total score.

I dedicated myself to this machine, playing for hours during my near-weekly visits to the Silverball. One day I caught fire and sailed past the high score, landing somewhere around 180,000 points. I proudly alerted the owner of the establishment that I had shattered the previous high score. He grunted and waddled over to the game, not investing one second in actually verifying my claim. He pulled the laminated scorecard from the top of the console and handed it to me. I wrote in my name and current high score. He placed the card back atop the machine before skulking off to stare at some broken flippers or whatever it is that pinball machine repairmen are interested in. I stood there and admired my accomplishment.

My championship glory would barely last a week. I returned to the arcade to stare at my card like a dog outside an Outback Steakhouse, only to find that my high score had been wiped from the laminated card! My handwriting had been replaced by a childish scrawl that claimed someone scored 400,000 points. Un-fucking-believable.

There was no way on earth the child who filled in the new score actually beat my score. The handwriting was aggressively juvenile to the point of parody. All it was missing was a cutesy backward "R" and maybe a smear of pudding. Maybe a parent let their kid write their triumphant high score on the card. That makes more sense but THEY WERE WRONG.

This particular Gold Strike machine was not so hot in terms of upkeep. The flippers had a poor response time and not a lot of muscle behind them. And the scoring on the game itself was a throwback to when pinball machines rewarded you with ten points for knocking down a target. At some juncture there was a wave of pinball point inflation that rivaled post-WWII Hungary. (I'm not sure if this is historically accurate; we didn't study stuff like history at Middlesex County College.) I knew how hard it was to set my score and I knew that nobody else was dedicating their existence to running up the score on a perfectly unassuming pinball machine from the mid-1970s.

As I saw it, I had three options:

1) I could accept the unfairness of this situation.
2) I could say something to the manager, which would make me the biggest loser on earth. "Hello, sir. Yes, I'll wait for you to set down your tin of fried calamari. Do you remember me from last week? I set the high score on Gold Strike. You don't? Okay, well, I did. It seems that another patron mistakenly believes they beat my high score. Please don't throw your calamari at me, sir. I'm a paying customer and I don't appreciate it. Okay, if you're going to throw calamari at me, please don't dip it in the marinara sauce first."
3) I could dedicate my existence to beating a ridiculous high score that I knew wasn't real in the first place.

I am nothing if not my mother's son, so I chose option #3 and promptly got to work.

I would play Gold Strike and only Gold Strike every time I visited the arcade, logging hour upon hour on this dumb relic of a machine. I was locked in, eyes on the prize. Imagine those training montages from *Rocky* movies, except with slightly less physical exertion and slightly more terrible pizza.

I carry a very specific defect in my head, one that can declare anything an accomplishment. The task itself is beside the point; the act of crossing something off my "to do" list is everything. Some days it's about hitting a writing goal or getting myself to the gym. But there are days where I could categorize closing out a sleeve of Oreos as an achievement: "I'm pretty proud of myself—there were, like, nine Oreos left! They would've gone back in the pantry but thankfully I took care of business." I brought this busted mindset to this pinball dilemma, working to break a record that nobody ever set.

I got better and better at the game over the next month. I developed an understanding of the machine's dead spots and quirks. And one day it all clicked into place: From the second I started playing I could do no wrong. My score kept climbing as I knocked down row after row of targets. The slight deadness of the flippers was now my ally. I was one with the machine, racking up extra ball after extra ball. I slowly nudged my score into the 300,000s. There was a point where I could simply feel the mass of momentum shift in my favor, as if the machine had decided it was time to get this over with. I was going to break the high score, erasing a child's twisted mistake from existence.

You're probably assuming that something ridiculous happened. Perhaps a crazed seagull flew through the arcade doors in search of a stray pizza crust and accidentally unplugged the machine? Or maybe the preacher's son from my childhood returned and started once again poking me with a cigarette? These are all shockingly probable considering my life, but none of them happened. What happened is I won. I edged past the 400,000-point mark and claimed the high score. I wiped the sweat off my brow and approached the front counter. There I stood, a guy well into his forties, proudly asking the manager to get off his stool and bring his marker to the Gold Strike machine. I was flying high as I wrote my name on the card. Who knew what else I could accomplish? Suddenly Kevin Garnett's wild declaration that "anything is possible" made perfect sense.

Two months later the Gold Strike machine was removed from the arcade, never to be seen again. The laminated high score card was also a distant memory. But I will forever carry this victory with me.

This was my *Dunkirk*. My *Hamburger Hill*. My *Full Metal Jacket*. My *In the Army Now*. And yes, I am 100 percent comfortable comparing playing pinball to serving in the military during wartime. My story might be harder, actually. It's not easy finding parking down the shore for civilians, but these military guys could drive their tank right onto the beach and nobody would say boo.

The type of game you play may change as you get older. Things that used to be fun now sound like potential death sentences, like a friendly game of pickup basketball. The notion of blowing out my knee while making a routine layup haunts me. But if you're afflicted with the competitive spirit, you've gotta find something to fill the demented void. A few summers ago, I found a game that was definitely not going to blow out any part of my body outside of my wallet. I became addicted to coin pushers.

"Now what is a coin pusher, Tom?" you find yourself asking the book you're holding.

Well, let me tell you, dear reader. Coin pushers are an arcade "game of chance" with two horizontal coin-covered levels (called "brooms") that rhythmically heave forward and backward like the ocean itself. These tiers are covered in valueless coins, with a sprinkling of poker-type chips and game cards scattered throughout. The chips and the cards are the prizes, not the coins. The coins are nothing more than the means to move the game forward. The player manipulates a trigger that spits out more coins, and the goal is to get these coins to land in spots that force everything to tumble downward when the broom recedes. Which in turn hopefully causes the coins on the lower level to fall down into the chute, taking some chips and cards with them. There is definitely some skill required in the coin pusher racket. You need timing to strategically maneuver the coins to sweep the cards and chips down into the chute. After playing you take the cards and chips to the arcade counter, where they can be redeemed for prizes that cost a fraction of what you spent on the game. And there you have it, the most boring paragraph ever written! You broke the spine on the book, too late to return it!

These machines are actually illegal in plenty of states because some consider them a form of gambling. I disagree with this, primarily because when you gamble at a casino, you can win actual money. Those who are triumphant at coin pushers are rewarded with spoils like sticky rubber spiders and scented pencil erasers. The only thing you are ultimately wagering is your sense of self-worth.

In short, coin pushers are the gaming equivalent of watching a squirrel struggle to climb a tree while holding a pizza crust. It's fun at first, but after a while it's pretty goddamn boring. But like so many things, if they enter your life at the right (wrong?) time you could get hooked quite easily. And although I've never been hooked on watching squirrels skitter up trees with pizza in their mouths, I got hooked big-time on these ridiculous machines.

I became addicted to the coin pushers a few summers ago. Terre and I had rented a house down the Jersey Shore not too far from the boardwalk. It was the perfect combination of isolation and over-stimulation. Step out of the house and you're on a stretch of private beach, but walk ten minutes and you've got your pick of any kind of food that can be dropped into a deep fryer. Seriously, the Jersey Shore boardwalks are out of control with their foods. Yes, I know that we all know about fried Oreos and fried Twinkies. They are as common as a pair of horn-rimmed glasses at a Wilco concert or a misspelled tattoo at a Tool show.

Nowadays the animals running these stands will fry up virtually anything they can fit into their trans-fat-fueled heart attack machines, including Pop Tarts, apple pie à la mode, and sticks of butter. And I fall for it every time, doing the same dance, year after year. I will be walking down the boardwalk and notice a new dumb thing advertised on the menu. I imagine how amazing it will be, then step up to the counter and order a fried box of Frosted Mini-Wheats or whatever innovation these beach-loving food jockeys developed during the off-season. Once they start preparing the food, I promptly look away because I will literally throw up if I watch some hairy-armed Jersey boardwalk guy sweatily touching my food. And I say that with impunity because I too am a sweaty Jersey boardwalk guy, albeit with a tasteful amount of arm hair. After a couple of minutes they plop my order on the counter and I snatch it up and skulk away like an untethered C.H.U.D.

After finding a remote corner of the boardwalk where nobody can judge me, I sink my teeth into the fried trash and immediately realize that if I continue to eat this, I will open a portal to the Worst Version of Myself. My life would become nothing more than a series of bad food decisions, ending up with me wearing a DON'T TALK TO ME BEFORE I'VE HAD MY FIRST SLICE OF FRIED CHEESECAKE T-shirt as I flip through the new issue of *Home Grease Cookers* magazine, pricing out a new bedside fryer. Sure, the old one still works just fine but the new one has a USB port!

Dystopian visions such as this—combined with the real-world awfulness of the food—compel me to take two lowly bites before tossing the remainder into a garbage can that will get picked through by a colony of soon-to-be-diabetic seagulls.

I'm not sure what made me drop that first token into the Wizard of Oz coin pusher. I have zero affinity for the movie, and the machine straight-up warned me to run away by playing the chorus of "Follow the Yellow Brick Road" on an incessant tinny loop. But I looked at those brooms surging forward and backward. I spotted a couple of cards and chips that were a millimeter away from falling into the chute. All I had to do was drop a few coins in the right place and they would be mine. This machine taps into every get rich fantasy we carry our whole lives; no matter how low you feel, you're always one lucky break away from hitting the jackpot! I gave in, and before long I fed that monster every dollar I had. I played for a solid hour that first night, and in that brief amount of time I caught a glimpse of a secret world operating within our shoreline arcades. This is the world of the coin pusher.

Before you can grasp a full appreciation for their (my?) kind, let me explain a few Wizard of Oz coin pusher ground rules. The machine pays out with either chips or cards. The chips are more common, so their value varies between fifty and one hundred points. The cards are another story. There are seven different cards, each depicting a different character from the movie. They are valued at five hundred points apiece, but if you can acquire a set of all seven character cards, you're talking about thirty thousand points. That's more than 8.5 times the value of any seven random character cards.

The catch is that the Toto card is infinitely more rare than the other six cards, making it extremely difficult to complete the full set.

The machine spits out Dorothy and Tin Man cards as if they were drunks getting tossed from a rowdy bar, but the Toto cards are few and far between. The result is a culture where dedicated players roam the arcade, checking every machine in hopes of spotting a stray Toto card. These are the Toto Rovers. I have seen children and the elderly alike scan the machines, hoping to see that little dog's face on a card.

My initial schooling with the Toto cards came on my second night of playing. A middle-aged guy sat down at the machine next to me while I played. He was a stereotypical Jersey Shore guy, a fella who is desperate to let everyone around him know that he JUST MIGHT be connected. Which means that he DEFINITELY isn't connected. "You know this is just gambling," he said to me as I focused every fiber of my being on dislodging a Cowardly Lion card from a logjam of coins. I told him that yeah, it probably was. I should've just told him to hit the bookstore in five years for a copy of *It Never Ends* to read my answer but I didn't because I wasn't sure I was going to write a book and I also wasn't sure that this guy could read. I'm sure he knew most of the alphabet, but those letters at the end are tricky! What is that squiggly one trying to say?

He then proceeded to tell me that he had lost about a half million bucks in Atlantic City over the years and that he needed to watch out with games like this one because he has "the bug." He said he should probably keep his daughter off them as well because she might have "the bug" too. But for all his fatherly talk he was completely ignoring his daughter's relation to "the bug" since she was running around the arcade holding a plastic cup overflowing with game tickets. I understood the concept of "the bug." I had it when it came to radio and writing and comedy and ice cream sandwiches. But I never saw a day where I would catch the bug from these machines.

The guy asked me if I'd ever pulled a Toto card. I hadn't gotten one as of yet, so he told me all about how rare the card was, explaining that "this is how they get you." He blathered on for a good while longer, but then his kid called him over to a machine a few feet away.

She spotted a Toto card! He bounced her out of the game chair and started playing.

Before long a few excited teenagers watched him try to nab the Toto card. I could overhear his conversation with the kids: He told them he lost $300,000 in Atlantic City over the years. I'm not sure why he rounded his losses downward for the teens but that's his burden. The guy slid into the role of pack leader pretty quickly, educating the boardwalk youth with wisdom like "I'm gonna spend two hundred bucks on this piece of shit game to get some fucking Toto card and they'll give me a fucking stuffed animal that I could've bought for twenty bucks." The kids covertly laughed at his expense a little bit, but the look on his daughter's face was pure and beautiful; she was thrilled her dad just might win her a big prize. I was repulsed and touched at the same time, kind of like watching *Antichrist* and *Fly Away Home* in a second-screen experience.

One of the kids started filming Faux Mob Dad's quest for Toto with his phone and the other kids chanted, "TO-TO! TO-TO! TO-TO!" Of course, they were being mostly sarcastic, but when the guy eventually got the Toto card to drop, everybody cheered with absolute sincerity. The daughter freaked out, jumping around excitedly as her proud dad handed her the Toto card.

If that wasn't enough excitement, another guy a few machines over was moments away from getting his own Toto card to drop. Everyone's attention shifted over to him, and after a bit of playing, his card fell and everyone cheered . . . except the card didn't fall all the way to the bottom slot. It was stuck somewhere in the guts of the machine. This sent Faux Mob Dad into full-on expert mode. He summoned one of the bored teens working at the arcade to pop open the machine. The kid opened the panel and there was the Toto card, lodged between two large chips deep in the machine. Faux Mob Dad then shifted into attorney mode, making the arcade into a seaside *And Justice for All*. "I'm out of order!? This whole boardwalk is out of order! These Skee-Ball machines are out of order!" He explained to me in a stage whisper that the fix was in, adding that "this is just like it used to be at the after-hour poker places in Manhattan. They'd get you all fucked up on drinks so you wouldn't realize that the decks were all loaded with face cards!"

I felt my interest in the machines grow with every passing second. The rush from watching those guys nab Toto cards was undeniable. I wanted my own Toto card, but the machine I was playing was bereft of anything resembling Toto. Thankfully Faux Mob Dad came to the rescue. He quietly tapped me on the shoulder and led me to another Wizard of Oz machine. "See that card?" he said. "That's a Toto, buried under those coins. You can see his little tail sticking out." But he wasn't looking to land a second Toto that night. It was my turn.

I sat down and started playing. I fired away, shooting coin after coin. I was going to get that card no matter how long it took or how much it cost. I could feel "the bug" that my not-connected new friend had referenced. I don't know why. Once again, I hate *The Wizard of Oz*. It feels like a movie that was filmed for the purpose of one day becoming a lousy grade-school play. But there I was, pumping five-dollar bills into the machine in a quest to obtain a card that depicted my least favorite type of dog from one of my least favorite movies.

When that Toto card finally dropped, nobody was around to cheer me on. Faux Mob Dad and his daughter had left the arcade and the sarcastic teens decided to spare me their mockery. I pulled the card from the chute and immediately welcomed the bug into my brain. From that moment on I was a part of the coin pushing community.

My daily routine soon became clear: I would head to the boardwalk for lunch, which usually consisted of a ridiculously large slice of pizza at one of the seven thousand pizza places on the Seaside Heights boardwalk before making my way to the arcade. I would play the machines for a good while, casually talking to the old ladies who were spending their summer the same way I was, feeding dollar after dollar into a gaudy machine that wouldn't stop playing a tinny version of "Follow the Yellow Brick Road" over and over.

I was getting good at the game; I could determine which machines were about to pop (the coins were just begging to fall) from the ones that looked too good to be true (too many layers of coins stacked at weird angles could create the illusion of appearing ready to drop). Look, I know the preceding sentence is the saddest thing I will ever write, and that's coming from someone who documented his audition for the New Monkees. All I can say is it was a rough summer, okay? I was stressed into oblivion from all sorts of professional and personal drama and I needed something that would help my very tired brain to calm down for a little bit.

For whatever reason, this dopey Wizard of Oz machine did the trick. I needed something that resembled doing something while not actually doing much of anything. I was experiencing what golfers claim to feel when they're out on the links, which I guess is a combination of peacefulness and competition? I don't know and I don't think I ever will because golf creeps me out on a cellular level. Golfers seem to be on some eternal victory lap, as if they're forever celebrating their own greatness. And the notion of fat cats making deals and world-shaping decisions while playing a game that requires wealth to participate is an undeniable celebration of exclusion. So seriously, fuck golf.

I issued a challenge to my listeners on *The Best Show* many years ago, stating that I granted them permission to shoot me if any one of them ever caught me golfing. I'd like to take this opportunity to clarify a couple of the finer points:

1) When I say "golf" I am talking the traditional game of golf: eighteen holes, driving a cart around, smoking cigars, and hanging out with assholes like Tom Brady or Kid Rock. I AM NOT TALKING ABOUT MINIATURE GOLF! Mini golf is NOT golf!
2) On second thought please don't shoot me under any circumstances.

The cold truth of why the coin pushers appealed to me probably boiled down to getting older. Not old, mind you. Just older. Sometimes it just feels good to sit down and do something that requires a minimal amount of effort. It wasn't the best feeling to be the youngster of the coin pusher community, but it wasn't the worst feeling either. After a lifetime of running hard after everything, after the years of fighting both inside and outside my head, it was a relief to just sit at a game and shut off my brain. "You'll never make me feel like a failure who could've made better career choices, will you, Wizard of Oz machine?" I would ask the game under my breath. And every once in a while the machine would whisper back, "Of course not, Tom. I love you. Now how about pumping another fiver into my slot?"

After a week of playing a couple of hours a day, I got pretty good. The Toto cards were no longer an unobtainable mystery; I spotted them hidden beneath piles of coins with ease. I started to accumulate some serious points, which meant I needed to decide on which prizes I was going to claim. I had sailed past a pile of rubber spiders or a plush Minion filled with gasoline-soaked rags. I could pick any prize that the arcade offered. But the problem was I really didn't want any of the stuff they were offering. I didn't need a toaster oven or some dopey Hummel figurines. I realized that I wasn't doing this for the prizes. I was a lost soul on a journey, looking for a sense of who I was and who I hoped to be. And I realized I was now the JFK of the coin pushers, a youthful new face that electrified the geriatric arcade community.

And what a community it was! There was the kindly arcade manager, a woman who wore the strain of supervising a haven catering to cranky bathing-suited maniacs across her exhausted face. There was the old lady who played the Wizard of Oz game every day. And that other old lady who asked me to watch her machine while she went to the bathroom was there too! Come to think of it there were a fair number of old ladies. But we were all there, all looking for our answers somewhere over the rainbow.

By summer's end I had accumulated about 1,600,000 points. The reward tickets still sit in an envelope on my desk. One day I will return to the arcade on the Seaside Heights boardwalk, points in hand. For one reason or another I won't be able to redeem them for a prize that I actually want. Or maybe they will tell me that the points have expired. There's also the chance that the entire business will have gone under, rendering my tickets worthless. Whatever the case, I will accept that reality and I will *complain*, because it is my purpose. My birthright. My family crest depicts someone hiding behind a second family crest to mutter their dissatisfaction with the first crest. The sound of my moanings will be low and steady, the complaints never ending, flowing back and forth just like the ocean waves caressing the New Jersey shoreline.

CHAPTER SIXTEEN

THE FINE ART OF PITCHING

ONCE I HAD achieved a slight foothold in show business, the next goal became obvious: It was time to sell my own show. If you are struggling to recall whether you've seen one of the many shows I've created, I'll drop a spoiler alert on you right here. You haven't because they haven't happened. I've come close but I haven't made it all the way through the gauntlet of getting a show picked up to series. That's how it goes, I get it.

I don't hold any real resentment or bitterness about it because first, that's the way the cookie crumbles, and second, I have gotten paid good money throughout my career for writing some seriously dumb jokes, so I don't really have a lot to complain about in the scheme of things. Nobody's dropping bombs on my head—they just chose to allow me to drop (comedy) bombs on your head (television). And besides, this line of work has allowed me to do *The Best Show* for years without worrying about getting paid, so I will always be grateful for that.

That previous paragraph isn't completely true. It is *mostly* true, but I want my own show and it haunts me that I haven't gotten it yet. I am far from done chasing this dream and I will not rest until I see my name next to a "created by" credit or the sound of dirt hits my coffin with a dull thump.

The first comedy joke pitching I ever did was not for television or movies. It was for legendary fake newspaper the *Onion*. At that point in my life the *Onion* was equivalent to *SCTV* or *Mr. Show*, the absolute tippy-top of the comedy mountain. Before the online version of the paper was commonplace I maintained a very expensive subscription to the physical edition of the paper for a few years, and I felt like a little kid getting a piece of mail addressed to them every time an issue arrived. I was in awe of the world they had built, but the notion of actually writing for the *Onion* was as foreign as getting to write "lap patter" for Santa.

Thankfully the reach of Rock, Rot & Rule extended all the way to Wisconsin, where the *Onion* staff was then located. A couple of writers—most notably the brilliant Todd Hanson—took a liking to my comedy. After a legitimately thorough tryout that entailed submitting page after page of potential jokes, I was invited to pitch for realzies.

I immediately went to work, writing dozens of headlines for the promise of eternal glory and twenty dollars, the going rate for a freelance headline. The submissions were reviewed at their weekly office-wide pitch session, and after a few rounds, I received word that they wanted to use one of my headlines! The headline they purchased was RAY MANZAREK GOES 51 MINUTES WITHOUT MENTIONING JIM MORRISON.

I was over the moon. I had made the grade! I would be a part of the *Onion*! So imagine my shock when I opened the paper to see the headline had been altered to read:

ROBBY KRIEGER GOES 51 MINUTES WITHOUT MENTIONING JIM MORRISON.

This is going to sound petty but I need to get this out of my system. Someone at the *Onion* clearly outsmarted themselves with their punch-up. I know exactly what they were going for: On paper it's funnier to name-check a lesser-known member of the Doors, and Ray Manzarek was a relatively well-known name. But Ray Manzarek was the member of the Doors who constantly flogged the legend of Jim Morrison. Every interview he conducted was littered throughout with "me and Jim." It was maddening to see this guy forever celebrating "the Lizard King" to this obsequious degree. By comparison, guitarist Robby Krieger was relatively normal; he talked about the band but didn't seem to be operating under some illusion that Jim was some kind of demigod.

Look, I get the value in the obscure name-drop. I have made a living making jokes about Bobby Blotzer (the drummer for the metal band Ratt). One long-running *Best Show* joke revolved around a supergroup called "Mick Nick Pick Mick Nick," a band whose members consisted of Mick Mars from Mötley Crüe, Nick Rhodes from Duran Duran, Pick Withers from Dire Straits, Mick Box from Uriah Heep, and Nick Hogan, the son of Hulk Hogan. But this time the obscure comedy reference was not the right choice. So I say to the *Onion* staff circa 2001: Ya blew it! I know how small and vindictive this makes me come off, but I told you at the start of the book that I would be settling a few scores, so consider that score SETTLED!

I placed a handful of headlines in the *Onion* over the next year or two, including:

> 8-YEAR-OLD CAN'T UNDERSTAND WHY HE ISN'T ALLOWED ON ROOF
>
> MICHAEL JORDAN NOT EXACTLY SURE WHAT PRODUCT HE JUST FILMED A COMMERCIAL FOR
>
> SCHOOL SUPERINTENDENT PAUSES FOR APPLAUSE THAT NEVER COMES
>
> NATION'S SHIRTLESS, SHOELESS MARCH ON WASHINGTON FOR EQUAL SERVICE RIGHTS

It was always a thrill to see the final product, especially in the hard copy of the paper. I will forever be in debt to the *Onion* for believing in me, and they will forever be in my debt because I know they didn't pay me for at least two of those headlines.

HERE'S A SHOWBIZ truth that you might not know, even if you're currently in showbiz. Everybody thinks they have a great idea for a television show. And they probably do! But the thing is that IDEAS ARE CHEAP. Jim told me this back at the sheet music store and he was right. Most anybody can sit down for an hour and drum up a premise for a TV show that would be as legit as anything on television. I'll prove it by pitching out three ideas off the top of my head:

- CRIME SHARE: A show about an Uber-type driver who solves mysteries they stumble across while driving their car around the gritty streets of whichever city will offer a tax break for filming
- THE CRIME SOLVER DELIVERER: A show about a Grubhub-type delivery person who solves mysteries they stumble across while driving their car around the gritty streets of whichever city will offer a tax break for filming
- CRIME TO MAKE THE DONUTS: A show about a pastry chef who solves mysteries they stumble across while running an artisanal bakery on the gritty streets of whichever city will offer a tax break for filming

Look, I didn't say they were good ideas. But all three of them are as bad or good as shows that have actually gotten produced. When you reduce a beloved show or movie to one sentence, you can see how something you thought was good could've just as easily been very very bad. "A space alien lands in the suburbs and hangs out with some confused kids while the FBI chases them around." That's *E.T. the Extra-Terrestrial*. It's a classic because Spielberg made it, but just imagine how awful it would be if it starred Hulk Hogan and Jim Belushi. Actually, that version sounds like an upgrade on all fronts. I'm picturing Hogan as E.T., but what if we switch out Reese's Pieces for grey market steroids! Now that's a movie I want to see!

What I'm trying to say is that ideas are important, but the value comes from the execution of the ideas. I have come up with some good ideas over the years, pitches that would've been good shows if we had gone the distance. I've also worked on developing the ideas of others, trying to transform their rough brilliance into a finely polished gem. No matter where the idea was generated, there is one truism that is constant and unavoidable: You will need to go pitch your idea.

What is pitching? It goes something like this: You work on an idea, kicking it around until you know who the characters are, what the story is, where the series or movie will go over time, and what it is you're trying to say with the story you want to tell and sell. Once you have answered all these questions, you then figure out how to present your show to executives and producers in the hope that they will want to make your idea. The act of explaining all this in a short time span—anywhere from ten to twenty minutes' worth of talking—is the act of pitching.

Pitching requires a skill set that many writers find themselves sorely lacking. You have to be affable and charming and positive and excited and mostly without sarcasm, and you need to convey all your thoughts and ideas in what amounts to an oversized sound bite. There isn't any room for weird detours that make sense only to the pitcher. Rambling needs to be kept to a minimum, but unfortunately writers tend to ramble. We are a messy and sweaty lot.

I was the messiest of all writers when I started out, a complete disaster when it came to pitching. There were times I would go into a room with my then–writing partner Joe Ventura and I would say maybe eight words. I was paralyzed with fear and Joe was unfailingly confident, partially due to his work in advertising. Joe was accustomed to going into a conference room and laying out his ideas. I was used to writing out my pitches for basketball magazines or explaining my ideas for *Monk* in a room that could be politely described as "casual." Joe was a master at pitching to strangers, so I considered my value to be that of the "silent partner," the one who would write half the stuff when nobody was looking but didn't say boo when actually sitting across from the executives and producers.

It was embarrassing on a fundamental level but I accepted it because I didn't really have any other choice. What was I going to do, start blathering just to hear the sound of my own voice? "Hey, I'm here too! Do I have anything to say? Well, no. Joe actually said all the important stuff. Thank you for the bottle of water!" No, I knew my role and I was perfectly fine with it.

Joe and I sold a couple of movies that never got made. There was the aforementioned *Flyin V*, which is still one of my proudest achievements, and there was *Jeff the Demon*. We had a star and a director and a studio on board for *Jeff* but then the star made a movie that people didn't see and suddenly no one wanted to make movies with them.

Joe and I did have a nice dinner at a fancy restaurant with Dwayne "the Rock" Johnson while discussing a different project, a dumb kids' movie he was contemplating. We sat at a round table in the corner where everyone could see us. We were eating with the Rock! I did okay in the talking department that night but I was still intimidated by him. He was incredibly cool and smart—there is literally no mystery as to why he is such a huge star. At one point, Warren Beatty came over to the table to introduce himself to Johnson, declaring what a huge fan he was. It was something else watching Beatty—one of the all-time Hollywood alphas—gingerly approach the table and convey his respects to the future president of showbiz. I called Beatty a cuck and told him to get the F away from our table. (I didn't do this.) Needless to say the movie didn't happen, so all I've got is the memory of that salmon dinner to keep me warm at night. I do remember that I wanted to dig into the basket of bread sitting in the middle of the table but I refrained because the Rock made it clear that he wasn't having any bread. (Who is the cuck now?!?!)

I eventually started to develop my own ideas for television, which meant I was going to have to pitch all by myself. Just remembering how I felt at this time can make me throw up. If you recall Nicolas Cage's onscreen portrayal of Charlie Kaufman in *Adaptation*, you'll get an idea of what it was like when your guy walked into a room to pitch during the early days. The first problem was the sweating. Holy moly, would I sweat. It was like someone turned on a lawn sprinkler mounted beneath my forehead. And the worst part was I WASN'T THAT NERVOUS! I wasn't scared of these people! I belonged there! But my body would invariably decide that the best time to run a test of its cooling system was during a meeting with the executive VP of development at Warner Brothers.

The sweating just knocked me off my game. I was embarrassed and humiliated. It made me feel like the fraud that I knew I wasn't. And look, I've been a fraud at different points in my life. There was the time I pretended that I'd seen *The Shawshank Redemption* during a conversation with friends. I knew that someone crawled through a sewer or a toilet in the movie, so I said something along the lines of "Yeah, that sewer scene . . ." I'm sure everyone knew I was full of shit but they were probably too embarrassed to ask why I would lie about having seen *The Shawshank Redemption*.

Something clearly had to be wrong with Ol' Sweatpile, right? Why else would he be perspiring like that? One time I started leaking from my face during a meeting and I told the executives to not think about the dripping liquid as perspiration, but to instead call it "excitement juice." This got a troubled laugh but they didn't buy my show.

Here's a bonus piece of advice to anyone in a showbiz-type meeting: Be careful who you make jokes about because you never know who the other people might know. It sounds like obvious advice, but one time Joe and Wurster and I were all in a room pitching a ridiculous project called *Rock School*—a movie that would be based on the Yo La Tengo music video for "Sugarcube," which Joe co-wrote with our friend/super director Phil Morrison. If you're not familiar, the video features Bob Odenkirk and David Cross as instructors at a rock school, desperately trying to teach the members of Yo La Tengo about the ways of rock.

In the course of our discussion one of us made an offhand crack about Kevin Costner. The executive stopped everything to declare that she was good friends with Costner and that he was a great man. The meeting promptly ground to a dead stop. The takeaway for that one was that you simply cannot assume that the person you're talking to is or isn't friends with Kevin Costner. It is a lesson I have never forgotten, and I hope you will take it with you to your grave.

If you're wondering about *Rock School*, it was insane. I remember the script made us laugh so much but was guaranteed to make any movie executive confused and unhappy. It wasn't that the script was too inside baseball. It's more like the script was playing basketball at a baseball game. The story had to do with a John Oates–type performer becoming the dean of a performing arts school to secretly further his comeback, and we fit into the screenplay as many ridiculous moments as possible; at one point a song parodist at the school sang their version of Smash Mouth's "All Star," with the focus being *The Blair Witch Project* (a movie that was already culturally dead by that point).

The lyrics were:

> Hey now, you're a Blair Witch
> Gonna scare you today
> Hey now, you're a Blair Witch
> Gonna make you run away

All those branches and stones
Leave you in the corner, all alone

Rock School was the closest thing there might ever have been to a Scharpling & Wurster movie. If you ever feel like something is missing from the world we are all living in, you are right. We are short exactly one dumb comedy about a washed-up rocker trying to steal a performing arts school's operating budget so he can record his comeback record. Oh, the comedy that will die on our laptops . . .

I eventually got better at pitching because I managed to figure out one detail in regard to my general unease. Pitching isn't a natural state for me, and it isn't natural for most writers out there. The person who goes into a meeting and jumps up on the coffee table and sells the pitch in the room is either a genius or a fraud. There are probably five geniuses in any given era, so I really can't concern myself with equaling them. The frauds are generally hucksters who know how to sell but have no idea how to write. Their worst nightmare is actually sitting down to write, whereas that is precisely when your boy shines.

But to bridge that very real confidence gap, I decided that I would stop acting like a writer and start acting like the host of *The Best Show*. You know what I mean: the version of Tom who gets heralded for hanging up on callers. It might seem weird that I don't do that all the time, but I don't. If I stayed in "radio mode" 24/7 I would be a very lonely soul. That version of me is still me, but it's me in a heightened state.

I would pretend that I had a microphone in front of me when a meeting began. All I needed was to get the ball rolling, and that little trick helped me get past the hump and the meeting off to a good start. If the notion of talking into a microphone doesn't automatically make you feel calm, then try imitating a confident person who you admire, even just for the first minute or two. The goal is to get things started, and once the ball is rolling you can resume being your normal confident self. Holy crap, this book is a memoir AND a self-help book! Go back to the bookstore and pay for it again!

WITHOUT A DOUBT the most memorable meeting I've ever experienced was pitching a movie with Horatio Sanz. The idea was Horatio's, so I'm not going to spill the beans here in case he ever plans on doing something with it, but I thought it was very funny. One of the things I wanted in my career was to make a mainstream Adam Sandler–type comedy, and this was my best shot. I know that a lot of people who only know Horatio from *SNL* might think he's "the guy who couldn't stop laughing" but trust me, he is one of the funniest people I've ever seen. On certain nights at the UCB Theatre, Sanz could create a funny line or moment that would bring a room filled with the funniest people—Amy Poehler, Adam McKay, Tina Fey, Jon Glaser—to their knees. I knew that if we ever got something rolling it would be a lot of fun.

Our idea wasn't ready to pitch but Horatio's management wanted us to shop it around immediately. We headed to Los Angeles and climbed aboard a merry-go-round of meetings. One meeting in particular stood out on the itinerary: We were going to pitch at Happy Madison, Adam Sandler's production company. I was excited because that is where the movie belonged.

Since I'm the guy who wrote a script for a third *Grown Ups* movie without anyone asking, you can probably guess I love Adam Sandler. I do. The prospect of writing a movie for his company was a dream. That said, I was slightly relieved that we weren't pitching to Sandler himself. We were set to meet with one of his producers, a gentleman named Jack Giarraputo. He seemed like a nice enough fella, one of those lucky humans whose cosmic lottery ticket came in the day he met Adam Sandler as a student at NYU. The rest was history; Jack and Sandler produced a ton of movies together and enjoyed the kind of success the rest of us slobs can only dream of. Anything I say here that sounds less than nice comes from pure unfiltered jealousy. Would I have wanted to meet my future meal ticket when I was eighteen? YES, I WOULD HAVE LIKED THAT A LOT. But Middlesex County College wasn't exactly a pipeline to the entertainment biz. I would've ended up trying to make a movie with the biggest stars to come out of MCC, either Danny Pintauro (the kid from the sitcom *Who's the Boss?*) or Ahmad Khan Rahami (a suspect in the 2016 New York/New Jersey bombings, who the MCC Wiki entry clarifies "did not graduate").

Horatio and I pitched the movie and it was clear that Giarraputo wasn't into it. I did a little sweating that day, still not completely out of the drippy phase of my career. But all told it wasn't too bad. After we concluded, Jack looked at Sanz and said, "You wanna say hi to Sandler?" We were both led into a massive room at the center of the building. Guitars lined the walls and at the back of the room was a desk, on which Adam Sandler was typing away. The Sandman in all his glory!

Giarraputo introduced us and Sandler was legitimately nice. He started talking shop with Horatio, pointing out that he noticed the little moves that Sanz made on *SNL*, some real game-within-the-game stuff that I couldn't relate to but found truly interesting. Sure, they weren't buying our movie, but getting to watch this conversation was a nice consolation prize. My bubble was burst when Giarraputo interrupted to point at me and say, "Hey, Adam! Who does he look like?"

Oh no. No no no nononoononooooooo.

The notion of telling someone that they look like someone else is forbidden in both my life and on my radio show. It is a dangerous game that offers nothing but downside. There are almost no exceptions to this. If I told someone they looked like Rihanna, one of the three most stunning people on the planet, they could very well say, "You think I have a big forehead?!" before storming off. But here I was on the receiving end of a round of "Who Does Tom Look Like." Actually, it was a round of "Who Does Tom Look Like—the Celebrity Edition" with special guest Adam Sandler, the star of so many of Tom's favorite movies.

Sandler looked at me for a couple of seconds. "I don't know," he answered.

"You can't see it? Look at him."

He looked at me again. "I'm not sure."

"Come on! Look at him!"

By now the sweat was pouring from my brow like a burst water main. I had gone into this meeting hoping to maybe sell a screenplay but instead I found myself standing in Adam Sandler's office with some jerkoff imploring the Sandman to stare at my face until he could determine who I looked like.

"I don't know," Sandler stated again, this time in a voice definitive enough to say that he was done with this game.

Giarraputo stepped forward and stood next to me, proudly exclaiming, "Apatow!"

Apatow?!?

Judd Apatow was a name I knew by this point; he had rewritten *The Cable Guy* for Jim Carrey and worked on *The Larry Sanders Show*. He was not yet the writer-director who made movies that were maybe twenty minutes too long. I had no idea what he looked like. But now after fifteen years of exposure to Judd, I am aware of one thing: I DON'T FUCKING LOOK LIKE JUDD APATOW.

I have no idea what Jack Giarraputo was all twisted about that day. But Sandler now looked at me a fifth time and said, "Uh, yeah, I guess," in the most lifeless voice possible. Anyone on earth would've gotten the hint that this game was over. But Jack replied with another "Come on!" hectoring Sandler to finally acknowledge the Apatow doppelganger standing in front of him.

Eventually the "Who Does Tom Look Like" game ended and we were set free. I never forgot this moment. I eventually ran into Sandler fifteen years later but didn't have the courage or interest to remind him about this night. (I also didn't mention *Grown Ups 3* because I am a coward.) I did say I noticed he was wearing a blue suit in both *Punch-Drunk Love* and *Uncut Gems*, to which he replied with a smile, "Yeah yeah, every twenty-two years I put on a blue suit and make movie magic." That moment was so much better than selling a movie to Happy Madison. Or at least that's what I tell myself every night while I struggle to fall asleep.

For the record, the most recent time I pitched a show, I "sold it in the room," which means exactly what it sounds like. And on a fun note, the executive who bought the show from me was later diagnosed with COVID-19!

CHAPTER SEVENTEEN

REVENGE OF THE SHOW AND DEATH OF MY FATHER

I ENDED *THE Best Show on WFMU* on December 17, 2013.

The final episodes were extremely satisfying. I announced the end of the show in October, which gave us seven weeks to wrap up things the right way. The shows were fun and often guest-filled affairs, and the Scharpling & Wurster calls were a parade of the show's greatest characters. Everything paid off like a *Sex and the City* slot machine.

The final episode was particularly special. Instead of overstuffing it with guests, we kept things lean and mean, just me and Wurster in the studio together, two people making each other laugh. When I finally signed off, I said goodbye and played "You're Innocent When You Dream" by Tom Waits.

I actually played the first twenty seconds of it before yanking the record off the turntable with a scratch worthy of a Steve Guttenberg movie trailer. Imagine ending the show with a fucking Tom Waits song! He sucks shit! After this one final curveball I said, "*This* is how we end *The Best Show on WFMU*," and played "Gimmie Gimmie Gimmie" by Black Flag, an infinitely more appropriate send-off.

The show always felt like a fight, and after thirteen years, the fight was over. We won!

The outpouring of appreciation was immensely gratifying. There were articles and interviews as people bid farewell to a show that meant a lot to its listeners. I was touched. But the funny thing about all this farewell stuff was that I knew *The Best Show* wasn't over. *The Best Show on WFMU* was over. After thirteen years it simply wasn't sustainable to do the show for free. But out of respect for everything WFMU stood for—listener-sponsored radio that wasn't based on financial gain—I didn't mention anything about returning on a different platform. I wanted to honor those tenets on the way out the door. The closest I came was to cryptically say during the final episode that the show was a victim of its own success and couldn't continue on WFMU, but that we weren't done yet. Which isn't very cryptic when you think about it. It's actually kinda clear, but that's how it played out. It's not like I was well-practiced in ending radio shows.

I ran into John Oliver at an event shortly after wrapping it all up. He has always been a vocal supporter of *The Best Show on WFMU.* His immediate response when I told him I was taking my program off a noncommercial station was "Well, it's about fucking time!"

Some people were certain that I was going to cry during the final moments of the last episode. I didn't think I would, but I wasn't sure, because I am an easy crier. Just about anything can send me into spasms of sobbing. Here are some examples of benign things that have made me cry:

- *Pee-wee's Big Adventure,* when Pee-wee runs back into the flaming pet store to rescue the snakes even though he hates snakes
- LeBron James returning to play for the Cavs
- Any video of a dog getting reunited with its owner
- *Pee-wee's Big Adventure,* when Pee-wee dresses like a nun and gets his bike back

- Certain videos of humans getting reunited with their families
- Any superhero movie where the slob citizens watch the superhero get knocked out and then unite to confront the villain, even though they don't have powers. Someone will usually say something like, "Hey, you can't treat Superman like that!" and pick up a bat to fight before getting knocked down by the villain
- Anytime anyone gives me the slightest amount of approval

As I hosted the final show, I kept wondering when the emotions were going to arrive. When would I break down into fits of sobbing? But the tears never came. I was a little surprised but it made sense because I wasn't sad! It wasn't goodbye forever; it was merely time to leave WFMU and see what the future held.

A good chunk of 2014 was spent figuring out where the best home for the next version of *The Best Show* might be. I took meetings with networks of all sizes. Public radio was interested; podcast networks were interested. There were a few people with start-up money who wanted me to consider using *The Best Show* as a guinea pig for their speculative platforms. Ultimately none of those places truly fit the bill. I didn't want the show to live on a public radio network that would inevitably bristle at me doing Gary the Squirrel for twenty minutes on their precious airwaves, and we had accomplished far too much for the show to be reduced to a corporate experiment.

One Los Angeles–based podcast network was interested in having the show as the flagship program of their East Coast expansion. It would've been a solid fit, but they wanted me to build my own NYC-based studio, which wasn't financially feasible. Reality sunk in: I was going to have to do this myself.

Once again my DIY instincts took over. I inherited these chops from both my family—who have been self-employed for generations—and the overall indie rock aesthetic I absorbed after joining the scene in my early twenties. DIY rules demand that if you want to accomplish something, don't wait for permission. The upside is that you control all your own business: no label head to run anything by or editor to nix an article. But the downside is that if you want it done right, you're on the hook for everything. When it's hard it's *so* hard. It is simultaneously exhilarating and exhausting. I knew the headaches I was inviting, but I had fought too long and hard to build up *The Best Show* and I just couldn't trust anyone else with my baby. I trusted the executives and producers I spoke to, but I didn't trust their bosses, the anonymous executives who ultimately wouldn't care about the show. I couldn't risk it, so I got to work and learned how to build both a studio and a business.

Brendan McDonald made it possible to do the show. Brendan is the producer of *WTF with Marc Maron* and has been a longtime friend. He helped figure out all the important things like assembling a studio, getting equipment, staffing up, and building a streaming platform on the Internet. I will forever be indebted to him for sharing his talent and time. Brendan, if you're at the bookstore buying this, show them this passage and the bookseller will give you a 5 percent discount on this book or a free pastry at the café. BUT NOT BOTH.

One of the first pieces that the show needed was a producer. I tweeted out that I was looking for a New Jersey–based engineer who had tech experience, and I received exactly one reply, from a young man named Jason Gore. It wouldn't have mattered if I had gotten a thousand replies because Jason would've beaten them all out anyway. Brendan and I sat down with him at one of Jersey City's worst diners and we talked about our plans. After Jason left, Brendan turned to me and said, "That guy is the real deal." He then said, "Let's order dessert." Having worked with Jason for a few years, I know that Brendan was as right as can be. Jason is one of the few people I've met who can handle his business on either side of the mic. He's insanely funny and can fix virtually any technical problem.

(Brendan was wrong about the dessert, however. The chocolate pudding was somewhat chalky.)

I also hit up a former colleague at WFMU to help out. Pat Byrne is another top-notch human, a hard worker with an amazing sense of humor. I first knew Pat as a kid who would call *The Best Show* on occasion. He would try to prank me but it was clear that Pat wasn't just a garden-variety trickster. He had weird ideas of his own, like his plan to make a film documenting him walking from Verona, New Jersey, to the George Washington Bridge. I was confused at the time about this idea (and I am still a little confused) but I liked him. Pat is one of the kindest souls out there.

And then there was AP Mike. Mike had been the call screener for *The Best Show on WFMU* since around 2004. At first, I wasn't sure what his deal was. He was quiet and unassuming, just a regular guy from Bayonne with amazing taste in books and movies. His musical opinions are a little more suspect; he's a huge Deadhead, which I still can't abide by. Over the years, I realized how talented Mike is. He plays along with a joke with more aplomb than 99 percent of comedians. Mike plays the role of a producer forever on the chopping block perfectly—to the point where people think he's actually a buffoon. But he's far from it. Mike is a well-read guy who has contributed immensely to the show through his call screening and hilarious observations over the years. A valuable piece of the *Best Show* puzzle.

Okay, enough of this "Tribute to *The Best Show* Staff." Time to talk more about meeeeeeee!

Most of 2014 was spent building up the show and by the end of the year we had a studio (located in an apartment building in Jersey City), all the equipment necessary to broadcast, and a killer streaming platform (courtesy of Martin Celis, another technical genius I forever bow down to). The return of *The Best Show* was right around the corner, and I couldn't wait. I had sunk a lot of my personal income into making this happen, so I was definitely on the hook. I obviously wanted the show to succeed, but now I needed it to succeed.

The show returned on December 17, 2014, almost a year to the day that we wrapped up on WFMU. It was fantastic to be back. It turned out that I needed a break from the show, if only to appreciate what it meant to me. The absence of a weekly platform to be funny and connect with the listeners meant at least as much to me as it did to the audience. I seriously missed it. If you are lucky enough to figure out the reason you have been put on this planet, it can be torture to say goodbye to that thing, even for just a year. But now I had a studio, I had my own network, I had an amazing staff, and Wurster and I were firing on all cylinders. The show was back!

Two weeks later my father died.

So THAT WAS a real fucking curveball, right?!

It happened suddenly. One Sunday afternoon I was at home in bed, trying to take a nap because I hadn't slept the night before. I was alone; the house was completely quiet. I reached that first fragile level of sleep, where the slightest noise can break the spell. For me it was a phone call from a number I didn't recognize. I ignored it and tried to drift back to sleep. The phone rang again. Same number. I picked up. It was the woman who lived across the street from my parents. I had never spoken to her on the phone, so I immediately knew something was wrong.

She told me that I should get to the hospital as fast as I could because my father wasn't doing well. I'm not sure if she said anything else because I ran out the door as quickly as possible. I had just talked to my father two days earlier and he seemed fine. I pulled into the hospital parking lot and ran inside. I immediately saw my mother and sister, both of them crying. They didn't need to say a thing. I knew.

For anyone who has yet to lose a parent, it is above all a strange experience. Every emotion rips through your brain at once and you feel your definition of life change before your eyes. Everything you understood as fact now means nothing. I don't recommend it!

My father was one of the all-time nice guys. I received my fight and fire from my mother, but my father gave me my sense of humor and my creativity. He was funny in a sly and unassuming way, and one story always resonates with me. My family made a point of seeing Star Wars movies together. It was a fun thing we all did and I never forgot it. My dad straight-up took me and my sister out of school so we could go see *The Empire Strikes Back* opening afternoon. My mind is like a sieve and countless memories have been reduced to dust but I can recall every part of that day, including the moment when we spotted our shop teacher also sneakily waiting in line for the movie. I remember the day so vividly because it is one of the memories I have run through my mind a million times. I knew it was special as it was happening and never let go of it.

We did the same thing for *Return of the Jedi*, skipping school to see the final installment of the original Star Wars trilogy. If you don't remember, the movie features a song called "Lapti Nek," a spectacularly terrible piece of crap performed by Jabba the Hutt's house band. As we drove home, my father made a bet with us: He predicted that "Lapti Nek" would top the charts. I think the bet was for ten dollars, but the money was beside the point. Why on earth would he initiate such a ridiculous wager? Even as a child hypnotized by all things Star Wars, I knew that "Lapti Nek" sucked shit. There was no way that dumb song could ever beat out chart-toppers like "Down Under" or "Ebony and Ivory"!

Fast-forward about six months. My family is eating dinner. Mom brings up the bet; *Return of the Jedi* had come and gone without "Lapti Nek" lighting up the Billboard Hot 100. She wanted to know when he was going to pay up. My father smiled and said, "We never set a date on when it would happen." So yes, the bet my father had with us is still active, and if "Lapti Nek" happens to hit number one I am going to figure out how to pay him.

My dad also informed my whole "slobs versus snobs" philosophy. I embrace that I am Jersey trash and my dad carried that chip as well. He never went to college and I think he felt the implied inferiority that gets dumped onto those who didn't pursue a higher education. He actually countered it by embracing it as a point of pride, bragging that the only books he had read as an adult were the Johnny Cash autobiography *Man in Black* and Erich von Däniken's "aliens have been visiting Earth for thousands of years" epic *Chariots of the Gods?* If my father had taken it upon himself to start a book club it would've been the weirdest—and quickest!—book club in history. I don't condone celebrating the act of not reading books, but I get it. He was a proud guy who made himself smart in his own way, through his own efforts. I'd rather listen to my father talk about things he learned through actually living his life than hear some Harvard windbag blather on about investing in ascots or whatever it is that rich people talk about. (And I'm not talking about all Harvard grads—just most of you. You know if I think you suck!)

The planning of the wake was a special level of hell I had yet to experience in my life. But we got through it as a family. After one particularly grueling afternoon, we all went to a pizzeria that my parents frequented. I'm not sure if the rest of the country can relate, but there is a very specific kind of New Jersey/NYC pizzeria that I have been eating at my entire life. The business is generally divided in two: One half is the pizzeria, which features a few tables and the pizza counter, along with a mounted television playing Fox News. The other half is the "restaurant," with more tables, a wall painting depicting an unevenly proportioned Italian *villaggio*, and a mounted television also playing Fox News. These pizzerias usually feature a stack of free "autos for sale" magazines that you could look at while eating during the pre–cell phone era along with one or two autographed headshots from local meteorologists and/or Uncle Floyd, who apparently eats a lot of pizza.

That day we took a seat in the back and sadly cobbled together an order. We sat quietly, not much to say about anything. We were all cried out. After we ordered I stepped outside to get some fresh air. The pizzeria owner must've seen me looking sad and asked me if something was wrong. He knew my parents as well as any slice slinger would know their regular customers. I pulled myself together and told him my father had died a day or so earlier. He expressed his condolences and I sat back down with my family.

The owner came over to the table and immediately zeroed in on my mother. He also conveyed his condolences to her, which was sweet. But then he kept going. "This is so terrible. So, so terrible. I can't believe it," he said. "He was such a good man." We all nodded in agreement. But Pizza Man didn't get the hint and started laying on the grief thicker than he sauces up a Sicilian pie. "This is the worst. Just the worst." His intentions were pure, I am sure of that. He was trying to lend comfort to a grieving family. But it felt like he started to up his mourning game when he didn't draw the tears he thought he would get. "You'll feel this forever," he said sadly, feet still planted firmly in front of our table. "He's gone forever." I wanted to yell, "Don't you have a calzone to heat up or something?" but I simply waited for him to stop. Which he didn't.

Pizza Man transitioned into his eulogy for my father. Looking at each of us with a weirdly scolding countenance, he told us, "Your father was a good man." His familiarity with my father didn't go much further than my dad's enjoyment of chicken parm subs, so I wasn't sure what he was going for. Thankfully our food came out and Pizza Man left us to our meal. It's a testament to the strength of my mother that afterward we talked about this insane moment and she thought it was funny. Dad wasn't the only parent with a sense of humor.

THE TIMING OF all this was devastating to say the least. After all the preparation and planning, my heart had been torn out of my chest. *The Best Show* was the last thing I was interested in and everything felt like a complete waste of time. I couldn't imagine getting back behind the mic and having frivolous fun. It was a struggle, all of it.

But I had to try. It had taken a lot of effort to bring the show back. I returned to the studio the following Tuesday to give it a shot. My crew understood that if I couldn't hold it together we would just pull the plug.

I was at a total loss for words. What am I supposed to talk about, the best and worst ice cream sundae toppings? It all felt pointless, but staying at home being sad didn't feel right either. I sat in my chair before the show and made notes with the hope that I would be prepared enough to get through the night. I looked at the tables that the equipment rested on. The mixing board, the turntable, the CD player atop two wooden tables positioned in an L formation. They were the backbone of the studio, and I then realized that my father helped me put them together. I had purchased some fixtures from the IKEA a few miles from the new studio and like the nitwit I am, I struggled mightily to assemble them. I'm not exactly a dummy when it comes to handywork. I can fix a running toilet and I can usually assemble basic furniture, but for some reason these tables weren't coming together.

So I did what I have done so many times throughout my life: I picked up the phone and I called my father to ask for help. My parents never really listened to the show, but they were both thrilled that I had something that made me happy. All they ever wanted was for me to be happy. I know they were relieved that I had pulled together a life for myself after all the mental problems. I had become an adult and could stand on my own two feet ... except when it came to assembling tables. As soon as I explained my dilemma, my dad did what he always did. He was at the studio with his toolbox later that night. Within a minute my father figured out what I was doing wrong with the tables and we built them together. He was always there for me until the day he wasn't.

I got through the show by owning where I was with my emotions. I talked about my dad and I played "Fly Like an Eagle" by the Steve Miller Band, one of his favorite songs. I remember the eight-track tape he had of that album with its bubbled label and unnatural mid-song skips. The music made sense and provided a little comfort in a very trying spot.

Man, I miss my father.

THE RECONSTITUTED *BEST SHOW* found its footing. I fell into a groove and was actually able to lose myself in the show a little bit. It was imperative for the show to return as strong as we had ended it, so getting to hide behind a creative endeavor was a gift. We righted the ship and the show took off once again, in no small part due to the tables that held everything up week after week.

CHAPTER EIGHTEEN

A STORY OF UNQUALIFIED TRIUMPH #3

IT'S CLEAR THE chapters documenting my unqualified triumphs are built on some pretty shaky ground. The first one, about the *Sex and the City* slot machine, was undeniable in its unqualified triumph-ness, but the one about the Paul Simon video? I don't know. I guess potentially getting Rhymin' Simon to read a video treatment in which he gets his leg crushed by a barrel is triumphant, if only to make him mutter, "This is the dumbest thing I've ever read." I'm also having trouble coming up with more of these stories. Is my life really this bereft of unqualified triumphs?!

Maybe it's the use of the word "unqualified" that's hanging me up? I'm not sure, but I do know that you paid eighty dollars for this book, so I'm gonna do everything in my power to make you happy. So sit back and relax, maybe smoke a little bit of God's Green Herb, and enjoy the story of how I got my head straight at the start of a new year.

I appreciate the significance of days and dates. I am by nature a sucker for structure—a regular Structure Sucker, if you will. I love to set goals for myself at the top of every month, eagerly writing them out in my schedule book (yes, I use a physical book!), listing everything I will accomplish if all goes according to plan. At the start of the following month I transfer the list of things I didn't accomplish to next month and start again. I get fired up when July 1 rolls around because the calendar year is half over, and that means it's time to take stock and make plans to squeeze everything I can from the remaining six months. The same goes for birthdays and the start of September, which still represents the beginning of the school year to me even though my days of reciting the golden rule and dipping pigtails into inkwells are long behind me.

But no day holds more power for me than the start of a new year. Everything is possible on the first of January; we have all been gifted with twelve months to build and reshape and improve and explore. Sure, by the end of the year I often find myself saying, "Well, I *did* eat more pizza than the year before—that's an accomplishment, right?" but the effort is what counts. And I know that a "calendar year" is a human construct and that we are always given a chance to improve the next 365 days of our life no matter what the date is. But I am nothing if not human, so I seek comfort in things like calendars and candy bars. (Hold up, is *Calendars and Candy Bars* a better title for this book?)

Ten or so Januarys ago I really wanted to start things off right. On the day after the New Year began I went for an afternoon drive to listen to music and reframe my mindset, letting in nothing but positive vibes. If this sounds a little hippy-dippy, then so be it. I'm proud to admit that I am not against a nice candle every now and again, and I can enjoy a good tarot reading, especially if the cards tell me that I'm awesome. I drove down Interstate 78 in New Jersey, a highway that I've always found incredibly boring in its beauty; lots of mountains and trees that never moved the needle for me. Perhaps it's because I-78 always reminded me of the long drive on the way to boring family get-togethers as a kid. Whenever I found myself in the backseat of the family car driving down good old I-78, I knew that within an hour I'd be hiding in the coat closet of an Italian restaurant clutching whichever book I was reading and praying that my family simply didn't notice my absence.

But today the scenery really resonated with me. The rolling hills were endless and majestic. I felt connected to their beauty. I spotted a scenic overlook off the highway and pulled in. It was midafternoon around this point, the sun just starting to show signs of retreat. The air was crisp and cold but not punishing. There are certain winter days in New Jersey that are surprisingly accommodating and this was one of them. I ascended the road and parked in the lot, pulling up to the edge of the overlook. The vista was amazing, just mile after mile of wintry trees and nature spread out for as far as the eye could see. I was inspired. There were a handful of cars peppering the parking lot and a dozen or so fellow travelers walking around the edges of the lot, also admiring the site's awesomeness.

I pulled out my notebook and started writing down my goals for the year. I often make New Year's resolution lists, and I try to refer back to them from time to time. I listed everything I wanted to achieve that year. Some of the goals were attainable—"Write a screenplay"—and others were impossible—"Play bass for LCD Soundsystem." But it didn't matter. I just poured it all out. I listed my fears and negative traits that I wanted to leave behind. It was a purge, getting every thought and goal out of my head and onto a piece of paper.

Burning the paper listing your intentions is a way to "release" the thoughts and goals to the universe. I know—hippy tripe. But sometimes it's good to indulge stuff like this if it makes sense for you; it's not the worst thing to feel connected to something larger, even if you know in the back of your mind that it's ultimately a dramatic form of goal setting.

I fished a lighter out of my glove compartment and stepped out of the car. The air was bracing but felt good. I had tapped into the beauty of both the location and the moment. I read the list to myself, making sure to feel each goal and fear and trait on the deepest level before moving on. This was an opportunity to start the year off right and I was going to get the most from this moment. A couple of guys walked past me as I held the paper in my hand, giving me quizzical looks. Perhaps they weren't familiar with the concept of a New Year's Day positivity ritual but that's on them. I was loving it.

I finished the list and calmly stared at the rolling hills, absorbing as much of this magic moment as the day would allow. Another guy walked past, this time giving me a straight-up dirty look. *Whatever, guy*, I thought to myself and proceeded with my ritual.

I set a small rock on the paper and lit it on fire. As it burned, I felt my consciousness expand a little. I was taking care of business on a spiritual level. It was going to be a good year. The paper was eventually consumed by the flame and I doused it with some of whatever liquid I had been nursing in my car, either a Diet Dr Pepper or an iced coffee. I looked out at the view and tried to process every challenge that life could throw at me: *What can I do to make life better for myself? How can I make it better for my family? Are there ways I can strengthen my relationships with my friends? How can I help the planet?*

But before I could ponder any more wisdom, another guy walked right past me, once again giving me a look like he wasn't sure what I was doing. I threw a slight smile on my face and watched him walk toward a parked car at the end of the lot. His energy was breaking the spell for me a little bit, introducing negativity into my beautiful day. *Where does this guy get off giving me a dirty look? What I'm doing here is my business, okay? You don't see me judging you for walking around the edge of the parking lot before getting into a car with the other guy that gave me a dirty look and—*

Ohhhhhh.

In a flash everything made sense. I realized why I was getting the evil eye from all the guys hovering around the overlook.

I was doing my New Year's Day positivity performance smack in the middle of a cruising spot. That's why these guys were bouncing around from car to car! How could I have known that my little ritual would ultimately be nothing more than a massive cockblock for the

Central New Jersey cruising community? A simple Google search could've solved this for me within thirty seconds; when I entered in "New Jersey Interstate 78 scenic overlook," a review page on a cruising website contained all the info I could've asked for:

> "Gave a good BJ last week in the guys SUV. Going into the woods is risky."
> "I gave and received good head here. Almost always someone looking to get some here."
> "From 7:30 to 8:30 in the morning is great, also have done a few guys myself."

Two takeaways from this info:

1) I am definitely a little slow on the uptake.
2) Seven thirty to eight thirty in the morning?! I can barely bring myself to speak before 9:00 A.M. let alone meet new people!

I think it is awesome that this scenic overlook serves the community in a variety of ways. And to be honest, that spot was a total snore. There were zero vending machines for starters. If you're gonna go all the way to a scenic overlook, you should at least have the opportunity to buy some Skittles. And how long can you really look at a fucking mountain?

If I remember correctly, I had a pretty good year. For that alone I award this story full Unqualified Triumph status. Hey, maybe my victories don't resemble yours, but I'll take what I can get.

CHAPTER NINETEEN

THE DEATH OF AMERICA AND THE ALMOST DEATH OF TOM

IT TOOK MOST of my adult life for me to be finally ready to write this book. For years the idea of telling my story was appealing but something always stopped me from going forward. The truth of the matter was that I was terrified of facing who I actually am. My life felt like the trailer for the movie *Gladiator* writ small: "The child who became a mentally ill teen. The mentally ill teen who changed his name and became a radio host. The radio host who conquered a not-inconsiderable portion of the axis between alternative comedy and independent music," and so on.

Any sort of self-analysis was only going to unleash the years of shame and suffering that I worked very hard to bury. The reinvention of myself as Tom Scharpling certainly helped me cope with my day-to-day existence. I was able to live a more brash life, pushing myself onto the world as a writer/director/radio host. But it wasn't without a cost; underneath the surface was all the shame, just lying in wait. Whatever psychic box all that crap was crammed into would not hold forever. So even though I complained on the radio that "Al Roker has a book but I don't" mostly for comedic effect, the reality was that I could have never written a book about my life until now. Maybe I should've just written one about Al Roker's life.

All in all, it was smooth sailing for the new version of *The Best Show*. We built the audience back up, and the listenership was engaged. The show was making a little bit of money from advertising, which was strictly verboten during the WFMU days. Jon and AP Mike were firing on all cylinders, and the addition of Pat and Jason to the show created immense value both on and off the air. Everything was coming together nicely.

When I realized in September 2016 that the show would once again land on the night of a presidential election, I saw an opportunity to do a unique episode. The staff and I brainstormed ideas for weeks, trying to figure out what we could do to make the night special. We kicked around a few loose concepts but one idea stood out: We could do a live show on election night but pretend it was a rebroadcast of a show from ten years earlier. The notion of creating a fake episode of the show was exciting: If we got the details right the audience would fall for it hook, line, and sinker. It was a creative challenge but it would be worth it to gently prank the listeners. Little did any of us know that the world itself was about to get pranked and I would barely survive the night.

One of the bizarre side effects of doing a show on Tuesdays has been that inevitable collision with election nights. *The Best Show on WFMU* started in October 2000 and within a few weeks I was doing a program on the night that George W. Bush "defeated" Al Gore. The pattern continued in 2004 when GWB beat John Kerry. I left the studio that night to attend a celebratory party that liberal radio network Air America was throwing. I was still ramped up from having done three hours of my own broadcasting but my mood immediately deflated as soon as I entered the "party" around 12:30 A.M. By then it was clear that Kerry was gonna eat it. I got to see a bunch of Air America personalities stress-smoke while hoping against hope that certain Ohio districts would somehow break for Kerry. They didn't, and Bush won. (Spoilers!)

I had to attend jury duty the next day and in an act of patriotism I placed a Hershey's bar on the trunk of a car sporting a Bush bumper sticker as I walked toward the courthouse. And I know what you are all wondering, so here's my answer: YES, I OFTEN CARRY HERSHEY'S BARS WITH ME. And for those of you who thought that me "placing a Hershey's bar" was some sort of toilet-based euphemism, I can only say shame on you. This was not my proudest moment, but I was racked with hopelessness over the loss. Besides, it was November in New Jersey and that Hershey's bar wouldn't have gotten too melty. If the driver of the car had some graham crackers and a marshmallow on their person they could've made a s'more for the drive home. You're welcome, right-wing shitbag!

Things were different when Obama won in 2008. The night of the radio show felt like a party, albeit one that nobody wanted to jinx. Any premature celebration felt like playing with fire after the previous two elections. I drove to a bar in Jersey City after the show and celebrated with all my friends. I bought literally anything that had Obama's face on it for the next two weeks, so if you're in the market for a shitty laminated Obama placemat that I jammed into a closet once it became clear that he wasn't gonna stop dropping bombs on people, let me know.

The weeks leading up to the 2016 election felt relatively uneventful. Everyone on earth was preemptively declaring Hillary Clinton to be the winner. At one point, the *Huffington Post* gave Trump something like a 2 percent chance of winning. We were all effectively living in a bubble, unaware of the geyser of hate and resentment that the Donald had been tapping into. Despite the looming disaster, it felt like we could figure out a fun show to do while waiting for Clinton to win the election.

Look, I'm not going to pretend that I'm a huge fan of either Clinton; my politics are somewhere to the left of Lenin. But I obviously preferred her over Trump, who I had become way too familiar with when I wrote recaps of *The Celebrity Apprentice* for a popular culture website a few years earlier. We were at the peak of the "birther" movement around that time, and Trump was hammering Obama on a daily basis for not providing a birth certificate that met his exacting standards.

I was disgusted by Trump, so midway through the season, I declared that I would no longer promote his name or brand, instead referring to him only as "Fuck Face." The editorial staff didn't appreciate this stance, telling me that my choice of language was a little "schoolyard." Which in retrospect sounds perfectly reasonable. My apologies to the Trump family for my appalling lack of discretion. I unfairly lowered the bar on an otherwise civil discussion. You clearly deserved better and for that I am truly sorry.

With the election seemingly in the bag, we all prepared this very strange episode of the show. I announced at the start of the program that the staff was taking the night off but as a treat we would air a rare episode of the show from 2006. The program was impeccably performed and executed: We made sure that the specifics were airtight, tracking which albums had (and more importantly hadn't) been released, which celebrities were still alive in 2006, even nailing down which sodas and junk foods had ceased production that year. (For your information, French Toast Crunch went under and Trix changed their fruity shape.) I listened to episodes of the show from that year to hear what my voice sounded like around that time. The difference was notable: I talked from my head more than from my chest, creating a slightly nasal effect that evokes the voice that comedians of color use when they're doing their generic "white guy" impression. All the music I played was from a decade earlier, like the Dirtbombs and the Little Killers. Wurster called in as Philly Boy Roy circa 2006 and *Best Show* mainstays like Terre and Brett Davis called in pretending that we were all in the past. It was an amazing night . . . until it was announced that Trump had won Ohio. Suddenly the world got a little wobbly. What the fuck was happening here?

I had to pull it together and continue the program, acting as if it was 2006. Except the reality of 2016 was becoming increasingly horrible with every passing moment. Things only got worse as states on the bubble started landing in Trump's column. The fun concept of a clever time-travel show suddenly felt like a cry for help, as if I were begging to literally turn back time. The narrative of the show shifted as the nightmare became all too real. During the final hour of the show, I found a way to embrace the creeping reality of our new president. I started talking about how the future was going to become very very bad, the 2006 version of me foretelling of the doom that awaited us down the road.

The show was, without a doubt, one of the all-time high-water marks of anything I've ever been a part of. But nobody heard it. They were all at home crying over the election results, and when the program became available as a podcast the listeners didn't want to relive the horror of election night 2016. And I can't blame them. It was a terrible night. But as I said, my own personal pan pizza of horror was right around the corner.

As I wrapped up the show it was clear that Trump was going to win. I packed up and headed to the nearby diner with Pat and comedian Clare O'Kane, who had come down to watch the "festivities," also contributing a call or two throughout the show. We commiserated about the future of the country while eating terrible diner food, then parted ways. I headed back home, getting on the southbound New Jersey Turnpike. I couldn't bear to listen to the news—the television in the diner had let us know that Trump would likely take Pennsylvania—so I played music instead, blasting a legendary Australian band from the 1980s called the Scientists. Their sound is thick and swampy and numbed my brain in just the right way.

The New Jersey Turnpike cuts a swath from the top to the bottom of the state. Large portions of it are indefensibly gross, embodying everything non-Jerseyans disparagingly hurl at my home state. The image of the smokestacks belching out poison? The filth that is the Newark Airport? That's all a small stretch of the turnpike, a road that runs for 117 long miles. The vast majority of New Jersey is beautiful and lush; there's a reason why it's called the Garden State, after all. But I was most definitely driving on the portion of the turnpike that Bruce Springsteen had in mind when he wrote "State Trooper"—the bleak industrial doom factories stacked up alongside the highway like a dying city in a dystopian sci-fi movie.

I have driven this stretch of road thousands of times throughout my life, from when I went into Manhattan with my parents to the countless times I headed into NYC to see a band or comedy show. I'm all too familiar with every aspect of the New Jersey Turnpike: I love the rumble of the planes as they come in for a landing directly above your head, and I can't stand the traffic on the Exit 14A-C extension during a morning commute. I thought I had seen everything this stretch of road had to offer, but that would change tonight.

One thing I had never seen on the turnpike was a deer. I was used to seeing them on residential roads, but this stretch of highway offered nothing that could possibly entice anyone from the animal kingdom; it's all asphalt and barrier railings. Never in my life had I seen an animal on the New Jersey Turnpike until that night.

There weren't any cars or tractor trailers on the road, a rare occurrence even at 1:30 A.M. I was still listening to the Scientists and wondering what the country would look like with the guy who played Waldo's dad in *Little Rascals* as the leader of the free world. I wasn't on the phone; I wasn't driving distracted. I didn't have a single drink all night. I was going over 75 mph, desperate to get home and go to bed after this disastrous night. The music fit the mood perfectly. The Scientists are hard-edged and ugly, kind of like if Creedence Clearwater Revival was composed of death-obsessed Australian nihilists.

Suddenly there was a massive deer in front of my car. He was huge, with a tower of antlers atop his head. My car was going fast but everything seemed to slow down. The deer was mere feet in front of me, scampering horizontally across the lanes of the turnpike. It was impossible for me to swerve or slow down. We collided, me into him, him into me. I still see it in my mind as a series of snapshots. The sound was deafening, just an explosion of crunching metal. I managed to skid off the road and stall out on the shoulder.

I sat in stunned silence as my Honda Civic went into cardiac arrest, every light on the panel blinking. The airbags did not deploy. The front end of my car was folded like an accordion. And somehow I was not hurt. I have replayed this scenario in my mind countless times and it never makes sense. If the deer had jumped up just a little bit he would've gone through the windshield. If anyone else had been driving near me on the turnpike I would've plowed into them as I swerved. Every variable broke in my favor, and if a single one of them had been altered even slightly I would have died. I still cannot believe I survived the crash.

I sat in the driver's seat, my stereo somehow still playing the Scientists. The song was "When Fate Deals Its Mortal Blow." I shut off the car and everything went silent. (And I know it might sound like some bizarre sort of cosmic coincidence that a song entitled "When Fate Deals Its Mortal Blow" was playing during my crash, but most every song by the Scientists would've fit the drama of the moment. The next song on the CD was "Burnout," for example. And the track after that is "The Spin," which would've been even more appropriate!)

I got out and surveyed the damage. Fluid leaking everywhere from the engine, the smell of metal on metal. The front of the car shattered and folded up into a V. The deer was nowhere to be seen. I called Terre and told her I had been in an accident but assured her that I was okay. Before I could tell her more, the flashing lights of a cop car pulled behind my demolished vehicle. I hung up to tell the cop what had happened, but my voice simply stopped working. I literally could not speak beyond a strained groan. I have never experienced a case of laryngitis like that in my life. It was clearly stress-induced but I couldn't concern myself with why it was happening because I was face-to-face with a cop who was extremely skeptical of my story.

I really can't blame him, mainly because the notion of a deer on this stretch of highway sounded insane, like the kind of lie a driver would use to explain away a drunk driving mishap. The traces of hair and blood embedded on the grill ultimately convinced him that I was telling the truth. Of course the cop kept acting like a dick but at least he was a dick who didn't think I was a criminal. He called a tow truck and drove off into the night to presumably see how many White Castle hamburgers he could fit in his mouth at once.

The tow truck arrived minutes later and I hopped into the cab after the Civic was hooked up to the rig. My voice was now a strained screech, barely able to say a word. The tow truck driver asked me if I wanted to take my car to my mechanic or if he should just take it to the tow yard. Since I don't have a mechanic, I asked to go to the tow yard. We drove together in silence as he guided my car off the turnpike.

The tow yard was exactly what you'd expect: a vehicle graveyard surrounded by ugly rusted fencing topped with barbed wire. I wasn't sure why they needed barbed wire to keep people out because there was nothing worth stealing in this metallic shit pit. Maybe they needed the barbed wire to keep people from escaping?

Things got bad for me once I settled into the reality of what had just happened. My voice was gone and it felt like a cap had been placed on my comprehension. The tow truck driver let me out of the cab and I went into the office, which I can only compare to the waiting room in *Beetlejuice* but with more monsters. I couldn't handle much of anything by this point but I had to approach the counter and talk to the woman behind a plexiglass window.

The lady running the tow yard resembled the mom from *Throw Momma from the Train* crossed with the train from *Throw Momma from the Train*, and she was vaguely irritated by my presence. It took a moment to realize why: She was tracking the election results from a small TV on her desk. She gave me some paperwork and I sat down to fill it out, my brain still in a fog. I handed the documents back to her and asked if there was a bathroom I could use. She pointed to

a hallway at the far end of the room and grunted that I didn't need
a key. I opened the door to what was the most disgusting lavatory
since the days of CBGB. I splashed some water on my face and tried
to process everything that had taken place. The night started off
with such hope: Hillary Clinton was going to beat Trump, so we
had planned a fun episode of the radio show. But here I was in a tow
yard bathroom, my car totaled and the fate of the country a massive
question mark. I noticed something scrawled on the bathroom wall,
written with one of those brownish wood markers.

It read:

> PIG
> USE THE BRUSH
> CLEAN SHIT ON TOILET

An arrow pointed downward from the word "brush," aimed at a
toilet brush leaning against the wall. I mindlessly stared at it for
a few moments, trying to make sense of any of it. But the fates determined that I needed a soundtrack to accompany my descent into
misery. I heard the voice of the woman behind the counter hooting
and hollering through the bathroom door. She was excitely yelling
that "Mr. Trump is president! Mr. Trump is president! We got a new
president and it's Mr. Trump!" By this point I was convinced that I
had died in the car crash. Clearly I had croaked and was now stuck in
a waiting room somewhere in hell. So this was my fate on the other
side? To be called "pig" and use the brush to clean shit on toilet?

I stepped out of the bathroom and took a seat in one of the hard
plastic chairs while I waited for Terre to pick me up. I sat in a state
of shock, just staring at the floor. The woman at the desk must've
noticed and tried her best to console me from behind the plexiglass.
"I'm sorry you got in an accident," she offered. "And I'm glad you're
okay." It was an attempt at humanity and even though she was a
grade A monster for celebrating the election of another grade A
monster, I was in dire need of anything resembling kindness. I

looked at the floor until Terre arrived, wondering what the world would look like tomorrow.

I didn't get a normal night's sleep for two weeks. Every time I closed my eyes all I could see were the snapshots from the accident. The dumb face on the deer a few feet in front of my car. The sound of the crash. A weird airless feeling inhabited my being. My voice was gone, and I came down with a bad cold a day or so later. I was clearly in a state of trauma. I knew what was going on because I'd been there before: When something catastrophic happens, my brain immediately shifts into action mode and there is no room for processing feelings. It is as if my brain is a nervous busboy at a restaurant, constantly asking if he can take the plates away even though everyone is clearly eating. (Whenever I'm in this situation at a restaurant, I will always declare to my dining companion, "They must be trying to fill up the dishwasher so they can run a load." This one might not work on the page but trust me. If we are ever eating dinner together and I say this, you're gonna spit your espresso all over your flourless chocolate cake.)

I eventually recovered. I knew I was on the mend when my beautiful voice started to return to its typical stentorian self. Before long I was back to normal, doing the show and writing. I got a new car. Things can sometimes revert to how they were without much effort if you get out of your own way. But one thing wouldn't go away: the crash itself. It had to mean something. Why would everything go my way when it came to that collision? If one tiny element had been altered by a fraction, that deer would've crashed into my windshield and I'd be gone. I slowly came to feel that the reason I was spared being an election night casualty was that I still had a few things I needed to do with my life.

Another thought I took away from the car crash was that while I was extremely happy to have survived the accident, it would've been pretty epic to shuffle off this mortal coil the very moment that Trump became president. Imagine if that episode was my final statement to the people of earth. I would've beaten David Bowie's impressive "release a music video that I die in and then actually die two days later" magic trick. It would've been legendary! I can see the T-shirts, with TOM KNEW IT WAS TIME TO GET THE FUCK OUTTA HERE! emblazoned across the chest. Boy, that would've been something. Yes, I realize that I am dead in this scenario. But what a social media coup!

I thought about everything that I had yet to accomplish. The list was long and I was not the spring chicken I used to be. It was time for some action. Time to finally stare down some of these demons that I had been carrying around for years.

I'm sure some people reading this are like, "Get over it, things happen." All I can say to that is TRUST ME WHEN I SAY I HAVE TRIED. I tried to get over the hospitalization and the ECT. I tried to ignore it, to medicate it, to talk about it in therapy. Shame and guilt are a real motherfucker sometimes. They take hold of your psyche and your identity, making so many of your actions and decisions nothing more than a pathetic reaction to all the shame. It grows and grows and before long it's impossible to even trace all the emotions back to the source.

Rodney Dangerfield called his depression "the heaviness." Winston Churchill referred to his as "the black dog" that followed him. I get it. The cloud descends and brings with it a pinball game of emotions, ricocheting from guilt to shame to sadness to anger to resentment, and back to guilt. I wish I was stronger in the face of my past. I know how strong I am capable of being in most aspects of my life. But I have struggled to be tough enough to deal with this. The sadness is accompanied by a voice that tells me to give in, that my life has been a waste, that nobody loves me. It will do anything and everything to keep me in this state. If I could stand up to it I would. But I can't. I've tried.

But after almost fifty years of this life, I had to try one more time. It was time to tell my story. So I sat down and I started to write. And then I promptly stopped writing because it was SO MUCH EASIER to write about anything else. So I wrote a spec script for a show about a singer in a nu metal band. It's called *Punched in the Nuts* and it's very funny. But it isn't the story I needed to tell.

By the following October I was ready, and as 2017 ended, the writing of this book had begun.

CHAPTER TWENTY

IT NEVER ENDS: THE END

So NOW WE have reached the end of the book. The final chapter. The end of the story, as it were. What a weird thing, to boil the entirety of a long life into a series of anecdotes that can be consumed before your Newark-to-LA flight touches down. It is just as strange to turn all the sadness into laughter, as if my life was being retooled from a Paul Thomas Anderson movie into a Chuck Lorre sitcom. What a strange and unnatural process: The act of even selecting the stories was difficult. Evergreens like the Patti Smith elevator story were automatic, but deciding to finally write about some of this stuff was a real challenge. Like I mentioned, a huge part of me was fully prepared to take some of these stories to the grave. Would I have eventually told them to the skeletons and ghouls and goblins that populate the afterlife? Now we will never know.

As bizarre as it is to write a book, it's exponentially weirder to write about writing the book. By now you realize I wasn't doing it as an exercise in being "meta" or "clever." This is not a book about writing a book, but rather a book about the hurdles I needed to overcome to realize who I actually am.

The actual writing went smoothly at first. I had fun writing out the Billy Joel concert, a tale that was easy to put to words because I've told it so many times over the years. But it took me months to write about the hospitalization. My recollection was compromised by all that memory loss, the magnitude of which wasn't apparent until I started trying to put these stories on the page. I am in awe of writers who can tell a story about their past and recall every detail and name: "When I was in second grade Jeffy Van Voorst stole my favorite royal blue marker during social studies. I remember it well; I was wearing my Janet Jackson T-shirt that day and had just eaten half a strawberry Fruit Roll-Up in the hallway before class." Meanwhile I'm struggling to remember the name of literally any teacher from any year of high school. And it always seems like the most boring people have the strongest memories: How many times must we endure a Hall of Fame snooze like Garrison Keillor blathering on about the guy who owned the corner sweet shop when he was six?

Since my memory was lacking when it came to certain parts, it became clear I would have to talk to some of the people from my life about what actually went down. The frustration of having had so much of my past erased was constant throughout the process, and I needed help. I was hesitant to ask my mother for details because it was such a brutal time for all of us. I can only imagine what my parents went through, watching their kid maintain an unyielding determination to snuff out his life. I eventually talked to her about it one quiet summer night in her backyard. She was amazingly composed and could recall so many details with little effort (is that what it's like to have a working memory?). She told me how hard it was to have to leave me in the hospital after a visit, watching me cry as she walked away. After some poking she admitted that the ECT treatments put my family in a financial bind; they had to basically pay money that they didn't have up front to get the procedures rolling. She demonstrated yet again how smart and strong she has been for me throughout my life. I can't think of another person who would have the fortitude to simply force their sickness onto the back burner so they could take care of their family. You might think your mother is the best but you're wrong. Compared to my mother, yours is an eighteen-gallon Hefty bag stuffed with twenty gallons of oily rags.

Armed with the details my mom provided, I wrote a few chapters to show prospective book people what this memoir would look like. For a few years I had been politely refusing the encouragement of a literary agent named Christopher Hermelin. He was a *Best Show* listener and politely reminded me over and over that the only reason Kelsey Grammer has a book and I don't is because HE ACTUALLY WROTE A BOOK. I was flattered by the encouragement but ultimately deferred because I still wasn't ready. But once I had the three chapters locked down, I contacted Christopher and proposed a unique arrangement.

I told him that I had written some of the book, but that I wasn't comfortable sending it to him. I wasn't sure what kind of reaction I would get from these chapters. Perhaps he would love them, but I was terrified that he would judge me for my past. Part of me wanted to tell my story, but another part of me wanted to bury these stories deep in a hole. I told Christopher that he could meet me in Midtown Manhattan on a day I had a voice-over session for *Steven Universe* scheduled.

I am aware I didn't write about my being the voice of Greg Universe on *Steven Universe*, one of the most profoundly game-changing shows in cartoon history. If you haven't seen it, Greg is a balding rocker and father of the titular character. Show creator Rebecca Sugar was a *Best Show* listener and developed the character with me in mind. I can remember the email she initially sent me, telling me that she wanted me to do a voice on the show she was writing if and when it got off the ground. I wrote back a polite "Yeah, sure! Let me know when!" fully believing that nothing would ever come of it, because most projects never break through the nightmare of development. But a year later she wrote again telling me the show was happening. I was now wondering what I had said yes to, but thankfully I loved everything about *Steven Universe*: so much heart and humor and love alongside legit action and storytelling. It has been a privilege to work on it and watch the series grow and impact generations of fans aching for LGBTQ representation.

Christopher met me outside the studio. I handed him the pages and told him that he could read the chapters while I did the voice-over. When I was done with the session, I would meet him at a coffee shop and we could discuss what he thought and whether or not these chapters were any good, with the understanding that I was taking the pages with me. I didn't want there to be any trace of me writing anything if it didn't seem like a viable book. I could shred the printout when I got home and it would be like none of this had ever happened.

I went into "the booth" and yelled all of Greg's lines—I have two settings as a voice-over artist: "screaming" and "screaming while running"—before catching up with Christopher at a nearby café. I was relieved to hear him say he liked the pages and that I was already a few chapters into writing an Actual Book. I felt buoyed by his feedback and told him that we would talk about the next step.

But I still took the pages with me.

IF I WAS going to tell certain parts of my story, I would have to take a serious dive into my past. I needed to know details about my time in the hospital. I had a handful of memories, but I wanted more. I wanted documents and medical records. I needed to see what my experience was like through my doctor's eyes. Certain questions lingered: How many volts were run through my head? How extreme was my ECT treatment compared to other patients? And what about the memory loss? Was there any consideration for the toll the treatments took on my brain?

Throughout my adult life I have—surprise!—experienced serious bouts of depression, and so many roads lead back to the months I spent in mental hospitals. While I have never seriously attempted to kill myself since my teenage years, let's just say I have spent a considerable amount of my adult life staring at the Atlantic Ocean, wondering how long it would take for my car to sink. It is a constant struggle that semi-regularly flares up and kicks my ass. I have been in therapy for most of my life and have tried different medications, so I am not white-knuckling any of this. I take it seriously and I would love nothing more than to actually put my past in my past. This felt like an opportunity to try.

I decided to visit Princeton House Behavioral Health, the place where it all went down. The facility is an unassuming one-story medical building that looks like a nursing home or a grade school. Over the years, I would sometimes find myself deep in a depressive swoon, and it made sense to drive to Princeton House and just stare at the building from my car. So many of my problems were fixed on the other side of those doors. So many of my problems were created on the other side of those doors as well.

I never had any desire to actually walk into Princeton House but now I needed answers. I had mailed a letter to an administrator asking about the possibility of touring the facility but never received a reply. I followed up with a couple of phone calls and was roundly rejected: Only patients and relatives of patients were allowed inside. By this point I had given up on actually seeing where everything happened; all I wanted were my medical records so I could hopefully grasp some clarity on my treatments.

The woman I spoke to at the admissions desk was disinterested in my plight. She reiterated that a tour was out of the question and deflected my request to speak to any doctors about my stay at the facility. I asked if the psychiatrist who had treated me was still working there and she immediately said no, he had left a few years earlier. I was striking out left and right. When I asked about the possibility of obtaining my medical records she told me all their documents had been moved to a new building a few miles away. I jotted down the information this human crab apple told me and drove to the new location of the hospital records.

The Penn Medicine Princeton Medical Center was the opposite of Princeton House, a massive institution with endless corridors and a lobby that would've made more sense at the United Nations building. I got sent on a wild goose chase by a well-meaning security guard before locating the tiny office that handled medical records.

I told my story to an infinitely nicer woman, who handed me some document requisition paperwork. I filled everything out and handed it back to her. She retreated to another room before returning a few minutes later, telling me with a sad face that all my records were gone; the hospital has a policy of destroying everything after twenty years. I wasn't surprised; my past was a mystery and mysteries don't always like to get solved.

My final option was the scariest. I needed to contact the psychiatrist who had prescribed and administered the electroconvulsive therapy more than thirty years ago.

IT WASN'T HARD to track him down: While he didn't work at Princeton House anymore, he had an office in a nondescript building less than a block away. I left a couple of voice messages but never got a reply. The doctor was getting up there in years—he wasn't exactly a spring chicken when he treated me back in the late 1980s—so I wasn't sure how active he would be at this point. My questions were answered when my phone rang one afternoon in June 2018.

"Tom?"

All my synapses fired at once as I heard his voice. It was him. A surge of emotions came rushing back. The doctor seemed uncertain as to why I was trying to contact him, which threw me for a bit of a loop. I was a patient of his, and a unique one at that. There wasn't anyone even remotely close to my age getting ECT throughout the month-plus I spent in that hospital, and I remained a patient of his for a couple of years after the treatments. But this torrent of memories only flowed one way: He had no idea who I was.

I explained everything I could remember to him. I told him when I was hospitalized. I mentioned numerous details from Princeton

House. I talked about my parents, who he had gotten to know quite well throughout our time together. But none of it registered.

"Oh gosh, I'm sorry. I just don't remember who you are. Did you try contacting the hospital?"

I told him yes, I had, but all my records had been destroyed. He gave a sad little sigh and said again, "I'm really sorry."

I tried to jog his memory in any way possible. I told him that I remembered the taste of the metal after the ECT treatments. I brought up our many sessions and described his office to him. But nothing seemed to work. I finally mentioned his appearance on David Letterman, the one he proudly played for me in his office on a washed-out VHS tape.

"Yeah, yeah. That was me. Boy, that was a long time ago."

The reality sunk in. The psychiatrist whose treatment erased huge stretches of my brain had forgotten who I was. The hospitalization and treatment that had impacted my life in every way was nothing more than a forgotten memory for him.

I thanked the doctor for his time, then sunk onto my couch, paralyzed with hopelessness. I was immobile for days. To his credit he did say "ciao" to me before he hung up. And he was pretty good on Letterman if I remember correctly. Not as good as I was in the handful of sketches I did on *Late Night with Conan O'Brien,* but not half bad.

TO BE FUNNY you need to have some understanding of the darker side of life, even if you choose not to indulge it. I have a pretty solid awareness of the power of my own negative thinking, but the truth is I don't see myself as a negative person. Laugh it up, but it's true. Yeah, I can moan about the dopiest things on *The Best Show,* from my dissatisfaction with the pizza in Toronto to the jorts that Kevin Smith wears like a second skin. But there's a huge difference between complaining for sport and actually being negative. I consistently work to make people feel good about their lives. I try to help others as much as I possibly can. Sometimes this comes from a place that is not entirely healthy—my compulsion to try to fix the lives of everyone around me is truly flawed—but most of the time it is borne from love and caring.

I like to build people up. I like to encourage everyone to be their best. I like to believe in people. For the longest time I thought I was at my core a wildly positive person. But after around eight hundred years of therapy I finally learned that so much of my positivity was a reaction to the negative way I actually saw the world.

I grew up understanding sadness and futility. I didn't think anything would ever work out. I was truly convinced there was a curse on my family, that we were all doomed to fail. The positivity I would promote was not my default setting, but a technique I developed as a conscious counterbalance to the bleak worldview that was hardwired into me. I don't like it but it's there and I accept it. If I can't have it excised from my soul, at least I can work to override it.

I said that I chose the title of this book because some things never end. Events happen over and over again throughout a life, sometimes changing form a little bit between reoccurrences but still maintaining a presence as the years pass. But some things do end, both good and bad. We can work past our hang-ups and foibles, but we can also watch the people we love die way too soon. Things change on both sides of the spectrum. Perhaps the full title for the book should be *It Never Ends Until It Ends*.

My life has changed in so many ways over the years. Relationships have fallen into my lap, blossomed, and then faded. I've been the one to get my heart broken and I've been the one who had to move on. My marriage to Terre is over; the strain of so much baggage—both hers and my own—brought me to a point where I just couldn't do it anymore. It was devastating but it was unavoidable. I am happier now but I also carry a ton of guilt about that happiness.

I've gotten a chance to meet so many of my heroes and in some cases I've gotten the opportunity to work alongside them. I was given an evening time slot on a listener-sponsored radio station and turned it into a weekly document of my life. I have had people I loved die and I've nearly died a few times. (I didn't tell you about the time I nearly drowned. Or the time I saw a bat fight on the streets of Toronto. Next book!) The only reason I got to experience any of this is because it hasn't ended yet. I appreciate all of it even if I didn't show it at the time, and I'm grateful for the continued opportunities to eventually get it right. Writing this book is the latest gift I have been given and I'm glad I didn't get smeared on the New Jersey Turnpike before I got a chance to do it.

So many of us carry trauma or shame. It is an unfortunate foundational truth for too many people. We live lives filled with sadness and embarrassment because we simply don't realize that we are not alone. And look, nobody reading this will have the same story that I have, but what we all share is the ability to identify who we are and how we ended up where we ended up. If you're carrying around shame, you can face it and you can ultimately move on. It's a struggle but you can do it. Get yourself safe and get the help you need. Reach out. Tell your story and try to be proud of your story. Then start figuring out a new story! You are not your trauma, so set it down and move forward. Because when it ends, it ENDS. So take advantage of whatever your life is while you've still got it.

ACKNOWLEDGMENTS

Wow, that was some book, huh? Admit it: You didn't think I had it in me! And truth be told you were partially right; the act of writing a book required endless stretches of loneliness and isolation balanced with a desperate reliance on everyone around me. I tapped into the strength, wisdom, and generosity of people in my life to turn this terrifying task into an incredibly rewarding experience. I wouldn't have made it to the finish line if it wasn't for their kindness.

I might miss some people so I apologize. I probably should've kept a running list of everyone that helped, but if I missed you this time you will get thanked twice in the next book.

Infinite gratitude to Phil Morrison, Robert Biegler, Ronnie Bronstein, Nick Thorburn, Joe Ventura, Rebecca Sugar, Brendan McDonald, Claire Evans, Jon Daly, David O'Reilly, Puloma Basu, Rob Hatch-Miller, Andy Breckman, Gail Bennington, Chris Gethard, Sean Clements, Adam McKay, Hayes Davenport, John Hodgman, Dr. Mary Laney, Clare O'Kane, Ben Gibbard, Jake Fogelnest, Adam Resnick, Patton Oswalt, Jo Firestone, Emma Healy, James Robertello, Gerard Cosloy, Jason Stern, Don Fleming, David Garcia,

Rosemary Carroll, Laurie Anderson, Matt Fraction, Matt Berry, Anna Gebbie, Marc Maron, Candace Mills, Leah Severson, Lisa Jane Persky, Peyton Reed, Mal Ward, Marc Marrie, Matt Aselton, Josh and Bennie Safdie, Brett Davis, Brett Boham, Chris Tomson, Ezra Koening, Mindy Tucker, Dave Wyndorf, Tim Cronin, Jim Romeo, Rob Meisch, Sharon Horgan, Jemaine Clement, John Oliver, Michael Bellino, John Telenko, Katherine Telenko, Kurt Vile, Michael Koman, Chris Cooper, Jeff Feuerzeig, Penny Lane, Tim Heidecker, Todd Abramson, Marcia Neumeier, Nicole Lawrence, Nathan Fielder, Paul Scheer, Alanna Santini, Mark Proksch, Andrew Weinberg, Mary Houlihan, Michelle Mae, Martha Kelly, Dan Bejar, Mary Lattimore, William Tyler, Jesse Thorn, John Darnielle, and Sarah Sahim.

Thank you to everyone who has helped with *The Best Show* over the years, including Pat Byrne, Jason Gore, Michael Lisk, Martin Celis, Jeff T. Owens, and Amy Gottschalk. And thank you to everyone at WFMU for all the early support. Of course, a ton of gratitude for all the *Best Show* listeners and supporters. You like me and I like you! Well, most of you.

I would be dead without the constant care and dedication of Dennis Kim, Jim Ehrich, and Mitch Smelkinson.

Garrett McGrath made me want to make the book as great as possible. Thank you to him and Abrams Press for all their hard work: Annalea Manalili, Sarah Masterson Hally, Deb Wood, Devin Grosz, Kim Lew, Gabby Fisher, and the rest of the team. Sammi Skolmoski is a next-level comedy wizard whose dedication and insight kept me believing. And my amazing literary agent, Christopher Hermelin, told me years ago that I should write a book and stayed on me until I finally gave in. Thank you, Christopher, I am forever in your debt.

Three of the most important people in my life are Jon Wurster, Julie Klausner, and Jason Woliner. They are the funniest humans on the planet and they all helped me immeasurably. Thank you.

As I wrote this book I couldn't wait for my friends Lynn Shelton and Neil Mahoney to read it. Two true talents who inspired me and made my life better in so many ways. Unfortunately, they passed away before I finished. We all feel your absence every day.

Theresa Telenko is one of the most amazing people on the planet and I am lucky to have learned so much from her. Thank you, Terre.

I thank my family for allowing me to tell these stories, especially Jill Giuliano, Sue Giuliano, Charles Kenney, and Charlie and Julianna. It breaks my heart that my father didn't see this book come to life. He would've been as proud of me as I was proud to call him Dad.

And this book would never have gotten finished without the love and support of Julia Vickerman, a true angel and beacon of gratitude. Thank you.

I realize I never told you the story of how I cheated my family's Secret Santa for five years straight.

OH GREAT NOW I HAVE TO WRITE ANOTHER ONE!